*Mongrels or Marvels*

Stanford Studies in Jewish History and Culture

edited by *Aron Rodrigue and Steven J. Zipperstein*

# Mongrels or Marvels

*The Levantine Writings of Jacqueline Shohet Kahanoff*

*Edited by Deborah A. Starr and Sasson Somekh*

STANFORD UNIVERSITY PRESS
STANFORD, CALIFORNIA

Stanford University Press
Stanford, California



The following have been published previously in English:

"Childhood in Egypt," *Jerusalem Quarterly* 36 (summer 1985), 31–41. Reprinted with permission. © 1985, Jacqueline Shohet Kahanoff.

"Passover in Egypt," *Bulletin of the Israeli Academic Center in Cairo* 23 (June 1998), 26–29. Reprinted with permission. © 1998, Jacqueline Shohet Kahanoff.

"Such Is Rachel," *Atlantic Monthly* 10 (1946), 113–116. Published under the author's maiden name, Jacqueline Shohet. © 1946, Jacqueline Shohet Kahanoff.

"Journey to a Better Land" and "A Line in the Sand" are excerpted from *Jacob's Ladder* (London: Harvill Press, 1951), 331–337, 351–371. Published under the author's maiden name, Jacqueline Shohet. © 1951, Jacqueline Shohet Kahanoff.

"Cairo Wedding," *Tomorrow* 4:11 (July 1945), 19–23. Published under the author's maiden name, Jacqueline Shohet. Reprinted with permission, Creative Age Press. Reprinted with permission. © 1945, Jacqueline Shohet Kahanoff.

"Reunion in Beersheba," *American Israel Review* 1:1 (October 1957), 25–28. Published under the pseudonym Louise Sasson. Reprinted with permission, American Jewish League for Israel. © 1957, Jacqueline Shohet Kahanoff.

"A Letter from Mama Camouna," *Keys to the Garden*, ed. Ammiel Alcalay (San Francisco: City Lights Books, 1996), 23–33. Reprinted with permission. © 1996, Jacqueline Shohet Kahanoff.

The following have previously been published only in Hebrew: "A Culture Stillborn, Part 2" © 1973, Jacqueline Shohet Kahanoff; "To Live and Die a Copt" © 1973, Jacqueline Shohet Kahanoff; "Wake of the Waves" © 1962, Jacqueline Shohet Kahanoff; "Rebel, My Brother" ©1959, Jacqueline Shohet Kahanoff; and "Welcome, Sadat" © 1978, Jacqueline Shohet Kahanoff.

"Ma'adi," "Alexandria," "Europe from Afar," "A Culture Stillborn, Part 1," "Ambivalent Levantine," "To Remember Alexandria," "My Brother Ishmael: On the Visit of Anwar Sadat," and "From East the Sun" are © 2011 Estate of Jacqueline Shohet Kahanoff.

Library of Congress Cataloguing-in-Publication data will be found at the end of this book.



Printed in the United States of America on acid-free, archival-quality paper

Typeset by Bruce Lundquist in 10.5/14 Galliard

"We are not so far removed from your ideal as you think, my father," Samuel said, "even if our reality does not fit with your dream. You have wished us to celebrate within ourselves a kind of marriage between East and West. Was there ever a perfect marriage? Cross-breeding produces mongrels or marvels, and that is what we risked."

*Jacob's Ladder*

*Contents*

*Acknowledgments*

The idea to work together to edit an anthology of Jacqueline Shohet Kahanoff's writings emerged from our conversations in 2000, and our collaboration began in earnest in January 2002. Over the many years that it has taken to see this project through, we have received the assistance and support of many individuals and institutions.

We are most grateful to Josette d'Amade, Jacqueline's sister, and Laura d'Amade, Jacqueline's niece, for their support of our efforts and their permission to print Jacqueline Kahanoff's writings. We have enjoyed the d'Amades' friendship and have shared and compared family stories. We hope that this volume brings honor to Jacqueline's memory.

We thank Eva Weintraub, Jacqueline Kahanoff's literary executor, for granting us access to her veritable treasure trove of notes, documents, and manuscripts. We spent weeks combing through these files, discovering long-forgotten pieces as well as unpublished diaries and manuscripts. Marginalia and notes provided leads to additional articles, and documents in these files confirmed the pseudonyms under which Kahanoff published while her parents were still in Egypt. It was through this research that our broad picture of Kahanoff's career as a writer emerged.

We are very grateful to Ammiel Alcalay for his comments on this manuscript and his enthusiastic support of this project. We also thank Ronit Matalon for meeting with us and discussing our mutual interest in bringing greater visibility to Kahanoff's writings.

We appreciate the care with which Norris Pope and Sarah Crane Newman at Stanford University Press have treated this manuscript. We are privileged to have had the opportunity to work with such dedicated editors.

Although all the pieces included in this volume were originally written in English, some of the original manuscripts were not found among Kahanoff's papers. After careful consideration, we decided to include five such pieces: "A Culture Stillborn" (part 2); "To Live and Die a Copt"; "Wake of the Waves"; "Rebel, My Brother"; and "Welcome, Sadat." We thank our accomplished translators Jennie Feldman and Gabriel Levin for undertaking the Borgesian task of translating from Hebrew back into the original English. Thanks are also due to Talia Shiff for her research assistance and to Rebecca Kleinhandler and Elizabeth Chasia for their assistance in transcription and copyediting.

The Department of Near Eastern Studies at Cornell University and the Department of Arabic Language and Literature at Tel Aviv University provided us with much-needed support, permitting us to get together in person on multiple occasions to conduct research into Jacqueline Kahanoff's oeuvre, to discuss which pieces to include in this book, and to draft the introduction. In 2003 the project received an international collaboration grant from the Society for the Humanities at Cornell University. We express our gratitude for the generous assistance that enabled us to produce the truly collaborative work before you.

We are most grateful for the support we have received from Terrie Somekh and Elliot Shapiro. Terrie welcomed Deborah (and Elliot) into the Somekh home on many occasions while we worked on this project. She also graciously ceded some of her vacation time in London in June 2003 so that we could work on this project together. Elliot valiantly endured two trips to Israel under challenging circumstances so that we could spend long days hashing out our plans for this volume. Terrie's and Elliot's love, good humor, support, and encouragement not only made this project possible, but helped make the process enjoyable as well.

DEBORAH A. STARR
ITHACA, NEW YORK, USA

SASSON SOMEKH
TEL AVIV, ISRAEL

## *Editor's Introduction*
## Jacqueline Shohet Kahanoff—A Cosmopolitan Levantine

DEBORAH STARR AND SASSON SOMEKH

In the mid-1950s a Jewish couple in Cairo whose two adult daughters had moved away—one to Israel and the other to France—let out their spare rooms to Tunisian and Algerian nationalists temporarily living in the Egyptian capital. The couple developed a particularly close relationship with one Algerian guest. Together they would frequently engage in lengthy discussions on topics ranging from philosophy and literature to the politics of national self-determination—Arab nationalism and Zionism alike. The couple learned their guest's identity only after he was arrested by French authorities. Their esteemed house guest had been Ahmed Ben Bella, the mastermind of the National Liberation Front (FLN) who later became the first prime minister and then president of the Algerian Republic.

The events described in this story are as difficult to imagine happening today as they were in Israel in 1959 when Jacqueline Shohet Kahanoff, the couple's Israeli daughter, published an essay describing her own discovery of her parents' encounter with Ben Bella. This essay, "Rebel, My Brother," like many of Kahanoff's other notable pieces, reflects upon a lost world of cultural interaction between Jews and Arabs. *Mongrels or Marvels* collects some of the engaging works of this distinctive essayist and novelist.

Born in Cairo in 1917, Jacqueline left Egypt in 1940 for the United States, where she remained for the duration of World War II. She then spent several years living in Paris before moving to Israel in 1954. Although Jacqueline first found her voice as a writer in America, Egypt and Israel provided the two primary geographic, cultural, and psychological anchors in her work. Her representations of both interwar Egypt and Israel in the first decades after the establishment of the state provide insights into important historical and cultural moments. Her writings about the past reflect an impulse that extends beyond preservation and transmission of a lost culture—although her work is important in this regard. Her writings, particularly the narrative essay genre with which she is most closely associated, also reflect an effort to engage with contemporaneous social realities.

To this end, in her Israeli pieces Kahanoff draws upon her experiences of cultural interaction in interwar Egypt to form the basis of a social model she terms *Levantinism*, a word derived from the Levant, the geographical region of the Eastern Mediterranean and the Arab East. In its adjectival form as popularly understood in Israel at the time Kahanoff was writing, "Levantine" connoted a corrupting, orientalizing force to be resisted at all costs. Kahanoff, on the other hand, vaunted the antiparochialism inherent in the admixture of multiple cultural influences and put forward Levantinism as a positive social model.

As a writer and public intellectual, Jacqueline Kahanoff had a significant effect on Israeli culture. However, she never wrote in Hebrew. Throughout her life she wrote in rich English and occasionally French, although the work that defines her career was composed during her years in Israel and published in Hebrew translation. Paradoxically, much of this significant body of work has never been published in English to date. This volume is intended to introduce this important writer to a wider audience and to make her work available in the language in which it was written.

In what follows, we aim briefly to introduce the reader to Jacqueline Shohet Kahanoff's life and work. First we outline the significant events in her life, particularly as they shaped her perceptions and affected her career. We also describe the Egyptian bourgeois cosmopolitan society within which she was raised and that forms a recurrent topic of her writings. Then we provide an overview of the trajectory of Kahanoff's career and the range of her literary production. Kahanoff is best remembered for a cycle of essays titled collectively "A Generation of Levantines" (1959), in which she advocates for the "Levantinization" of Israeli society. We therefore map the concept of Levantinism as it develops through Kahanoff's career, as well as analyze and interpret its shifting valences. Although her proposals were met with some resistance within 1950s Israel, her work has had a lasting effect on several generations of Israeli writers and intellectuals, so we end by attempting to assess the scope of this effect on Israeli literature and culture.

## East to West and Back Again: Personal and Intellectual Trajectories

Jacqueline was born in May 1917 into a well-to-do Jewish family in Cairo. Like many of the Jews of modern Egypt, both sides of the family were relative newcomers to that country. Jacqueline's maternal grandparents, the Chemlas, immigrated to Egypt from Tunisia, and her father's family, the Shohets, hailed from Iraq. Through the late nineteenth and early twentieth centuries, the Jewish community in Egypt grew and flourished because of immigration from throughout the Mediterranean basin, the Arab world, and Eastern Europe. In 1840, the Egyptian Jewish community was estimated to number five thousand to seven thousand, and by the year of Jacqueline's birth, the community had grown to nearly sixty thousand.[1]

Despite the fact that both of Jacqueline's parents, Joseph Shohet and Yvonne Chemla, came from Arab backgrounds, the family spoke French in the home. Indeed, French was prevalent among middle-class and upper-class Egyptian Jews and served as a lingua franca in their professional and social dealings with educated Egyptians and members of other minority and foreign communities of their class. Among the Jews who had arrived in Egypt within one or two generations were also some families that spoke Ladino, Italian, and Yiddish at home. In Rabbanite and Karaite families,* whose presence in Egypt predated the waves of immigration, Arabic was the primary language.

Jacqueline received her formal education at the French Mission Laïque school in Cairo. Her schoolmates and friends also spoke French, in the main, but had some knowledge of English as well. Jacqueline achieved

* Rabbanite Jews follow Talmudic law and comprise the majority of world Jewish communities; Karaite Jews, a small community, follow the laws of the Hebrew Bible, rejecting Talmudic law.

an excellent command of English from her early exposure to the language at the hands of her British nanny and governess.

Unlike her father, Jacqueline, as well as a great number of the Egyptian Jews of her class and generation, never felt at home in the Arabic language. Although many Egyptian Jews could speak Arabic in the local dialect, most of them didn't learn the written language, *fusḥa*, which was taught at school or acquired by traditionally educated Muslims through memorization of the Quran. This linguistic situation presented yet another difficulty for the new immigrants in becoming full members of the cultured community of the Egyptian nation. Since Jacqueline was not educated in literary Arabic, she was not familiar with the great works of Arabic literature, nor was she aware of the literary efforts of modern Egyptian authors who were influential in shaping Egyptian culture during her formative years. Many years later, according to a story she related to friends, as an adult living in Paris she studied elementary Arabic because she felt embarrassed as an Egyptian not to know the language and literature of her home country.

Jacqueline never felt at home in Hebrew either. In her youth she had not been educated in Hebrew, as it was common to offer formal religious education only to boys. The only religious ceremony she mentions in her writings is the Passover seder, commemorating the Exodus of the Israelites from Egypt under Moses. In her essay "Passover in Egypt," included in this volume, she describes the time she realized how little she knew about her own religion when she tried to explain Jewish practice to a Muslim friend. However, her writings as an adult demonstrate great affinity for biblical sources. The representations of Abraham, Hagar, Rebecca, Jacob, Rachel, and Joseph that pepper her work offer insightful reflections on the characters and the biblical narratives. Also, although she was intrigued by and sympathetic to the Zionist project of rebuilding the land of Israel, an effort she witnessed firsthand when she visited Palestine as a tourist in 1937, she, like most Egyptian Jews, did not envision settling there and therefore did not endeavor to learn Hebrew for that purpose. Jacqueline learned Hebrew to a functional level only after her immigration to Israel in 1954 at the age of thirty-seven. Throughout her adult life in Israel, however, she remained self-conscious about her command of the language and never wrote in it. Her writings intended for an Israeli audience were composed in English and then translated for publication into Hebrew.

The options for intellectually curious women were limited in Egyptian bourgeois society, a complaint Jacqueline frequently made in her writings. Upon completing her secondary education in 1937, she attended courses in law in the French school designed to prepare students for a career in the Mixed Courts, the judicial system for noncitizen residents in Egypt. Even at the time of her enrollment, the courts were being disbanded under the stipulations of the Montreux Convention. Jacqueline and several of her female friends also volunteered at medical clinics and tried their hands at running their own services in the impoverished Jewish quarter, *harat al-yahud*. As she writes, their efforts were thwarted. She retrospectively disparages these endeavors as dilettantism, characterizing them as diversions undertaken by young women marking time until marriage.

Despite these various activities, Jacqueline intimates in her essays and in interviews that she had always, even as a child, wanted to be a writer. In "A Culture Stillborn," included in this volume, she describes her earliest efforts at writing fiction published in a short-lived Francophone literary journal in Cairo. Unfortunately, these early pieces have not been located.

Like many educated women of her generation, Jacqueline found her escape from social strictures in marriage. At the age of twenty-two she married a physician, Izzy Margoliash, and in 1940 the young couple sailed to the United States, where he joined a medical practice in San Francisco. For the next decade she lived there and, among other places, in Chicago and New York. In the United States during World War II she was able to pursue an education and her dreams of becoming a writer. She attended Columbia University from 1942 to 1945 and received a bachelor's degree in general studies and a master's in journalism. During this period, she separated from Margoliash and took an apartment with her childhood friend Denise Mosseri, the daughter of a wealthy and influential Egyptian Jewish family, who helped support her intellectual pursuits. New York proved to be a productive environment for the budding writer. While there, she wrote and published her first short stories in English and began work on a novel, *Jacob's Ladder*.

During and immediately after the war, Jacqueline also took courses at the New School for Social Research and began circulating with European intellectuals, including Claude Lévi-Strauss, Raymond Aaron, and Claude Vigée, who had reached the American continent as exiles escaping from the growing Nazi threat. Many of the ideas and concepts evident in her later work are drawn from the intellectual universe she discovered in the United States, even if her writings about the country are disparaging of the bleak, industrial landscape and the racism she witnessed. Although many of her later works reflect upon the multicultural society of the Cairo of her youth, those representations are shaped by the intellectual discourses she encountered when she lived in the United States.

Jacqueline's attachment to French culture did not recede during her many years in the United States, nor during a brief period in London where she apparently completed the manuscript of *Jacob's Ladder*, published in 1951. Following the novel's publication, Jacqueline moved again, settling in Paris to be near her younger sister, Josette. However, she was creatively frustrated. "In France," she wrote, "I couldn't write, except in diary form. I had nothing to say to the French."[2]

In 1952 in Paris Jacqueline married Alexander Kahanoff, an acoustical engineer by profession, who had been a friend from her youth in Cairo. The couple decided to settle in Israel and arrived in that country in 1954. Israel at that time was a new state grappling with severe security concerns, as well as with the problem of the displaced Palestinian refugees wanting to return to their homes. Furthermore, Israel was confronted with the need to provide residences and employment for more than a million Jewish refugees arriving from Eastern Europe and Middle Eastern countries.

The Kahanoffs settled in Beersheba, at the time a small town surrounded by desert approximately seventy miles from Tel Aviv that was mainly inhabited by newcomers. During her two years there, Jacqueline Kahanoff began publishing again. She served as a freelance writer for agencies such as the Jewish National Fund, United Israel Appeal, and the Youth Aliyah movement and also published her first journalistic pieces for Israeli newspapers. In addition, she wrote articles for the American Jewish press featuring stories about newcomers to Israel from

Middle Eastern countries. Out of fear of reprisals directed against her family still living in Egypt, these early articles were published under the pseudonyms Dina Monet, Louise Sassoon, and Dimona. After her parents left Egypt in 1958, she started publishing under her married name.

In the spring of 1958 she published an article, "Reflections of a Levantine Jew," in the American journal *The Jewish Frontier*. Nissim Rejwan, an Anglophone Israeli intellectual of Iraqi origin, who also published an article in the same issue of the journal, took note of Kahanoff's work. Rejwan takes credit for introducing Kahanoff to Aharon Amir, the man who was responsible for presenting her to the Israeli public by translating her fluid English prose into Hebrew.[3] Amir, a noted translator, poet, and public intellectual, had recently begun a journal, *Keshet* (Rainbow), which was to have a long and influential run. Amir used his new journal as a platform for introducing Kahanoff's work, featuring her four-part series "A Generation of Levantines," beginning in the second issue. Amir's inclusion of Kahanoff's essays in his journal positioned her as an intellectual figure in Israel only a few years after her arrival in the country.

## Literary Production

Kahanoff once noted that "the role of an artist is, I think, to reflect the multiplicity of a lived and living truth, through the prism of an individual experience, inseparable from an individual style."[4] However, she found the form of personal artistry that she espoused to be a source of both inspiration and limitation. She admitted: "The conflict between an urge for self-expression and a deep distrust of self-exposure is one I have never quite solved. One consequence of this is that I've written quite a lot, but published relatively little, mostly in fragmentary form."[5] The texts included in *Mongrels or Marvels* are intended to assist the reader in patching together the fragments without attempting to create an uncharacteristically seamless whole. We have arranged this volume chronologically by content, starting with the pieces that draw upon anecdotes from Kahanoff's childhood in Egypt and ending with reflections on her place within Israeli culture and society. This organization permits the reader to follow the trajectory of Kahanoff's life, piecing together the recurring themes and issues that span her career. Reading through her masterful works this way, we are struck by the narrative shape she gives her life through her writing. To assist our present-day readers, throughout the book we provide footnotes to historical events and personages of Kahanoff's day, and offer a glossary of terms and concepts at the end of the book that might have been familiar to an Israeli readership but are less well known to an English-speaking audience.

Kahanoff is best known for her nonfiction essays that interweave anecdotes from her personal and family experiences with sociocultural analysis and critique. Through these narrative essays the reader most clearly hears the writer's voice and comes to see her distinctive vision of society. The work with which her name is most closely identified, the "Generation of Levantines" cycle, included in this volume ("Childhood in Egypt," "Europe from Afar," "Rebel, My Brother," and "Israel: Ambivalent Levantine"), defines the genre. In it, through reminiscences and family stories, Kahanoff depicts the multicultural society she experienced in Egypt and employs it as a model for the development of Israeli society.

Her narrative essays were published in Hebrew translation by Israeli literary and intellectual journals. Many of the significant pieces written in this genre are collected in a Hebrew anthology of her works titled *From East the Sun* [*Mi-mizraḥ shemesh*] that appeared in 1978 shortly before her death. That volume, edited by her Hebrew translator Aharon Amir, long constituted the bulk of her legacy in Israeli cultural memory, although at the time of this writing, it is out of print.[6]

Kahanoff also produced fictional work. Indeed, her first extant published pieces, published under the name Jacqueline Shohet, are works of semiautobiographical or, to use her term, "sociologically honest" fiction.[7] Her literary works were warmly received while she was living in the United States as a young woman. She published her first story, "Cairo Wedding," in the journal *Tomorrow* in 1945.[8] The following year, her story "Such Is Rachel" won second prize in a new writers' contest held by the prestigious *Atlantic Monthly*, which published the story.[9] Both stories, included in this volume, reflect situations in which young women strive to break out of patriarchal social strictures.

During the same period in which she succeeded in publishing these stories, Jacqueline also received a Houghton Mifflin fellowship to complete *Jacob's Ladder*, published in the United States and England in 1951. The novel is a coming-of-age narrative of Rachel, the character who first appeared in "Such Is Rachel" and whose family is much like Jacqueline's. The primary conflict in the novel is Rachel's revolt against her English governess, a struggle that occurs against the backdrop of Egyptian resistance to British rule. These works all reflect an innocence, nostalgia, and touch of the exotic that may well have appealed to readers emerging from the shadow of World War II. Readers will find two excerpts from *Jacob's Ladder* in the following pages ("Journey to a Better Land" and "A Line in the Sand").

The tension Kahanoff describes between revealing and concealing herself as an artist through her writing is also evidenced in her production of fiction. In her essay "A Culture Stillborn" Kahanoff explains how her concerns over her family's misgivings about her early efforts prevented her from completing her second novel, a project she worked on for decades. This unpublished novel, *Tamra*, even in its unfinished state, projects a maturity lacking in her early work, and while it remains "sociologically honest," it represents a departure from the overtly autobiographical content of *Jacob's Ladder*. The excerpts from *Tamra* included in this volume ("Ma'adi" and "Alexandria"), depicting a youthful romance between a Jew and a Muslim, represent previously uncharted territory in Kahanoff's repertoire.

During her later years, Kahanoff returned to writing fiction, publishing a handful of short stories in the 1970s. We have included one of them, "To Remember Alexandria," which interweaves the world of memory with the realities of Israeli life.

Throughout her career, Kahanoff also functioned as an important cultural mediator, introducing international literary and intellectual trends to a broad Israeli readership. For example, an article titled "The Literature of Cultural Mutation" ("Sifrut shel mutatsia ḥevratit"), published in the Tel Aviv daily newspaper *Haaretz* in December 1972, discusses the works of Indo-Caribbean writer and Nobel laureate (2001) V. S. Naipaul, the Asian American writer Santha Rama Rau, the Belgian Chinese writer Han Suyin, and the Franco-Tunisian Jewish writer

Albert Memmi. Through the early 1960s Kahanoff regularly contributed articles of cultural and literary criticism to the important, widely read Hebrew newspaper *Ma'ariv*. These reviews discuss the works of such luminaries as Jean-Paul Sartre and Simone de Beauvoir as well as Peggy Guggenheim, Alfred Kazin, Malcolm Lowry, and John Steinbeck. Starting in 1967, she published a regular culture column, "The Spirit of the Times," in *Ba-Mahane*, the journal of the Israeli armed forces, opening new worlds to a generation of Israeli youth. She was also a frequent contributor to *At*, a popular Israeli women's magazine. Topics ranged from a critique of the French *nouveau roman* to meditations on food and culture, and from a discussion of literary archetypes to reflections on the culture of Portugal. While the short format of these popular columns makes them less weighty than her contributions to literary journals, it is through these media that Kahanoff reached her largest audience.

Of this wide-ranging and abundant body of work, a number of longer pieces are worth mentioning individually. In 1963 Kahanoff edited the anthology *Modern African Writing* (in Hebrew) and wrote the introduction to it, presenting the emerging voices of contemporary African poetry and prose to an Israeli readership. In the same year, she published a lengthy study in the journal *Amot* of the French poet Charles Péguy, a writer whose work engaged her for many years.[10] And in 1972 she published a series of articles on contemporary Japanese literature in the literary supplement to the newspaper *Davar*.[11] From this work we see the diversity and global scope of Kahanoff's interests during a period when other leading Israeli writers and intellectuals were engaged with imagining the individual within the state. This work also provides an important counterbalance to her narrative essays and offers a glimpse of the broader horizons she offered to her Israeli readers. We have included one such essay in this volume, "To Live and Die a Copt," a review of *Beer in the Snooker Club*, by Egyptian novelist Waguih Ghali. Ghali, like Kahanoff, wrote in English. The novel she discusses, featuring a romance between a Copt and a Jew, reflects upon the social changes Egypt underwent during the 1950s.

Discussions of Kahanoff's work generally overlook the fact that she was perhaps most prolific as a freelance journalist. Although her journalistic pieces were ephemeral, her work as a journalist adds an important dimension to understanding Kahanoff as a writer. As mentioned above, during her stay in the United States, she studied journalism at Columbia University. Her journalistic career, from which she earned her living, began in Israel in 1956 with a series of articles documenting the experiences of Jewish immigrants to Israel from the Arab-Islamic world, translated into Hebrew, in the daily newspaper *'al-Hamishmar*.[12] In that same year she published two series of articles in the *Jerusalem Post*: one on Moroccan Jewish immigrants living in an outpost community along the Israeli-Egyptian border,[13] and the other on the immigration to Israel of Jews from Egypt.[14] She continued writing as a journalist until the last years of her life, publishing pieces on a wide variety of topics in the Hebrew and English Israeli press, as well as in American Jewish publications, including *Hadassah* magazine, to which she was a regular contributor for more than a decade. The topics she covers in her articles serve as an index to her shifting interests in various aspects of Israeli society over the length of her career. In this volume, we have included one article in this vein, "Reunion in Beersheba," documenting the challenges faced by one bourgeois Egyptian Jewish family as they adapt to a more austere life in Israel during the mid-1950s.

Kahanoff's most substantial journalistic piece was a commissioned book-length report published in 1960 on the Ramat-Hadassah-Szold Youth Aliyah Center for a series by the Fédération Internationale des Communautés d'Enfants (FICE), then a UNESCO-sponsored organization. This project, which documents the organization and pedagogical techniques of the center and provides case studies and statistics, grew out of Kahanoff's experience writing reports for social service agencies during the 1950s. In the preface to the volume she writes: "Born in the Orient and educated in the West, I myself know the difficulties of resolving different worlds within oneself. . . . I became interested in Youth Aliyah not so much because of what it had done for children from Germany twenty-five years back, but because of what it was doing right now to help the children from Iraq, Yemen, Morocco and Egypt find a common language with those from Poland, Hungary, and Rumania."[15]

Another piece with a lasting influence is Kahanoff's "To Die a Modern Death," published in two parts in 1967 in *Keshet*.[16] The essay expresses Kahanoff's reactions to the progression of her father's illness while she attempts to navigate the Byzantine, technocratic Israeli health system in the interests of his care. The piece is a sustained appeal for the reintroduction of dignity and humanity into end-of-life care and remains an important teaching tool for the training of social workers in Israel.

In the late 1970s Kahanoff also documented her own battle with cancer in a series of articles published in *At*.[17] From her sickbed, Kahanoff witnessed the world changing around her. In November 1977, Egyptian president Anwar Sadat visited Israel, the first Arab head of state to do so. Sadat's visit and the subsequent peace negotiations leading to the Camp David Accords in September 1978, and culminating in the March 1979 peace treaty between Egypt and Israel, were particularly momentous for Egyptian Jews living in Israel.[18] As the borders opened between the countries, many Egyptian Jews returned to visit their old home. Kahanoff was in no physical condition to join them; however, she mustered the strength to compose two short reflections on these developments, both of which are included in this volume. The first, "My Brother Ishmael: On the Visit of Anwar Sadat," appeared in the December 1977 issue of *At* within a special section of essays welcoming the Egyptian president at the time of his visit. The second, "Welcome, Sadat," Kahanoff composed as an afterword to *From East the Sun* published in 1978. Kahanoff also personally sent copies of this essay and the book to Egyptian First Lady Jehan Sadat. These reflections on Sadat's visit and the possibilities of peace between Egypt and Israel are the last works she wrote.

## Reflections on Levantinism

As mentioned above, Kahanoff's reputation as a writer is most closely identified with the "Generation of Levantines" essays and the critical rubric of Levantinism that she began to develop in her work during the late 1950s. The Levant has a long history of cultural contact and exchange. As Kahanoff's friend and colleague Nissim Rejwan notes, the term *Levantine* describes individuals who embody this admixture: "to be a Levantine is to live in two worlds or more at once without belonging to either."[19] Kahanoff's Levantinism functions as both history and social theory, oscillating between description and prescription, the past and the future. The past she documents is the Egyptian Levantine society of her youth, and the future is an imagined pluralist society within Israel, which in her later work is extended to a utopian cosmopolitan society spreading throughout the Levant. Her representations of the past are fraught simultaneously with reverential nostalgia and distaste, yet in her writings she returns to that society over again as a flawed but once functioning model of pluralism. The United States and France proved disappointing to Kahanoff, as she felt alienated by segregation and elitism, respectively. Nevertheless, we can trace her intellectual formation and the origins of Levantinism to her work published during her years in the United States in which she first depicts the multicultural but deeply divided patriarchal milieu in which she was raised.

When Kahanoff arrived in Israel in the mid-1950s, she found a state emerging out of an ideological movement, a society in formation. Kahanoff's notion of Levantinism developed in this context. Through Levantinism she takes up the utopian spirit of the Zionist project, but her proposed social model calling for the revival of "the Levant as a geographic entity, comprising many genuinely native peoples and cultures" sits uncomfortably with Zionist ideology, which espoused the abandonment of the diasporic past in order to create a modern Israeli identity.[20] Kahanoff chose to make Israel her home, and her writing demonstrates a commitment to improving the functioning of its society. Yet, although she lived and wrote in an era that valued the collective, she refused to conform to dominant ideologies, maintaining her individualism and her critical voice.

Kahanoff did not invent the term *Levantine* nor its application within the Israeli context; rather, she inverted its meaning and reclaimed it. As critic Gil Hochberg articulates, the Levantine is "a *borderline figure* that marks the slippery lines between West and East and as such is found to be inferior not only to Europe but also to Europe's imagined Other, the Orient."[21] When in the early 1950s Israel experienced large waves of immigration of Jews from the Arab and Islamic worlds, there was much consternation over the effect their cultural integration might have on the relatively new state. This vision was anathema to the Socialist Zionist parties under the leadership of David Ben Gurion, who viewed Levantinization, or the infusion of "oriental" tendencies into Israeli culture, as a corrupting force. Absorption of these immigrants was conducted with a patronizing attitude toward their cultural heritage, and educational programs assumed developmental backwardness in terms of both skills and intellectual potential.

By labeling her model Levantinism, Kahanoff appropriated the loaded term that had taken on these negative connotations as a tool for redressing the discriminatory policies it fostered. In the words of one critic: "From the first publication of her essays, Jacqueline Kahanoff caused a revolution in the term 'Levantinism.' This was a 'revolution' in the meaning from a shameful word to a possible description of honor for people who exist in dual cultures."[22] As we see in the writings included in this volume, throughout her life Kahanoff indeed validated hybrid cultural identities.[23]

But her writings on Levantinism transcend a feel-good multiculturalism in order to explore its potential to function as a model for constructing a just, pluralist society. Kahanoff's writing is nuanced and engaging, and her sober tone radically contrasts with the hysterical pitch of those who predicted Levantinization as the corruption and downfall of Israeli culture.

However, Kahanoff maintained an unrealistic optimism toward the social possibilities of the Egyptian, bourgeois Levantine model. Her perspective is perhaps attributable to her departure from Egypt before the cosmopolitan society she writes about went into steep decline. She left Cairo for the United States in 1940, returning to visit her family in 1946, at which time Egypt was in great upheaval as pressure mounted on the British to evacuate their troops from Egyptian soil once and for all. The Jewish community was not much affected at this stage by the anticolonial struggle, however, and Western influence was still very much in evidence. Kahanoff did not have any firsthand knowledge of the effect on Egyptian society of the events of 1952—the burning of Cairo in January and the coup d'etat in July—nor of the repercussions of the 1956 Suez conflict on the communities of foreigners and Jews.

In the wake of the radical transformation of the regional balance of power following the 1967 Arab-Israeli war, Kahanoff recast her conception of Levantinism into a vision of a cosmopolitan society encompassing the entire region. Her writing from this period hews closer to mainstream Israeli political rhetoric than her earlier writings. In an unpublished essay, "From East the Sun," dating from 1968, which we have included in this volume as the author's afterword, Kahanoff writes, "Reconstructing a pluralist Levant may offer a workable alternative to imperialism, neocolonialism, Christian, Moslem, or Great-Power rivalries and domination, by suggesting a framework in which people have the right to be free, different, and equal, rather than one in which the 'superior' would subject, eliminate, or at best tolerate others in the name of universalism."

This vision is likely to strike the present-day reader as culturally imperialist. Indeed, although Kahanoff devoted a great deal of effort to unmasking legacies of European imperialism and internal forces of colonialism within Israeli society, she never recognized her own colonizing tendencies toward Arab-Islamic culture. Her social model is derived from a notion of a Levantine subculture composed primarily of minorities that served as a bridge between East and West but had little direct contact with the majority culture outside of their milieu. The disconnect from Arab culture is present in many of her writings but is particularly evident in a passage from *Jacob's Ladder* included in this volume, "A Line in the Sand," in which the young protagonist, Rachel, tries and fails to overcome her stereotypes of Muslim Egyptians. This passage is striking both for its honest portrayal of the prevalent cultural stereotypes and for the unsettling effect it produces in today's reader. When in her later work, such as the 1973 essay "A Culture Stillborn," Kahanoff begins to contend with the role of Arab culture in the formation, fostering, and demise of Levantine society in Egypt, we see a world of limited possibilities that appears doomed to fail.

Although her efforts to create a social model are circumscribed by these limitations of vision, Kahanoff's work demonstrates a deep commitment to social justice. Throughout her life Kahanoff advocated for gender equality. Her voice of resistance to the patriarchal society in which she was raised is perhaps most evident in her two early short stories "Cairo Wedding" and "Such Is Rachel." In the 1970s, fired by the success of political feminism in the United States and Europe, Kahanoff again turned her attention to women's roles in society, from technology and the economy to culture and the arts. Many of these pieces first appeared in publications geared toward women. Yet, interestingly, despite the very personal tenor of much of her work and her keen awareness of gender issues, in her writing she rarely reflects on her experience as a female intellectual in Israel.

## Kahanoff's Legacy

Jacqueline Shohet Kahanoff died in Tel Aviv in October 1979 at the age of sixty-two. Although her career as a writer of essays and fiction in Israel spanned less than two decades, her work has had a lasting effect on Israeli culture. Much loved by her peers, she was a welcome guest and sometime hostess to literary salons in Tel Aviv during the 1960s. Her essays were read during her lifetime by a generation that produced such Israeli literary luminaries as A. B. Yehoshua, Amos Oz, David Grossman, and Yehoshua Kenaz.

Other Israeli Hebrew writers have viewed their acquaintance with Kahanoff's writing as an integral part of their literary formation. The main influence of her essays was their ideational content; the literary form that she introduced to the Hebrew-reading public, the narrative essay, has not to date been emulated. Her ideas concerning the desirable place of Israel among its neighbors and vis-à-vis the modern world continue to permeate the writings of a younger generation of Israeli novelists, poets, and essayists. In particular, Kahanoff's brand of Levantinism has inspired writers such as Ronit Matalon and Nissim Calderon. Indeed, Matalon signaled this influence by including a character named Jacqueline Kahanoff in her novel *The One Facing Us* and reproduced two of Kahanoff's "Generation of Levantines" essays within the narrative.[24] Levantinism, as transformed in meaning by Kahanoff, has encouraged Jewish intellectuals in Israel of Middle Eastern origin to search for artistic means by which to express their own complex identities. According to Ammiel Alcalay, the publication of Kahanoff's collection of essays *From East the Sun* in 1978, and the rediscovery of her work by a generation coming of age during the late 1970s, arrived at a critical juncture in the development and expression of Mizraḥi identity in literature and film.[25]

Kahanoff's lasting influence on Israeli culture today can be illustrated further by the fact that in 2009 the Van Leer Institute of Jerusalem, one of the foremost Israeli research institutes in social and cultural studies, advertised the launching of a biannual scholarly publication titled *Journal of Levantine Studies*. In past years, it will be remembered, the adjective *Levantine* was hardly ever used in connection with high culture. The change of heart to a great extent can be explained by the cumulative effect of Kahanoff's writing on Israeli society three decades after her death.

Kahanoff is a notable example of an intellectual who did not belong to the cultures in which she operated but whose influence was nevertheless significant. She was born the year of the Balfour Declaration, but she was never a full-fledged Zionist; she was born two years before the 1919 Egyptian Revolution, but she was never a full-fledged Egyptian. While Kahanoff's life and its vicissitudes, as represented in her writings, are interesting in and of themselves, the influence that her mature works have had on a large cross-section of the Israeli intellectual elite makes her unique.

Although Kahanoff's work had its greatest effect on the Israeli literary scene, it is important to remember that she was a multinational writer with global vision. She began her writing efforts in Egypt, publishing in Francophone literary journals. As described above, her literary efforts in the United States between 1945 and 1951 were warmly received, and she continued publishing in American Jewish journals throughout her life. Even once she had settled in Israel, she maintained an interest in literary and cultural trends in North America, Europe, Africa, and Asia—an interest reflected in her writings throughout her career. It is this breadth and the universality of her vision that make her appealing to audiences outside of Israel as well.

The title of this volume, *Mongrels or Marvels*, is drawn from Kahanoff's novel *Jacob's Ladder*. In a passage near the beginning of the novel, which serves as the epigraph to this volume, Samuel, a successful businessman in Cairo with a Western education, addresses his elderly father, Jacob: "You have wished us to celebrate within ourselves a kind of marriage between East and West. Was there ever a perfect marriage? Cross-breeding produces mongrels or marvels, and that is what we risked." Like this troubled marriage, Kahanoff's writings evidence an ongoing struggle between her Eastern and Western desires and impulses. Her works simultaneously express a resistance to assimilation, to the loss of cultural difference. It is the complexity of this hybridity—dismissed as mongrelization by the Israeli society in which Kahanoff produced her works and embraced with wide-eyed wonder by Kahanoff herself—that we wish to evoke in our selection of title.

## Notes

1. Gudrun Krämer, *The Jews in Modern Egypt, 1914–1952* (Seattle: University of Washington Press, 1989), 10.

2. "Mi-mitzrayim ve-'ad henah," *Ma'ariv*, Oct. 4, 1967: 36.

3. Nissim Rejwan, *Outsider in the Promised Land: An Iraqi Jew in Israel* (Austin: University of Texas Press, 2006), 68–71.

4. "Mi-mitzrayim ve-'ad henah," 33.

5. Ibid.

6. A posthumous Hebrew anthology of some works not included in *From East the Sun* [*Mi-mizraḥ shemesh*] (Tel Aviv: Hadar, 1978) has served to introduce the scope of Kahanoff's writings to a new generation of Israeli readers: *Ben shene 'olamot*, ed. David Ohana (Jerusalem: Keter, 2005).

7. "A Culture Stillborn," included in this volume.

8. *Tomorrow* 4, no. 11 (July 1945): 19–23.

9. *Atlantic Monthly* 177, no. 10 (1946): 113–116.

10. *Amot* 1, no. 5 (June–July 1963): 44–58; 2, no. 1 (Aug.–Sept. 1963): 50–65.

11. This five-part series, called "'Al ha-sifrut ha-yapanit," was published in *Masa*: "Nikudot le-hashva'ah 'im sifrut eropa," Sept. 22, 1972: 3; "Tor hazahav shel nashim kotvot," Oct. 6, 1972: 4; "Hashpa'ot ma'araviyot b'ad ve-neged," Oct. 20, 1972: 4; "'Olamo shel mishima," Nov. 3, 1972: 4; and "Kawabata—omanut be-tamtsitah," Nov. 17, 1972.

12. The three-article series, called "Gesher el 'ole ha mizraḥ," was published under the byline Dimona: "Hem Zekukim la-ozen kashevet," Aug. 3, 1956; "Lo hevinu et Regina?," Aug. 10, 1956; and "Ba-gilat 'kevar ayn b'ayot,'" Aug. 17, 1956.

13. The two-article series, called "Facing the Gaza Strip," was published under the byline Dina Monet: "Young Moroccan Immigrants Pioneer the Negev," Oct. 12, 1956: 4; and "The Sten Gun and the Book," Oct. 14, 1956: 4.

14. The series of five articles in the *Jerusalem Post* appeared under the byline Dina Monet: "Egypt's Jewish Community Played Decisive Role in Country's Modernization," Dec. 21, 1956: 5; "Jews Emerged from Egypt's Ghetto: School and Health Services Were Community's Top Concerns," Dec. 23, 1956: 4; "Nasser's

Nazi Experts Efficient: Cairo Jews Thought Israel Foundering," Dec. 24, 1956: 4; "Jewish Refugees from Egypt Difficult to Locate: Chaos and Terror Mark Mass Exodus," Dec. 27, 1956: 4; and "Absorption of Egypt's Aliya in Good Hands," Dec. 31, 1956: 4.

15. *Ramat-Hadassah-Szold: Youth Aliyah Screening and Classification Centre* (Jerusalem: Publishing Dept. of the Jewish Agency at Goldberg's Press, 1960), 13–14.

16. "Lamut mitah modernit," *Keshet* 9, no. 2 (winter 1967): 5–27; *Keshet* 9, no. 4 (summer 1967): 108–123. Reprinted in *Mi-mizraḥ shemesh*, 225–270.

17. "Yoman maḥelah," *At*, Mar. 1977: 40–41; Apr. 1977: 52–53. Ruth Peled offers a fictionalized account of Kahanoff's final days in her novel *Mehalekh Aḥaron* (Tel Aviv: Sifriyat Poalim, 1985).

18. For more on this topic, see Joel Beinin, *The Dispersion of Egyptian Jewry: Culture, Politics, and the Formation of a Modern Diaspora* (Berkeley: University of California Press, 1998), 207–240.

19. Rejwan, *Outsider in the Promised Land*, 81.

20. Quotation from "Afterword: From East the Sun," included in this volume.

21. Gil Hochberg, *In Spite of Partition: Jews, Arabs, and the Limits of Separatist Imagination* (Princeton, NJ: Princeton University Press, 2007), 46.

22. Yaira Ginossar, "'Otzmat ha-kfilut," *Iton* 77 (May–June 1978): 14.

23. Hochberg discusses, interprets, and expands upon this idea in *In Spite of Partition*, 50–54.

24. The English edition of the novel includes only one essay by Kahanoff. *Zeh 'im ha-panim elenu* (Tel Aviv: 'Am 'oved, 1995); *The One Facing Us*, trans. Marsha Weinstein (New York: Metropolitan, 1998). For discussions of Matalon's citation of Kahanoff, see Hochberg, *In Spite of Partition*, 54–66; and Deborah Starr, *Remembering Cosmopolitan Egypt: Literature, Culture and Empire* (London: Routledge, 2009), 134–146.

25. Ammiel Alcalay, *After Jews and Arabs: Remaking Levantine Culture* (Minneapolis: University of Minnesota Press, 1993), 249.

*Mongrels or Marvels*

*One*

# Childhood in Egypt

*This essay, first published in 1959, represents the colorful debut installment of Jacqueline Kahanoff's "Generation of Levantines" cycle. Out of her sense of alienation from the traditions of the East and exclusion from European modernity, Kahanoff forges a hybrid "Levantine" identity that she hopes will be imbued with the power to effect change. For Kahanoff, this identity is an expression of her cosmopolitan aspirations for her generation "to become free citizens of the universe."*

When I was a small child, it seemed natural that people understood each other although they spoke different languages, and were called by different names—Greek, Moslem,* Syrian, Jewish, Christian, Arab, Italian, Tunisian, Armenian. I was aware that Arabs were more numerous than other people, and poorer: they were servants, peddlers, and beggars who showed arms without hands, legs without feet, eyes without sight, and called out to Allah to send them a meager *piaster*. The children scavenged in garbage pails for something to eat. Rich Arabs were pashas, but then many of them were Turks, and the Turkish ladies were princesses. One only caught a glimpse of them when they passed in their carriages. They wore a little bit of white veil around their heads and chins, while the Arab women were all wrapped up in black.



* Kahanoff consistently uses the spelling "Moslem," which was common at the time she was writing. The editors have elected to retain this spelling in Kahanoff's texts. In the introduction and notes the editors spell the term "Muslim" in keeping with current academic standards.

Moslems prayed kneeling on small rugs when the muezzin called them to prayer from the top of a minaret; it was a sad, beautiful song that filled the sky when the sun fell and disappeared. But in the morning, it returned to shine on everything, and that was why one prayed to God: to thank him for the Light.

It was a friendly world, with something exciting always going on. Crowds milled about in their brightest clothes for *Bairam*, after the Ramadan fast, and peddlers sold them magnificent sugar dolls in bright tinseled paper clothes, with little bells jingling on their heads. There were processions when the Holy Carpet returned from Mecca, or when the King opened Parliament; then all the streets were covered with orange sand and decorated with banners and festoons of light bulbs that shone brightly at night. At Easter time some shops sold chocolate eggs. Later, the Greek grocery stores sold eggs dyed in the most beautiful dark shades of purple, orange, and green. There was one holiday, *Shamm al-Nissim*, the Feast of the Sun, when absolutely everybody celebrated the spring by having a picnic by the Nile.

Mother said that before going to sleep, it was good to remember all the nice things that happened that day, and there were lots of them, even on ordinary days. Sometimes camels came into town, carrying bundles of fresh-smelling greens in the rope bats flung across their humps, and it was funny the way they twisted their mouths, always chewing on something. Often my uncle Nono would invite me to see the new toys they had received at the store, and he said I could choose anything I wanted, although Mother scolded him for spoiling me too much. Or there were uncles and aunts who came from Paris or Manchester for weddings or business affairs. There were days, late in summer, when Nono and Uncle David distributed among their married children the good things they had received from Tunis—olive oil, and delicious big green olives, dates, and muscat grapes that were so good, that when we had a party to eat them together, everybody, even the children, were tipsy.

On Sundays, old Maria, our maid, sometimes took me with her to early mass in St. Joseph's Cathedral, where fat little angels floated among the pink clouds painted inside the domed blue ceiling. Father said I could go because God was everywhere, but that I must never,

never dip my fingers in Holy Water or make the sign of the Cross, because I was Jewish. Every people had its religion, he said, just as every bird had its song, and God loved and understood them all. Our religion, he said, was to await the coming of the Messiah, who would bring the day when people could love one another almost as God loved them all. I hoped that the Messiah would come quickly so that everybody could enjoy everything about other people's religions, as well as their own.

Our religion was also a mysterious language of prayers, called Hebrew, which only the men recited and understood. But, what was being Jewish most of all was to visit my father's parents, far, far away in the Abbassiyah quarter, where they lived in a little house surrounded by jasmine and honeysuckle. My grandfather Jacob, who came from Baghdad, sat in a long robe, with a turban on his head. He intimidated me because of his white beard and the prayer books which lay on a table at his side. My father gave me a little push, and I knelt before this old grandfather, who was also like a priest, to kiss his hand as my father had done, and received his blessing. When Grandfather Jacob's hand rested on my head, I felt that this blessing was something ancient and precious, a treasure, which the grandfathers of our grandfathers had received from God. Because of this blessing, I was in God's safekeeping and belonged to the people of the stories in the old prayer books.

There were no real pictures in this grandfather's house; that was forbidden, but there were two frames containing writing on the plain white-washed wall, which I always saw as I lifted my head after the blessing. Father explained that one was the Ten Commandments in Hebrew, which God had given to Moses when they waited in the desert before entering the Promised Land, and these commandments told people what was right and what was wrong. The other was the Balfour Declaration, in English, and it said that the time was soon to come when we would return to our Promised Land. This land was called Erets Yisrael, Father said, but now it is called Palestine, for we had lost our Promised Land. But we should remember that the Lord God of Israel had promised it to the sons of Jacob.

"To the daughters too?" I asked, and, smiling, my father said yes, to the daughters too, for Israel honored its women, the daughters of

Rachel and Sarah. I thought how beautiful it was that the people in my family had the same names as those in the stories.

My grandmother sat on a couch in another room, draped in gray silk, her legs crossed under her. She was religious, and wore over her black wig a kerchief decorated with many crocheted flowers which dangled on her forehead with each of her movements, and which made her look young. Although I was told she was not beautiful, to me, this ancient Jewish queen, who never shouted and before whom people lowered their voices, was more than beautiful. I wanted the years to fly quickly, till I became an old grandmother just like her. My father's parents were the only people I knew who were in total harmony with themselves, inwardly and outwardly, who accepted themselves as they were and did not want to be other than they were.

I remember one summer we were in a hotel in Alexandria, by the sea. It was full of English officers and their wives, and one lady asked me what I was. I did not know what to answer. I knew I was not Egyptian like the Arabs, and that it was shameful not to know what one was. And so, thinking of my grandparents, I replied that I was Jewish and Persian, believing that Baghdad, the city they came from, was in the country from which all beautiful rugs came. Later, my mother chided me for not telling the truth, and said that when people asked me such a question, I should say I was European. I suffered because I knew this was not the truth either, and I burned with shame when the English ladies who had been nice to me laughed about "the little girl who wanted to be Persian."

I knew that my father suffered too, but I could do nothing about it. The image of his parents became something precious and secret I kept locked in my heart. They were the pillars that supported the frail bridge which tied me to my past, and without which there could be no future.

Whenever we passed the Qasr al-Nil bridge, where the English barracks were, I thought of the desert far away where the past slept under the sand. This was the treasure I must find when I would be grown up and free, so that the past could come alive and become the future. Sometimes the bridge opened to let white-sailed feluccas pass on their way to or from the mysterious place where the river and the world began. I thought that if once I stood at the edge of the bridge, just when it opened in the middle, I would fall into a felucca and be carried to that beginning, or to that end, where the river flowed into God, which was like a beginning. But perhaps I would miss the boat, and drown, sucked in by the whirlpools. I was safe only when I stood on the bridge. I knew that the feluccas traveled between Aswan and the Delta, carrying onions and watermelons, but the mythical river was my real world, where no harm would befall me.

We moved to a different house, where the river flowed by my window, and beyond it the three triangles of the pyramids spoke mysteriously of the time when everything called history started, long, long before English tutors taught us to read *Alice in Wonderland* and French schoolteachers made us memorize all kinds of nonsense about our ancestors the Gauls. The Wonderland was here, where our ancestors had created what the books called "ancient civilizations" at a time when the Gauls were savages clad in the skins of wild beasts, whose flesh they ate raw.

We played by the river where Pharaoh's daughter had found Moses, and where He, who would be the Messiah, was perhaps already born, a little child sleeping amidst the reeds. The Messiah would surely usher in a time when there would be no Christians, no Moslems, and no Jews, no white, black, brown, or pink people, and no princes who rushed by in their big red cars, so hardened by the thick crust of their wealth that they could not see, hear, or smell the poor who crouched by the gates of the Qasr al-'Aini hospital, where the air was foul from the stench of their sores. Barefooted, the princes would then approach them, and the crippled, the sick, and the poor would rise, forgive them, and be whole again.

My friend Marie, a Catholic, said that the Messiah had already come, and that he was Jesus. I could not bear to think the Messiah had come, and failed, without God giving men another chance, as he had done so often since the time of the Great Flood. Perhaps, I thought, many false Messiahs had to come, to suffer and to die before every person could open his heart to Him who would come last. Jews were people who knew that another Messiah had yet to come, and that was why they waited. No matter what happened they would wait. That was their faith, their hope, their belief, that the Kingdom of Heaven would and could be on earth, in every man.

Marie spoke constantly of charity but accepted poverty as something to be compensated for in heaven. She was a Syrian, and like me, was half-native Levantine. She, too, was humiliated by our embittered British spinster teachers, but she never dreamt of revenge. She spoke of turning the other cheek, of meek resignation, of enduring one's sufferings for the love of Christ. I admired Marie; she also troubled and infuriated me. Marie never got angry. She told me I sinned through pride, and that people were not able to tell good from evil without the guidance of the Church. She pleaded with me and prayed for my conversion; she loved me and did not want me to burn in Hell because the Jews had killed Christ. I would retort, "When *my* Messiah comes, He will save everyone, even those who do not believe in him. And if he doesn't come, I don't want to be saved while other people burn in Hell. It's too unjust."

I racked my brain to find these arguments. I had had no formal religious instruction and had fitted together, as best I could, the notions I had gleaned from books, from the English translation of the Haggadah my father had given me for Passover and from what he told me of my religion. I was grateful for his trying. But one thing would often remind him of another, just like when people told stories in Arabic, so that I didn't know exactly where a story began or ended, and what was important and what was not.

When I passed by the English barracks, I would remember Gulliver, a sleeping giant, pinned down to earth by thousands of threads nailed to the ground by thousands of little people. It occurred to me that perhaps our thoughts were like those threads. If we kept winding them between our heads and our hearts every day for years on end, like an invisible spider spinning a web around the barracks, then one day, all of us could pull together, and the slumbering giant would awake. But alas, too late. The barracks would crack open, like the Philistines' Temple, and an avalanche of stones and pink-faced soldiers would be hurled into the Nile when its waters were high, and disappear forever, sucked in by the whirlpools. Then, when the English soldiers were gone, we would lock up our nannies and Misses in chicken coops, and parade them in the streets, lined with orange sand, like when the King opened Parliament, so that everyone on our street would have a good laugh before we shipped them back to His Majesty King George.

I wondered if other children had such thoughts, and feared that perhaps I was mad. I tried to reason with myself. The Messiah who would come would most certainly forgive even the British soldiers and the English Misses, so before He came perhaps I should forgive them myself, and if I did, perhaps they would just go away. But I couldn't forgive. I didn't really want to. The truth was that I loved hating them more than loving them, because it excited and thrilled me, while love was something tranquil and restful, like sleep. But, if people loved to hate, then there was no difference between the black, the brown, the white, and it did not matter whether or not the barracks were destroyed, because the Messiah who would come would fail, as Jesus had failed, as Moses had failed, and nothing would change, and if nothing could change, there was no sense even in being Jewish and waiting for the Messiah to come.

This riddle was in the Haggadah, which I loved because it taught me that we were the people who would be given the Promised Land. God himself had not been able to soften Pharaoh's heart, nor make him give up his wicked power over another people. God had had to force Pharaoh by threatening him with the Ten Plagues, and He hoped that after each one Pharaoh's heart would be filled with pity. But Pharaoh loved his power and his wealth, and rather than give them up, he let the crops which fed his own people be devoured by locusts, and the river which fed their fields be turned to blood, and the first-born die in the little mud huts which were like those of the fellahin.

After all that Moses had sacrificed for them, even his own people had worshipped the Golden Calf, which was very much like Tutankhamen's mummy case in the Museum of Egyptian Antiquities. Moses, who was the son of an Egyptian princess, died of sorrow, thinking of those who had perished en route and were refused entry to the Promised Land. We, his people, had not been worthy of the Promised Land, and would weep in exile until we learned to know what we had been chosen *for*. Then we would return to the Promised Land once more, the Messiah would come, and all would be peace and harmony. Everything would be different. We and the Egyptians would be free together, and no one would set us against each other.

To make this happy end possible, I had to find out why things had turned out so badly in Pharaoh's time. I could do this only by elaborating fantasies around symbols, because I did not know the words needed to express my thoughts. True, I was very young, but I also felt that none of the languages we spoke could express our thoughts, because none was our own. We were a people without a tongue and could speak only through signs and symbols. Our elders spoke of ordinary, everyday things, or about religion. Their religion was to say *maktub*, *inshallah*, "amen", "Our Father who art in Heaven," and to pray and fast sometimes; but it did not say anything about the things that were so difficult for us in life. Whether, for instance, it was right to want the British to go, and wrong to hate them, right to learn so many things from them and from their schools, but wrong not to want to be like the British and French, or our parents, or the Arabs. We were searching for something *within* ourselves which we had yet to find. Religion seemed to have nothing to do with how people lived, and this did not seem to worry them, although they said that religion explained life and told them what they must do.

At school, we learned other things, but there too, we learned nothing about ourselves or what we should do. We did not know how it had happened that Jewish, Greek, Moslem, and Armenian girls sat together to learn about the French Revolution, *patrie*, *liberté*, *égalité*, *fraternité*. None of us had experienced any of these things. Not even our teachers really believed these words had anything to do with our lives. They seemed to think it was right for us to want to be like French children, although they must have known that we could not really become French, and that they did not really want us to be their equals or their brothers, and that actually we were nobody at all. What were we supposed to be when we grew up if we could be neither Europeans nor natives, nor even pious Jews, Moslems, or Christians, as our grandparents had been?

It was impossible to question anyone about these things. One could not ask one's parents, who kept saying they spent so much money to give us an education and advantages they had not had (and this was true), nor our teachers, who would laugh at us without even trying to understand. I could not share my feelings and thoughts with anyone, not even the other children, because I had no way of knowing if they were really happy and if they really believed the world we grew up in was true and good, or if they only pretended, as I did, because they were frightened and could not speak out. It was only through fantasies that I could explain this inexplicable little world to myself, and be able to fit it into a larger world, where I could find my place.

In one such fantasy I imagined a ruby and a lightning rod. The ruby was an inheritance received from my grandfather. A gentle fire glowed in its depth, and whoever held it knew the answers to all questions, and was at peace. I would fall asleep, my hand clutching this imaginary treasure, but when I woke up at night, my hand was always open. The ruby was gone. I believed that a wicked priest had risen from a dream and stolen it. Nothing could check this priest's power once he possessed both the ruby and the lightning rod—except trickery and deceit.

The rod was light and fire, but it was a cold, hard, white light, and whoever touched it died instantly unless he owned a magic glove. When its rays touched men it made them work to build pyramids and bridges, and when it pierced the ground, the earth surrendered its riches. The lightning rod was in the movement of machines, trains, ships, and airplanes. It did things without thinking, while the ruby which had knowledge of all things, did nothing. The Master of the World used the rod to make life, and it was good when the ruby directed its action. The ruby was the jewel at the center of Pharaoh's crown, and the rod was the staff in his hand.

Pharaoh grew weary of holding the rod, as the power in it always wanted to strike, and from this power the wicked priest was born when Pharaoh slept. He persuaded Pharaoh to let him lock the rod in his temple, and replaced it by a stick. Then he stole the ruby, which he in turn replaced by another red stone. Pharaoh then became a statue, a dead, motionless god. But the people, seeing him with the ruby and the rod, did not know that he was dead, and that the wicked priest ruled by the rod alone. That is why they did not understand their own misery.

Pharaoh's daughter knew these things but, being a woman, she did not have the power to change them. She found the child Moses, and told him the secret. He became a novice in the temple, where he learned to use the power of the rod, which he caught and held in his own staff. He found the ruby too, and hid it in the desert, thinking that he could always return to it after he had defeated the wicked priest. When Moses challenged the wicked priest, he had to make his plagues more powerful than those devised by the wicked priest, but he could not stop them because he did not have the ruby. Even God could not stop the plagues, because if He made miracles men would not learn the meaning of their deeds and He would have to unmake the world He had created, starting from when he made the apple so tempting in the Garden of Eden that Adam and Eve *had* to eat it in order to learn right from wrong.

In the Wilderness of Sinai, Moses knew that even if he had not trusted in the ruby, but only in the rod, he would have died of a broken heart. After he died, mankind would be divided into two parts, those who remembered the ruby, and lived only to seek it in themselves, and those who knew only the power of the rod. The first were the People of the East, and because they rejected knowledge of the rod, they worked only if driven, grew lazy, sick, and poor, and waited idly for something to happen. The people of Europe knew only the rod which coldly lit their darkness; and because they created machines and electricity, they worked and made others work. They ruled the earth, but without understanding. I thought the Messiah would finally arise from those people who kept the memory of oneness, with each person yearning for that part in himself which was lost. The Promised Land was where they would meet and be one, the people of the ruby and the rod, in whom all things would be united.

When I reached adolescence, these fantasies lost their grip on me, or rather they expressed themselves more deviously through rational thoughts and political sympathies. I was not entirely aware that I was pretending to believe in certain ideas because they were already clearly formulated, while I could not express my own, partly for fear of appearing absurd, and partly because a reflex of self-defense prompted me to keep secret what was my own. This measure of deceit and self-deception, which disguised self-doubt was—and still is—characteristic of my Levantine generation. We thought ourselves to be Socialist, even Communist, and in our schoolyard we ardently discussed the Blum* government, Soviet Russia, the civil war in Spain, revolution, materialism, and the rights

* Léon Blum (1872–1950) was elected prime minister of France in June 1936. He was the first Socialist and the first Jew to hold that office.

of women, particularly free love. The only language we could think in was the language of Europe, and our deeper selves were submerged under this crust of European dialectics, a word we loved to use. We talked and pretended to act as we imagined the youth of French lycées in France talked and acted, without being fully aware that they were still within a traditional framework which we had lost, and for which we envied them. We blithely dismissed everything that was not Left as reactionary, and because we were culturally displaced and dispossessed, without yet being able to define our predicament, we did not fully realize that our motives were not those of French youth, and were neither as pure nor as generous as we had imagined them to be. Revolution, which would destroy a world where we did not have our rightful place, would create another, where we could belong. We wanted to break out of the narrow minority framework into which we were born, to strive toward something universal, and we were ashamed of the poverty of what we called "the Arab masses," and of the advantages a Western education had given us over them.

*

Our parents were pro-British as a matter of business and security, and we were pro-nationalist as a matter of principle, although we knew few Moslems of our age. We felt this nationalism was an inevitable step on the road to liberation and true internationalism and, sensing that we might be sacrificed to it, we accepted it as unavoidable and even morally justified. We hesitated between devoting ourselves to the "masses" and going to study in Europe, to settle there and become Europeans. In later years, many of us switched from one attitude to another, or attempted to achieve some compromise between them, the most usual being to help educate or improve the lot of the Arab masses either by social work or by preaching Communist doctrine. Some of us became cynics, bent on enjoying our advantages "while there was still time," but some of us were acutely aware of our dilemma and the difficult choices before us. We felt cut off from the people and the country in which we lived, and knew that nothing would come of us unless we could build a bridge to a new society. Revolution and Marxism seemed the only way to attain a future which would include both our European mentors and the Arab masses. We would no longer be what we were, but become free citizens of the universe.

There was in us a strong mixture of desperate sincerity and of pretense, a tremendous thirst for truth and knowledge, coupled with an obscure desire for vindication, from both the arrogant domination of Europe and the Moslem majority which, we did not quite forget, despised its minorities. We would be generous and get even with the Moslem masses by introducing them to hygiene and Marxism.

Few of us Jews were Zionists, because we believed that for humanity to be free, we had to give up our narrow individuality as other people were expected to or, at most, we argued that the Jewish people had a right to national existence as did all other people, as an inevitable preliminary to "international Socialism."

I said these things, as my friends did, but wondered if they too only half-believed and were biding their time before speaking up with their own voices. Our teachers expounded knowledge from on high, and most of us who sat, heads bowed, taking notes were Jews, Greeks, and Syrians, the Levantines, those whom the Moslems called with superstitious respect and suspicion, the People of the Book. We the Jews, and the Greeks, were always there, had always been there, changing the world more than we changed ourselves, remaining the same under our many guises. Other people passed us by, and we bowed our heads until their power spent itself. Our teachers, too, would depart, but we would pass on the ferment of knowledge, making history in our insidious, secretive way, without ever being totally undone by it. Perhaps in our own time, we would witness and share in the undoing of Europe's dominion, the fall of all its barracks, and even, perhaps, a return to the Promised Land. What would we, the Levantines, do in that world which would be ours, as well? In any case this new world would have to wait for us—we who were still in the schoolroom—to give it a different color and shape.

Throughout our Mediterranean world, and the vast continents it bordered, other young people were imbibing this knowledge from their teachers, never suspecting that the dormant seeds would suddenly burst out from under the silt of centuries. The Arabs and the other colonized peoples were the crossbreeds of many cultures by accident, while we Levantines were inescapably so, by vocation and destiny. Perhaps our ways would part, but together, we belonged to the Levantine generation, whose task and privilege it was to translate European thought and action and apply it to our own world. We needed to find the words that would shake the universe out of its torpor and give voice to our confused protests. We were the first generation of Levantines in the contemporary world who sought a truth that was neither in the old religions nor in complete surrender to the West, and this, perhaps, should be recorded.

In later life our paths sometimes crossed, and we could talk with our own voices, Greeks, Moslems, Syrians, Copts, and Jews; those who became Arab nationalists, and Zionists, Stalinists, and Trotskyites, Turkish princesses in exile, priests and rebels. We talked of our youth when our souls were torn, and were so divided within ourselves that we had feared we could never recover. Yes, we had mastered words, a language in which to frame thoughts that were nearly our own. We were moved to discover how close we had been to each other in our youth, although it was perhaps too late to make any difference. Our choices had commanded other choices, which locked us in a position from which, in the adult world, there was no retreat.

Today, when we can no longer meet and talk, we know that history is our childish fantasies come true, and that they sometimes turn into nightmares. In newspaper stories we recognize the names of those we knew, hear the echoes of things we said or thought long ago. We understand why each one of us chose his particular road, and at last we recognize ourselves in events which happen *through* us, and not only *to* us, even though we may grieve that between our dreams and our deeds, the wicked priest has cast his shadow to separate us, and that none of us can as yet turn about and start again.

*Two*

# Passover in Egypt

*The Jewish festival of Passover commemorates the Exodus of the Israelites from Egypt. The narrative of the Exodus and the celebration of Passover play a particularly important role in the stories modern Egyptian Jews tell of their experiences and of their dispersal. According to this essay, published in 1965, Kahanoff was already a school-aged child when she attended her first Passover seder held at the home of her maternal uncle, David Chemla. The seder also serves an important narrative function in her early fiction.*

This was an important event, also delightful. For the first time in my life my parents would take me to celebrate Passover with them in Uncle David's house, and what was better still, I would stay there three whole days with my cousins, Jacques and Roger. Their grandfather was the oldest brother of my grandfather, and the head of the family—that is, of my mother's family, which had come to Egypt from Tunisia. Jacques, Roger, and I had grown up together, and we had a lot of fun. Our grandparents' department store in Cairo was our kingdom, and we loved those days when the old men invited us to choose from the new toys which had just arrived. The toy department was our favorite, but we knew all the people who worked in the store, most of whom were cousins who had come from Tunisia with our grandparents.



On Saturday afternoons, all the family gathered in Uncle David's house. The older people sat talking around the table, which was covered with delicious almond and date-filled cakes, honey-dipped and fried, made by Aunt Mreima, Uncle David's wife. We children played in the long corridor, hollering as we raced up and down on roller skates or tried to balance walking sticks on our noses. In Uncle David's house we did pretty much as we pleased, so of course the idea of three days' holiday together was entirely delightful. My English governess grumbled that she'd have an awful time getting me back under control after those three days, but the English were that way; they couldn't bear the idea of people having a good time.

Still, Passover was also something serious, even mysterious. Every year, our house was turned inside out, some dishes put away and others taken out, and tons of all kinds of *matzot* stored away, enough, my mother complained, to last not a week but a year. My father bought me a book called the Haggadah, and as I turned the pages, looking at the pictures, he told me about the story which was ours. How extraordinary to think that we had all been in Egypt long, long before, at the time when the pyramids were built, those three pink triangles I saw from my balcony, on the opposite bank of the Nile! And when we played hopscotch on the promenade by the river, Kadreya, Marie-Thérèse, and I, it might have been at the very spot, down below the stone embankment, where Pharaoh's daughter found Moses in his little basket. I felt great pride that my people should be God's chosen people; after all, it wasn't for everybody that He opened a dry passage through the sea. I didn't think, for instance, that He would accomplish such a miracle for the British, when they would leave Egypt.

Passover made the streets of Cairo more interesting than ever. They were full of Arabs trotting at the sides of little donkeys or camels, which were always chewing on something, big bundles of fresh greens or flowers held in rope bags slung across their humps. Were the Arab Egyptians the same as those who lived in Pharaoh's time? They couldn't be, or the Jews would not have returned to Egypt. But if we had made peace, why did Jews still celebrate Passover and pray for the return to the Promised Land? I asked my father questions about it, but his answers weren't clear at all. In fact, when people talked about religion, it was difficult to understand what they said. For instance, gentle Marie-Thérèse, who was Catholic and brought up in a convent, was always sending people to roast in Hell because they didn't believe Christ was the Messiah—not only the Jews, but the Moslems, too. It wasn't her fault; it was religion.

Still, I was Jewish, and if Marie-Thérèse and Kadreya believed in their religions, I must believe in mine. Was Kadreya my enemy because she was an Egyptian? Or was it different now that Egyptians were Moslems? When I met Kadreya in the Gezira gardens, I told her the little I knew about the Passover story and all we had suffered at the hands of Pharaoh, until God opened the Red Sea for us to escape. "Ya allah," she said. "It's not possible. I swear that not my father, or his father, or my grandfather's grandfather would do such things to your father, his father, or his grandfather's grandfather. I love you; you are my friend."

"I love you, too," I said, "but it's all written in a book called the Haggadah. Father also says Palestine is our Promised Land. So perhaps I'm not Egyptian like you."

Kadreya began to cry, swaying back and forth as we sat side by side on the grass, our legs crossed, oriental fashion. I consoled her: "Perhaps there's an explanation in the prayer of Passover night. I'll tell you about it. Because, look, now that you are Moslems you aren't the same people as in Pharaoh's time, and you aren't like the Christians, always sending us all to burn in Hell."

Kadreya, thinking things over, suggested a conciliatory solution: "My father went on a pilgrimage to Mecca, and turns to Mecca when he prays, but Egypt is his country. Of course, you'll go on a pilgrimage to Palestine because Nebi Moussa, your prophet Moses, took you there. So Palestine is your Mecca, because that's how it is with religion, but Egypt is your country too, and we'll always, always, be friends."

What Kadreya said sounded sensible, but I had an inkling it wasn't all that simple. We had been chosen and promised that we should return again to the Promised Land. So perhaps it was against my religion, "sacrilegious," as Marie-Thérèse would say, not to want to return to live there? Perhaps just to go on a pilgrimage was not enough? I confided my doubts to Kadreya, who said: "If I could, I would give you the Promised Land, but you know, the English are there, like in Egypt." She sighed and added honestly, "But I'm not so sure about my brothers giving it to you. Men are different. Listen, I'll tell you something, if you promise not to tell."

Once I promised, Kadreya whispered in my ear, "I would like a religion where God is also a woman, not only a man."

I was shocked, of course, but when Kadreya and I met with Marie-Thérèse, we plotted our revolution like two conspirators, rewriting past history with a feminine gender and in the present tense to provide it with a happy ending. Somehow, the wicked priest who hardened Pharaoh's heart against Moses and his people became a redheaded stranger, who strangely resembled a British Chief of Police whom we often saw strutting on his pommeled horse. But Pharaoh's daughter saw through her father's wicked councilor and advised her father to get rid of him and send him back to his own country. Then Pharaoh's daughter, the princess, arranged a meeting between her father and Moses, and the three of them decided that if there wasn't room enough in the narrow green ribbon of the Nile valley for both peoples, then those who had come with Joseph would go back to the Promised Land in peace, and they would always be friends and allies with the Egyptians, against all the outsiders, the priests, the soldiers, the governesses, and the Chief of Police. Kadreya and I were pleased with this arrangement.

Finally, *Pesah* arrived. It was beautiful in Uncle David's house. The table was so long, passing through the French doors that separated the dining room from the living room in order to seat us, forty people in all. Everything shone: the crystal, the silver, the flowers, and the two big baskets, covered with gold brocade, in which were hidden all the things one would use or eat during the service. At the head of the table sat the old people, husband and wife. The younger married couples sat along the sides, and at the far end of the table the youngsters crowded together, with me sitting between Jacques and Roger.

I showed them my Haggadah, and when they came to the picture of Pharaoh's daughter, whose peculiarly flat breast, seen in profile, was naked, they said they had never seen anything so ridiculous. Snatching the book, they scrambled under the table and emerged by their parents to show them. Everybody in turn had a good look at the bosom of Pharaoh's daughter and laughed, making naughty jokes I only half understood. I hadn't thought *Pesah* and the Jewish religion were like that at all. Still, my father looked serious when they began the service, and I was proud of him because he knew the prayers so well and helped the old men, who often lost their place in the Haggadah. The voices of the men were like thunder, like the crash of waves, but mixed with laughs—because in my mother's family, except for food, the store, and family matters, they took nothing really seriously.

As the service bounced on, the baskets were uncovered, and at each part of the service one ate something: a piece of lamb, a hard-boiled egg, or little sandwiches of *matzot*, lettuce, and *harosset*, a delicious jam made of dates, honey, and all kinds of nuts. Everybody shouted: "Don't stuff yourselves with the *harosset*, there's a good dinner coming!" Then, all of a sudden, the young men in the family stood up, lifted the baskets high, and raced around the table, passing them to one another so that the baskets seemed to fly over everybody's heads. That was for good luck. Jacques, Roger, and I had great fun jumping up and down to be sure our heads bumped against the baskets.

But I didn't like the *Dayenu* prayer, with all those plagues that fell upon the Land of Egypt and the poor fellahin. When I told this to Jacques and Roger, they said that girls were silly. I retorted that they were just stupid boys, but they were rather tipsy and paid no attention.

The dinner was wonderful and very gay, but I was unhappy when my parents left; I would have liked to ask my father about the Egyptians and the Ten Plagues. The next morning, at the breakfast table, Jacques and Roger zestfully invented new plagues to send upon the Egyptians and played war, pretending they were driving the chariots of Pharaoh's army. I thought they were really savages.

Soon after I returned home I met Kadreya again, and she was eager to know all about Passover. But I couldn't tell her about the Ten Plagues that had devastated Egypt; I was too ashamed. Then I thought perhaps it would be bad for the Jews if the Egyptians knew about the Ten Plagues (they seemed to have forgotten), even if they were Moslems now, and I was also ashamed to tell her that we had returned to Egypt after we had reached the Promised Land. So I looked important and mysterious and told her that the Passover prayer was a secret part of our religion, and it was forbidden to tell about it. Kadreya was hurt, and she reproached me: "I told you my secret, but you, you won't tell me yours." We were never such good friends again, and in time we lost sight of each other.

Many Passovers have passed since then, and now we celebrate them in the Promised Land. But I often see the Nile's brown waters, and I remember Kadreya, who had wanted to give me my Promised Land. Most of all, I remember the innocence of children who reinvent the world and offer it to one another with a smile.

*Three*

# Such Is Rachel

*Echoing some of the elements of the previous essay, "Passover in Egypt," this short story depicts a young Egyptian Jewish girl's experience at the last Passover seder led by her elderly grandfather. In its attempt to assimilate traditional religious practice with feminist ideology, one could argue that this story is as much a product of the cultural hybridity Jacqueline experienced living in the United States during World War II as it is of her childhood in Egypt. This piece won second place in a story contest held by the* Atlantic Monthly *to encourage new writers and was published in the magazine in October 1946.*

Jacob Benzion's sons arrived in their big cars at their father's house in the Arab part of Cairo. The narrow street could hardly contain the cars, and the Moslem neighbors, gathered on their jasmine-bordered verandas to take in the sweet evening air, observed, "Tonight the old Jew has his sons and his grandchildren around him to celebrate Passover, the great feast of his people. May Allah gladden the old man's heart!" For many days they had seen the servant Muhammad coming back with baskets of food in preparation for the feast. The Arab neighbors smiled, pleased that the house usually so silent behind its high walls would overflow, this one night, with the voices of young people.



The Benzion sons, their wives and children, wearing handsome European clothes, smiled vaguely at the indistinct mass of their father's neighbors, and were ill at ease in the half-forgotten Arab surroundings. Arab children gazed at the cars, patting the steel flanks with shy, curious fingers, and their parents said, "Late into the night will we hear the Jews' prayers. Then the sons and their families will return to their European houses far across the river."

In the house, each of the Benzions went in turn to the armchair where the old man sat, his hands folded in his robes. They knelt, kissed Jacob's hand, and he blessed each of them. The eldest son, Isaac, knelt a little stiffly, as a man to whom his years were already a burden. Simon knelt with unthinking acceptance, and David, the third son, knelt with unswerving devotion to his old father and the old ways. The women knelt passively, as women do, a little reluctant to give this mark of respect to a man of another house. In the children, he felt the resistance in their necks, which refused to yield under his blessing, their shame to obey the oriental custom.

Only Rachel, David's thirteen-year-old daughter, coming up to him with her little brother, had no shame in kneeling, and when she had kissed his hand, she shifted her head slightly, so that after her lips, her cheek touched her grandfather's hand. He blessed her, saying the Hebrew words slowly, as if he wanted to bless her more than the others. When Rachel stood up again and pushed her brother before him, he felt pride, because the girl Rachel carried well her name.

Jacob examined David's son, a blond lad with merry golden eyes, brought to him for his first Passover, and he wondered what Passover would mean to this grandchild who had light hair. The boy knelt, kissed the old hand, but before his grandfather had had time to bless him, he escaped, laughing, to his mother. David rebuked his son in French, "Jack, are you not ashamed to run from under your grandfather's blessing? How often have I told you, you must venerate the head of your house?"

David's father, who understood French and English although he did not speak them, said to him in Arabic, "Your son is an *'afrit*, a little devil, but he meant no wrong. And, my son, this is a different world from the one we left behind us when we came from Arabia thirty years ago. The world changes, David, and you must accept the change."

Jack did not understand the Arab speech, but laughed again, because he knew that the old man in Arab clothes they called his grandfather had sided with him against his father.

The women gossiped in one corner, and the young ones in another. Rachel was silent, and Jack, observing everything with his intelligent golden eyes, saw his uncle Isaac glance nervously at the door left open. He tugged at his sister and asked, "Rachel, why is the door open?"

"Tonight, any man who's poor and hungry can come in and be one of us," Rachel said. "The door is open for all. The guest may be a barefooted beggar—he may also be the Messiah."

Jack pondered for a while. "But Rachel," he asked, "Miss Kelly said Jesus was the Messiah, that he had already come, so why are we still waiting for him?"

Rachel was angry. Always their English governess was saying such things to pull Jack away. Passionately, she told her brother, "What can *she* know about the real Messiah, the one who is ours and other people's too, the one who will save the Jews, and everybody, and not only the Christians as she says—He may come tonight—" And Rachel's eyes went to the door open on the little garden, with its jasmine and honeysuckle, where the Messiah might appear any moment.

Isaac also looked at the door open on the Arab street and he asked Jacob, "My father, why do we not close the door, so that we may have our Passover in peace, unheard by those outside?"

The old man said, "Isaac, these are kindly people, our neighbors, who mean us no harm. Do you not know that tonight our house must be open to any man with a need to be filled, for us to fill his need? Are we to shut our door when the Prophet may come? Ah, Isaac, how far has your heart strayed from Israel?" Then Jacob, shutting the anger within him, lifted himself from his armchair and told them all, "Now, my children, let us go in and start the prayers, and thank the Lord for having delivered us from Pharaoh's heavy yoke."

They followed him into the dining room, next to the parlor where they had sat. Rachel went in holding Jack by the hand, impatient to make him share the pain and pride of Passover, to win his soul, and give it to her grandfather. Jacob seated himself in the armchair at the head of the table, his sons on his right side, the women on his left, and at the opposite end of the table, the young ones, with Rachel and Jack in the middle, facing him.

*

Rachel gazed at the long Passover table. She saw beside her grandfather the engraved silver tray covered with glasses, tall ones for the grownups, small ones for children, the glasses brimming over with the ruby-red wine from Palestine. On her side of the table she saw the seder plate, a basket covered with red and gold brocade, under which were hidden all the symbolical things they would use for the prayer. She saw the centerpiece of roses, the roses still full and round and sweet-scented on their wire stems. She saw the silver goblet from which the Messiah would drink if he came to visit them. Her hand tightened on Jack's and she asked him, "Isn't it beautiful—don't you love it?"

Jack squirmed to free his hand. "You hurt me, Rachel. No, I don't like it a bit. The table is so big the servant won't have enough room to pass with the dishes. The chairs are almost against the walls."

Rachel dropped his hand, and her vision also dropped away. Jack had made her see the narrow limits set by plain whitewashed walls where before she had only seen the mystical beauty of the table. She watched the others getting ready for the prayer and in a voice now a little uncertain, she said, "Get your school cap, Jack, and put it on your head."

"Why?"

"Because you must have something on your head for the prayers."

"When Miss Kelly took me to church once, people took their hats off. We put them on—it's silly."

"Look, Jack, not all people pray to God in the same way. Why should you think one way is good and the other is silly? Go, Jack, please get your cap."

When Jack came back with the round navy blue cap of his English school on his head, he said, "Maurice and Charles have no hats, only napkins. Why, Rachel?"

"They never wear hats, and they think it's bright and funny to pray with a napkin falling off their heads all the time. They are just stupid."

Rachel's eyes left the napkined heads, rested on those of her uncles, with their European hats pushed back on their heads, went over to the vulgar faces of her aunts, the aloofness of her mother, and the tired dignity of her father's face under his felt hat worn straight on his forehead. She saw Jacob in the ample folds of his long silk robe, with its harmony of two shades of gray, and wearing on his majestic head a white turban draped around his red fez as he would have worn a crown. He was, to the girl, a serene old king of those days when the Hebrews had great kings, except that he ruled over subjects unworthy of him. She watched the slow dignity with which he washed his hands before starting the prayer, oblivious of the servant holding out the towel for him to dry his hands. Why was she not a boy so that she could be like him? Why had there never been great Hebrew queens?

Jacob Benzion began the prayer, the men chanting the old rhythm with him, "Praise to Thee, Eternal, our God, who has chosen us from among all people, and has given us this sacred feast to commemorate our deliverance from Egypt . . ."

They all leaned on their left elbows to drink the wine and Rachel made Jack sip his. She wanted to give him the meaning of Passover in words a child of eight could understand. Fearing the task before her, she thought there was so much she did not know and could not explain. Yet she knew the task was hers, for was she not the only one to know that when her grandfather died one worthy of him should be among them, so that something of his greatness would live on? She was only a girl, therefore useless. The last hope was Jack, the last child old Jacob could have brought to him for Passover. She dared not, she could not, fail. Her heart beat hard within her, and she cleared her voice to ask her brother, "Do you know who built the pyramids?"

Jack said, "The people who build houses."

"No, we built them. We, the Jews. That was long ago, when Egypt was different. There was a cruel king in Egypt then, and his name was Pharaoh. He made us carry those heavy stones on our bare backs, his soldiers flogged us, and thousands died building those pyramids we see every day. We were slaves, you see."

"You mean *we* were slaves?" He was unbelieving.

"Yes, we were slaves. But that's nothing to be ashamed of when you've gained your freedom and God is on your side."

"Perhaps you were a slave, but I'm sure I never was. I don't want to have been a slave, ever."

"We have the same mother and father, Jack."

"Yes, but you are like Father, and I'm like Mother, and I'm sure *she* was never a slave."

Rachel did not answer. Anguished, she thought Jack might be right. He was like their mother, and not like herself, her father, and her grandfather. Perhaps her mother's people had not been Jews in those times, but people like the Gauls she learned about in her French history book, carefree savage pagans, roaming in green forests, while the Jews strained under the heavy stones and the floggings, erecting pyramids in burning golden deserts. Perhaps, indeed, the unforgotten bitter splendor of those days was hers and not her brother's.

Rachel would not give up. "You'll understand later, Jack. But now listen to me. I can't tell you the story exactly as it is in the prayer book. Mine is in English, and I only know where Grandfather is in the prayer when he does something my book says we should do, then I find my place again. But you are a boy, and later you'll learn Hebrew and you'll know it all as it is. Shall I tell you the story?"

Jack had been ready to say he did not want to learn Hebrew, but Rachel's eyes were pleading, and he could no longer tease. He slipped his hand in hers, and said, in a fit of tenderness, "Please tell me the story, Rachel darling."

*

Jacob had lifted the unleavened bread and said, "Here is the bread our fathers ate in Egypt. This year we eat it here, next year in the land of Israel as free men." He watched his sons repeat the words, watched all of them nibble at the hard bread. Simon's wife shouted to her youngest son across the table, "Don't eat too much of it, Charles. You know how this stuff always hurts your stomach."

Jacob said to her angrily, "What matters your son's bellyache, woman? Were not our ancestors' bowels twisted by worse pains?" And watching his sons, he thought they were hardly better than this woman.

He saw Isaac, who refused to admit he was bound in chains; Simon, who did not even know he had chains; and David, accepting them with mystical resignation. He saw his sons' sons, who could hardly read the words in the prayer book, their mothers, waiting with vacant eyes to resume their gossip. He thought of his other sons who had gone west too far, too soon, and who had probably forgotten Passover existed. How could those still around him ignore the burning and longing in those words?

Wearily, he thought he should feel joy at this numerous family surrounding him, but he felt only the sadness of a dying hope. He remembered how he had brought them to Egypt, long ago, from Jeddah, in Arabia. He had wanted to transplant his tree, withering in the ancient dryness of Arabia, to the rich soil of Egypt, where fresh winds blew from west and north. He had wanted the tree to grow mighty in the forest of Israel, and have his old Judaism bloom again in the new climate. What had become of his vision when, full of faith, he crossed the Arabian desert in caravan with all his tribe? To giddy heights his tree had grown, but now, hollow inside, unable to draw the sap from its roots, how could it stand when came the tempests and the storms?

What of his sons, and their wives, and their children? They had grown prosperous in Egypt, but they had forgotten that Israel had always storms to withstand, and they were Israel. They no longer knew that wealth was only the means by which, in the abundant years, one generation eats enough, learns enough, accumulates enough for the next generations to live on in the lean years, the years of persecution and huddling in ghettos. They no longer knew that the hungry years spread over generations and were much longer than the seven lean years of which Joseph spoke to Pharaoh. When the time would come to pack and leave, as their ancestors had done in Egypt, would they find the strength to survive, these children who did not know that always the Jew is thrown back into the ghetto?

His voice low, he commanded, "David, read this part of the prayer. Your son, the youngest among us, should read these words, but since he has not been taught Hebrew, you must speak his words for him."

David bent his head under the reproach, and read, "Why is this night different from all other nights?"

Jacob began to read the answers, as in old times, when children were taught their great inheritance.

Simon said, "Why not skip this part of the prayer, my father? The children do not listen, and they cannot understand."

Jacob looked at the young ones, impatiently fidgeting on their chairs, the youth of his house who could not feel the words in which beat the heart of Israel. He told his sons, "If their ears hear not, and their eyes see not, still I will do that which the Law commands, for it is still our duty to instruct our children."

He read the four answers for the four types of children the Law describes—the wise, the ignorant, the stupid, the mean—and asked himself, "Around me, I have the ignorant, the stupid, and the mean, but who is wise among them?"

How long he had prayed for this wise one, the one to lead the house of Jacob after him! Year by year, generation by generation, child by child, face by face, he had watched for a sign that would tell him, "This is the Chosen one." Once again he searched their faces, but where was the Chosen one?

His eyes dwelt on David of the ancient wisdom, a lost exile to whom a new world was a prison. This was his dearest, but not the one to guide the house of Jacob, for in this age the truly wise one had to marry within him the past and the future, the old and the new, and David lived in the past.

And here was David's son, a blond head wearing an English school cap as a birthright, eyes sparkling with merriment, eyes on which the brooding thoughts of Israel never cast their shadows, a smiling child, subtly chiding the tradition of his fathers. This was the last child, the last hope, and this too was gone. For Jacob was past eighty, and life, ebbing away, could wait no longer for a child still unborn.

His eyes went from Jack to Rachel, in whom he had always seen the maiden by the well, whom Jacob, father of Israel, had loved. To this Rachel, his own, the new world was a well from which she drew her substance, and yet on her face alone had he seen his own emotion mirrored at Passover. In her, by an irony of fate, two worlds were made one, the beauty of an old tradition wed to the vigor of a new age, as he had wanted them to be in his Chosen one. In this maiden, to be given as bride to another old man's house, were squandered the gifts he had sought in the man who was to make great his house.

Time had come for Jacob to die, a bitter death with none there to take his place, with all hope dead. The house of Jacob would die with Jacob, crumbling as a castle of sand, for were they not, his sons and their children, sterile grains of sand to be blown away and scattered, useless, among other people? He read the Passover prayer, while in his heart the cry rose, "What, O Lord, has become of Israel? Is Thy Chosen People a rivulet to melt away meekly in the mighty seas of other people? Why hast Thou forsaken me, and my house, and Israel, O Lord?"

His vision of Israel's new greatness, again to spring from the loins of Jacob, the vision which had swept him across the desert, appeared now as utter folly, and nothing remained but a dark despair, an old patriarch who no longer heard the voice of his Lord. The old voice rasped and sobbed when Jacob recited the Ten Plagues the Lord had sent upon the Egyptians, and his hand, so steady when it had blessed, trembled now as he shook drops of wine out of his glass, one drop for each plague.

The change in the father's voice dried the prayer on the sons' lips. Isaac asked, "Are you ill, my father?" Simon said, "Rest yourself awhile, the prayer can wait." And David asked, "What grief assails you, my father, that makes you sing the song of triumph as a lament of death?"

"Grief lies heavy upon me," Jacob said, "and when God wills, time may soon come to rest, but now, let us still pray."

*

Rachel knew the sorrow which had quelled Jacob's voice. The old king was dying, knowing no head was proud enough to wear his crown. Ah! Had she not been born woman, she would have worn the crown, even if she were to pick it from the gutter, even if it were a crown of thorns. Yet, Rachel would not despair. When they had been slaves in Egypt, had not God saved them when they had reached the bottom of despair? Had He not sent Moses to lead them, and worked miracle after miracle until they had won their freedom? What God had done then, He could do again. He had not abandoned Moses, and now He could not abandon Jacob, and still be God. There would be a miracle, and perhaps even now could Jack be won.

She told her brother, "This part of the prayer tells how God punished the Egyptians and thanks Him for all He did for us. God sent Moses to Pharaoh to ask him to let us leave. Pharaoh always said, yes, he would let us go, but he always broke his promise, and treated the slaves worse than before. Ten times God had to punish the Egyptians. He changed the Nile water into a river of blood, sent wild beasts, millions of frogs and grasshoppers to eat up all the crops. He made darkness out of daylight, and killed the Egyptians' first-born. Pharaoh was so wicked, even then he didn't let us go. Then . . ."

"It's horrible, Rachel," Jack interrupted. "God couldn't have done those things."

"What else could He do if Pharaoh shut his heart to all pity?"

"But the little children, it wasn't their fault. How could God kill babies?"

"And our babies, Jack, what had they done when Pharaoh had wanted to kill them, and what had their parents done? Can't you see how wrong it is to pity the masters, when the masters have no pity for the slaves? Should we have stayed slaves forever?"

"I don't know, Rachel, it's all so cruel. And why did we have to come back to Egypt after all that? It makes me feel so ashamed."

"Every country has been to us as Pharaoh's Egypt, although never so bad, I think, and every country we had to leave. If we had never returned when things got better, long ago there would have been no place for us to live in."

"You mean those things still happen?"

"Yes, Jack, they do."

"When I grow up, I don't want to be a Jew. It's too horrible. Why do you, Rachel?"

"I'm born that way—oh, Jack, why won't you understand?"

Rachel knew she was defeated, and wished her heart could become a hard little pebble, to feel no more the steel fingers squeezing so much pain out of it.

While she had talked to Jack, she had not noticed her cousins listening to her. Now she heard them goad her. The girl Arlette said, "There's Rachel trying to make a convert. Well, you didn't, Rachel, did you?" And the boy Maurice, "And now when the old man calls us for that comedy of carrying the bread, he won't call you, Rachel, will he?"

Rachel did not answer. Instead, she asked God, "Why didn't You help me when I did try, so hard? But now at least, please, God, help me not to cry in front of everybody, and also make Grandfather call me to carry the bread this time, and not leave me out so all the others will laugh at me."

Jacob's eyes had rested on Rachel. In his torment the sight of her was soothing as oil upon scorched flesh. While saying the prayers, he had watched all that passed at the other end of the table. He thought, "As in the Temple one candle is lit with the flame from another candle, so has Rachel wanted to light her brother with her own flame. How could she, a little maiden, know the boy was already cut off from his people, already burning with an alien flame?"

Now he saw serenity flee from her face, and held-back tears flicker in her dark eyes as stars in somber night. Still only a child, she knew the deep grief of losing a soul beloved that one had wanted to bring in offering to the Lord. Had she known his vision and his despair, with love enough to divine his secret heart? Why else the anguish and the immense appeal in her eyes? And if it were so, his doubt must be her doubt, and his ache her ache. What mattered if, being a woman, she was useless to the house of Jacob! She was a soul kindred to his own, and he knew how the sharp steel of pain could pierce such a soul. She was worthy of being a son of his house, and as a son he would treat her.

When he reached the part of the prayer which told how the Hebrews left Egypt, and how the young boys slung the still unraised bread around their shoulders, to carry on the long passage, he said, "Let our two youngest boys come forth to carry the bread, as our ancestors did in Egypt, and Rachel, my child, you too come forth, and carry the bread." He watched the change on her face from grief to uncertain joy, and faith returned to the radiant eyes.

Isaac asked, "Why Rachel? She is only a girl."

Rachel stood against the wall, not daring to advance. Again Jacob called her, "Come, Rachel, do not fear, and carry our burden like a man."

He wrapped the bread in a napkin, and when she had knelt before him he tied it around her shoulder. Then he said, "Let my old hand bless your young head." And when he had blessed her he kept his hand on her dark hair, and turning to his sons, he said in answer to Isaac, "Women there are who count as men, for they are wise when men are foolish, strong when men are weak, brave when men are cowards. Such is Rachel."

The girl returned to her chair, holding the precious bread against her as if afraid to lose it. And Jacob's mind dwelt upon the words he had spoken, and the truth in them beyond the truth in his thought. Such indeed was Rachel, brave and wise, as the one he had awaited. Seeking a man, he had failed to see in Rachel the Lord's gift. In his pride, he had thought first of building the greatness of his house, and seeking a shepherd for his flock, he had forgotten Israel, the greater flock. For if the girl Rachel could not lead his house, she could do greater things for Israel in the new world open before her. And before Israel, what mattered the house of Jacob? Let it perish! If one was there to accomplish its purpose, it had not existed in vain.

But was not this too heavy a burden to lay on the slight shoulders of a girl? He had known the loneliness of one who lived for such a task, and where he had weakened, could he ask this child to remain strong? As the time had come in the prayer to eat the bitter herbs, symbol of the bitterness of their life in Egypt, he thought, "Can I take this child by the hand and tell her, 'The bitter herbs of earth shall be thine, but not the sweet wine of life; the pains and the searching will be thy lot, but not the laughter and the joy, for thou art chosen?'"

When the bitter herbs had reached the lower end of the table, again he watched Rachel. Jack tasted them and pushed them away, saying, "They're so bitter."

"Yes, they are bitter, but they must be eaten," Rachel said.

She ate hers, and then she ate her brother's. Their bitterness was hers, and her people's, and that of so many others. And when one refused his share of bitterness, another must eat both shares. Her grandfather had said she was strong and brave, and having no man, he had chosen her, a girl. There could be no other meaning to his words, and now she must learn to be worthy of him. Gravely eating the herbs, she looked up at him and smiled to show him she had understood him and was ready for what he wanted of her.

Jacob smiled back, now that he could no longer doubt. Alone the child had taken to herself the bitterness of those who carry forth the Lord's ordained task. Again, she had been sure when he had doubted, and alone, she had heard the Lord's call.

And when Jacob sang the hymn praising the Lord for all He had done to deliver His people from slavery, his voice soared sure and full, "Praise to the Eternal, for He is kind, and His loving-kindness is eternal."

*Four*

# Journey to a Better Land

*Houghton Mifflin awarded Jacqueline a fellowship to complete her first novel,* Jacob's Ladder, *published in 1951. The coming-of-age novel, from which this chapter is excerpted, follows the character Rachel Gaon, first introduced in the story "Such Is Rachel." This selection from the novel depicts a rare moment of tenderness shared between Rachel, suffering from diphtheria, and her parents. Rachel's governess, Miss Nutting, with whose authority she struggles through much of the novel, is pushed aside as the parents, Alice and David, step in to care for their daughter. Like the life-sustaining power of narrative wielded by Scheherazade in the* One Thousand and One Nights, *Rachel's father tells a story about his family's journey to Egypt that keeps his daughter alive through a critical night in her illness.*

Waking up one morning, Rachel, who had been out of sorts, felt much worse. She forced herself to swallow some breakfast, and went to school as usual. When she was asked to recite a lesson, she said she had not learned it, too numb to struggle through it. She wished only for night to come, to lie down, very still, forever. She knew she was ill, but would not say so. Let them find out, she thought, wishing to make herself ill beyond all struggle, to punish her mother, Miss Nutting, everyone. They could never forgive themselves if she died.



Alice called Rachel to her boudoir, wanting to know what had happened to the report card. She noticed her flushed cheeks and the dark circles under her eyes. "Let me feel your forehead," she said. "But you are burning with fever, darling!"

Rachel collapsed, her head in her mother's lap, and sobbed wildly with the relief of giving up her fight, now that at last she had forced her mother to be her mother. Alice rocked her child, and when she had quieted down, inspected her throat, which was swollen, red, and blotched with white.

"How long have you felt ill, darling?"

"Three days, I think."

"But why don't you ever say anything, Rachel?"

Three days, like Abraham and Isaac climbing up to the mountain for the sacrifice, Rachel remembered, and screamed, flinging herself against the wall in a new fit of sobs, "Don't ask questions, all the time! Oh, Mother, you take care of me! You must! Don't let anyone else do it!"

Rachel was put to bed in her mother's room, and when the doctor had seen her, he told Alice, "I'm afraid it's diphtheria. We'll only have the results of the test tomorrow, but we shouldn't wait to start serum injections. We can't risk losing another day."

"Diphtheria! But it's impossible! How can a child go about with diphtheria for three days, and say nothing?"

"Rachel showed great courage, but unfortunately, it makes matters worse. We must use serum immediately, but remember, Mrs. Gaon, diphtheria isn't as dangerous as it used to be before the serum was discovered."

All her courage gone, Rachel cried like a baby, biting her thumb as the thick, sticky fluid was forced into her. Before she surrendered to the delirious nightmare invading her, she made a last effort of will as she heard that Miss Nutting and Daniel were moving out of the house and going to the Smadjas. "Tell Daniel I love him, tell him not to be afraid," she urged Alice, "and tell Miss Nutting to show Daniel that she loves him while he's away from home."

"Why do you say that, Rachel? What do you mean?"

"Just tell them what I said," Rachel urged afresh, closing her eyes.

She lay still as all the events of the last months streamed behind her eyelids in terrifying combinations. Faces melted into each other—Miss Nutting, the Evil Magician, Marika. The river on which *Happy Days* traveled flowed from her own body,* changed into the biblical river of

* *Happy Days* is a boat on the Nile that is the source of escape fantasies for Rachel and her brother, Daniel.

blood, its banks lined with a thousand Marikas singing loudly, "I'm full of poison!"

She opened her eyes to make sure her mother was there, and pleaded, "Don't leave me, Mamma."

"I won't, Caline.* Close your eyes, and sleep, my beloved. We are here with you, and no harm can come to you."

The serum checked the infection but produced its own dangerous reaction. Hives spread over Rachel's body, and in dismay, Alice and David saw their child's flesh rise like bread in a hot oven, her face a shapeless red lump, with eyes reduced to narrow slits. The hives spread to her nostrils and tongue, and so swollen did they become that she could hardly breathe.

Outside the room, Dr. Nessim said, "I hope we can stop this swelling of the tongue immediately. There's also Rachel's heart, pumping so hard because all the blood is congested at the skin's surface."

Alice wept.

The doctor took her hands. "We'll fight hard, Mrs. Gaon. If only we can get her through this night, she'll be out of danger."

Alice and David sat, listening to the child's painful, uncertain breathing, giving her drink, and when Alice changed the compresses of aromatic vinegar intended to soothe the itching, David discreetly left the room, returning only after it was done.

Rachel closed her raw eyelids, her mind oddly lucid, so tortured by the itching that to scratch could bring no relief, and the smell of vinegar was hateful, inescapable, no matter where she turned her head. The soles of her feet were on fire, and the smell of vinegar was the smell of death. Who had died smelling vinegar, no matter how he turned his head? Christ on the cross. Perhaps His feet had itched, and He couldn't scratch because His hands were tied. His feet were also tied, so He couldn't even rub one against the other. He tried to twist His head away from the smell of vinegar, but no matter how He turned, the smell was there, and then He died. They said it was the Jews who had killed Him, but it wasn't true, it wasn't the Jews, it was the vinegar and the itch. She felt the bed sink under her, falling, falling, faster and faster. Therese had said that people who died

* Alice's private pet name for her daughter.

felt they were falling into a bottomless, black hole, and now Rachel was dying, falling, falling, with no one to help her, no one to hold her back.

Alice took her up in her arms. "I'm here, my love, don't be frightened," she said, and as the green slits of eyes stared at her, unrecognizing, she forced Rachel back to the pillow, shouting above her endless scream, "I'm Mamma, Caline, your mother, you must recognize me. You must!"

Rachel swallowed back her scream. "Don't leave me," she whimpered, "please don't leave me."

"We are all here, we won't leave you for a second."

Rachel tossed about the bed, and after he had given her an injection to sustain her, the doctor said earnestly, "Listen to me, Rachel. You must keep quiet, to help your heart. It's fighting very hard for you. Don't give it extra work. Keep still."

"I'm afraid to sleep, afraid I'll die, so afraid," the child cried, and squirmed ceaselessly as if to free herself from the mesh of death.

David watched his child who lived, struggling, suffering behind the leering mask; he watched the doctor lean anxiously over her, listening to her heart, feeling her pulse; he heard her breath start and stop, and each time it stopped he feared it would never start again. Now Rachel lay very still, her eyes closed.

"Quickly, Mrs. Gaon," muttered the doctor, "I'll give her an injection of strychnine and camphor, in the belly, the effect's quicker that way."

This time David did not leave the room as his daughter's body was uncovered; he saw the gleam of the hypodermic needle in the doctor's hand, saw the needle jab into the flesh. There was a small sudden cry from Rachel, who had seen nothing but had felt the jabbing pain. David felt sick and faint as he battled to get control of himself.

"It's going to be all right, Rachel," the doctor said soothingly, as she showed new signs of restlessness. Out of barely open eyes she saw her father bend over her and she felt him take her hand.

"Fight, Rachel, you must fight," the doctor urged her, and Alice turned to David, tears streaming down her face.

How could he help her to fight for her life, to free herself from the terror of death which possessed her? Holding her damp hand, he suggested diffidently, "Doctor, perhaps if I told Rachel a story, it would help her to forget her pain?"

He felt a slight pressure of Rachel's fingers and, without waiting for the doctor's answer, began, "Listen Rachel, this story is about us, about how your grandfather brought us safely to Egypt, and what happened to our caravan." He spoke hesitantly, hoping that his French would not fail him, but as he went on, the immense urgency of his desire to help her loosened his tongue.

"Your grandfather wanted to bring us to a better land, where there was more justice than in Baghdad. In Baghdad, if a Jewish peddler in the streets had the things in his basket slashed by a Turkish soldier's knife, and then trodden into the dust, he could not protest. If he did he would have been spat upon and kicked for accusing a Moslem of wrongdoing. So your grandfather wanted a better life for his descendants. He waited a long time for the word to be spoken. Then he took his sons and their wives and their children, his wife and all those in her house who were dependent on him, in all forty people. He sold everything he possessed, even the house we were born in and loved. He carried under his robes the wealth with which he was going to build his house in Egypt. It was sewn into seven belts, which he wore about him—the lowest and the easiest to reach held small coins, and the uppermost, nearest his heart, gold and precious stones.

"Now to come to Egypt we had to cross the Syrian desert. Your grandfather had hired armed guards to protect and guide our caravan. He himself remained at the rear to watch for any danger coming from behind. Halfway across the desert, the danger he had feared and foreseen came upon us. Robber Bedouins were hidden among the sand dunes, and as the caravan passed by, they attacked its rear. So he threw out to them the belt which held the small coins; by the time the robbers had dismounted their camels and begun to fight over it, he was able to give the alarm to the guards, who hastened to defend the caravan. Had he given the alarm too soon, the robbers would surely have killed him; when they realized they had been deceived, however, it was too late. The guards were more numerous and better armed than they were. They fled.

"But not before they had struck your grandfather a blow on the head, and although his turban broke its force, there was a great gash across his skull.

"The caravan continued its journey to Beirut and there embarked. Your grandfather nearly died crossing the seas, but he lived, and brought his caravan safely to its destiny, though he was already an old man. God was with Jacob Gaon, and God is with you now, Rachel, in your hour of need. You are also in our caravan, and one day you, too, must help to guide it and to protect it from all dangers as your grandfather did. You have not yet accomplished your destiny. Do not fear, do not doubt. You are not alone, God is with you."

David wiped off the sweat that had collected on his forehead. His words, which he had feared might falter, had streamed out of him unhindered, and he who usually found it so difficult to express himself had tonight found the gift of his tongue.

"Oh, Papa," Rachel murmured. "It's the most beautiful story I've ever heard. I'll always remember it." She breathed in deep gulps, as though the clean winds from the desert had blown through the stuffy sickroom.

"How do you feel, young pilgrim?" the doctor asked. "Your pulse is better, anyhow."

Rachel collected the strength to smile. "I feel as if I've been at an exam and my father had helped me with the answers," she said. "I'm not afraid to sleep anymore."

"You'll be all right when you wake up tomorrow, darling," Alice told her, helping to settle her more comfortably in bed, and kissing her.

Then as the adults listened to her even breathing, Rachel had a dream. Caravans wound their way to a pool of clear water, where the Messiah awaited them. There they dismounted and drank side by side, as the lamb and the wolf had done in the Garden of Eden, before Eve's sin and Adam's fall.

# *Five*
# A Line in the Sand

*This chapter from* Jacob's Ladder *(1951) depicts the final confrontation between the preteen Rachel Gaon and her overbearing British governess, Sheila Nutting. Both Rachel's brother, Daniel, and mother, Alice, are aware of the growing tension between the two but fail to prevent a confrontation. The chapter reflects Rachel's conflicted Levantine identity, torn between the British education imparted by her governess and the culture represented by both her grandparents and the Egyptian Muslim community around her. Against the backdrop of the Egyptian anticolonial movement of the interwar years, Rachel stages her own revolt for independence.*

On the surface, everything remained the same, while Rachel established her position, tested her ground. She must wait, watch, wear down the enemy.

Miss Nutting was exasperated that the girl's conduct was so exemplary, and that she could almost never catch her off guard. To everything she said, Rachel replied, "Yes, Miss Nutting," in a tone of infinite patience, which was in itself a mocking insult, a sly provocation. Sometimes she wondered why she simply did not go away. She did not wish to fight that final battle, and yet there was a fascination in knowing how and when the last blow would fall. She had usually stumbled into such dramas, but here was a protagonist with intelligence, perception, purpose, and even a strategy. She felt more weary than she had ever been in her life, and yet curious of this new Rachel, this fierce little person who intended her destruction. The most baffling was the strange tenderness, almost the sorrow she felt for Rachel between her fits of uncontrollable fury. Part of her was involved in a deadly struggle, while another detachedly watched.

In the tension between his sister and governess, more painful since it was hidden, Daniel was shaken and unhappy about something implicit which he could not wholly grasp. He had worried about Rachel, suffered when he was separated from her, exiled in another house, and had longed to be home, and to find everything as it had been. But nothing was the same, and in the new person he saw before him, he hardly recognized Rachel. He could not bear to witness Miss Nutting's decline, to be caught in this feline tussle between two women, each claiming his loyalty, and even Wednesdays brought him neither pleasure nor relief. Since his sister had become just another grown-up, they could not even find refuge in Tana-Gassi together.*

He asked Rachel once, as they watched *Happy Days* moored to the riverbank for the idle summer months, "Do you really want Miss Nutting to go away?"

"Yes, I do."

"But she's so unhappy, Rachel, and she was so good to me in Grandmother's house, nicer than anyone else. She does love us, and when she came, you said she only had us to love her in the whole world." Daniel was pleading with her, his childish face tortured.

"Yes, and look what happened! Miss Nutting will always be unhappy, she can't help it. What we can avoid is becoming as miserable as she is."

"You never said things like that before. Why aren't you the same, Rachel?"

"When I tried to be kind, she could hurt me. Now she can't. I don't want to hate her, I only want her to go away. When she goes, we'll be happy and free. You'll see, even if you miss her at first, you'll like it after a little while. I can manage it so we'll never have a governess again."

"I don't like children who don't have governesses. They have bad manners, and I don't want to be like them."

"You can go to the English school next year and become like the kind of children you admire," Rachel said dryly.

* Tana-Gassi is a world of make-believe that the children create together.

"What's going to happen? Are you going to tell her to go away? When? I feel so sorry for her," the little boy said tensely. Rachel took her brother's hand, and told him earnestly, "I know it would be better for you if I did it right away, but listen to me. In three weeks, we're going to Alexandria. We're always freer by the seaside, and we'll be together, so it won't be so hard for you. You don't have to do anything, or even pay any attention as the fight is between her and me. If I made her go now, mother would get us another governess for the summer. But if she goes later, mother will think it isn't worthwhile getting someone else before we return to Cairo, as you'll be going to school next autumn. I'll tell her that we can try out this way, that she's always got time to find another governess if she isn't pleased with our behavior. I'll take care of you, and we'll have at least six weeks at the seaside absolutely free, and we'll be so happy. You think I've changed, but I haven't really, Daniel, even if I've grown up and can't talk of Tana-Gassi as I did before. Don't think I don't understand how upset and sorry you are about Miss Nutting, because I feel the same way. But I want to get rid of her, as I would of a heavy stone around my neck. You'll see how wonderful it is to be free. You do believe me, don't you?"

"I do, I do! But it's the waiting!" Daniel cried out.

Rachel consoled and mothered him. "Didn't we wait before? We waited to be punished, all the time. Now we wait to be happy and free, it shouldn't be more difficult. So don't worry, darling. Everything will be all right."

Daniel wiped his tears, and smiled. Rachel had won him back, and although he preferred not to have to choose, he would still choose her rather than Miss Nutting.

The whole family moved to Alexandria, settling in a large villa with a fine garden and a portly gardener of whom Alice was very proud.

Rachel liked to sprawl on the beach in the early morning, lulled by the languid song of the waves, daydreaming, digging her feet and hands below the top layer of sand, already warmed and dried by the sun, to find the depths which still held the cool dampness of night. This was one of the secrets of the beach, captured at this early hour, when it was still deserted, and most intimately hers.

It annoyed her when Daniel shook her out of these trances. "Won't you play with me? Let's dig a big hole, until we strike water, and build a castle, or bury me like a mummy."

"Oh, can't you leave me alone?"

"Why won't you play when I want to? You shouldn't daydream, anyway. Miss Nutting is watching, and she thinks it's more natural when we play," Daniel said cunningly.

"All right, all right," Rachel said, angrily flinging sand away. They both laughed when the brims of their straw hats collided, as their heads bobbed in and out of the hole they dug, and it surprised Rachel that she still enjoyed these childish games. It was fun to "bury" Daniel and shape the damp sand around him, like a mummy case, on which she inscribed mysterious hieroglyphics, reciting incantations in a cavernous voice, until he squealed with terrified joy and broke through his coffin, to make sure he was not, after all, really dead.

Sometimes, she deliberately worked to charm Daniel, to test on him this power, yet unknown, surging in her. Then she told him the sort of things he liked to hear, but coquettishly, without her earlier artlessness. On a particularly hot, moist day, without any breeze, or the slightest ripple on the sea, they watched tall, dark men, naked save for their slips, clearing away thick strips of brown seaweed, which had drifted ashore during the night. They flung away the weeds, hanging like wigs from their rakes, and as they moved on, transparent patches of emerald appeared, in contrast with the solid blue of the sea beyond, like a dress fringed with precious stones. Nothing disturbed these clear pools, so still in the glossy belt of seaweed, and they could see the men's brown legs undulate in the transparent water.

Rachel sprang up, snatched handfuls of weeds from the velvety masses on the beach, and shook the sea drops on Daniel, laughing, "This is the hair of the sea, beautiful, curly brown hair, isn't it? There's lots of it. The sea has no governess to make her brush her hair ten minutes every morning. That's why it's all tangled up, and today, she's having a haircut." She squeezed the water out of little berries hanging on a bunch of delicate golden weeds, twined among the others.

"And those little balls, what are they?" Daniel's tone was expectant and scandalized. "Dandruff?"

"No, the sea is too clean and beautiful for that. These weeds are, more like feathers, and the shiny balls are pearls. The sea puts up her hair, like a queen or an actress."

"Don't touch those filthy things," Miss Nutting shouted from the cabin.

Rachel dropped the weeds, and told Daniel with exasperation, "She stops us every time we do something amusing. She's poison."

"Are weeds really dirty?" Daniel inquired.

"Of course not, but she thinks everything in Egypt is dirty, and must be washed in some smelly disinfectant. Soon, we'll be coming to the beach with a barrel full of Lysol, and pouring it around us when we swim, or who knows, perhaps she'll want to boil the sea, to kill all the germs." Rachel scampered off moodily, leaving Daniel to think how he would paint these weeds, one day.

Rachel did not understand her swiftly changing moods, why on some days she needed activity, and on others she was sullen, wanting to hide from people. Then she sought refuge on the cliff separating Bulkeley from the next beach, concealed in a nook. She watched the waves break furiously on the rocks below, and swinging her feet in space, she thought vaguely of all sorts of things, finding pleasure in scratching sand out of her hair, or licking the brine off her sea-polished skin. She liked to swim out alone, tasting intensely her freedom, to swim very far, and stay long in the water, until her lips were blue, and her fingertips crinkled. Then she ran fast across the burning sand at noon, and fell exhausted by the cabin not caring if she were scolded for swimming so long. Stretched on the sand, she could feel the beach, both sultry and crystalline, which she had known since childhood.

People moved each year to the beaches farther east, as the ones close to the city became too popular and overcrowded, but whether Sporting Club or Bulkeley, the beach was always the same, with the same children growing up, the same Abu Chanab following them in their migration,* to watch over them, and the same candy man to tempt them. He still tramped the beach, with the same glass case, but he no

* Abu Chanab is the nickname of a mustachioed beach merchant who hawks his wares on this stretch of beach.

longer sang, an older man now, who limped and complained of losing consistently at the races. The beggars, too, were the same, well-to-do beggars, who specialized in trading on the better people, and could afford the train fare to Alexandria.

There was a new grace about Rachel, both wild and passive, her green eyes contrasting strikingly with her sunburned skin, and although Miss Nutting did her best to keep her looking prim, she could not erase that indefinable expression of face and body, tender, sensuous, longing. The governess often remarked nervously, "Don't sway your hips when you walk. It's terribly vulgar, and you already look far too much like a woman."

"Do I, Miss Nutting? I don't do it on purpose, it just comes," Rachel said, smiling slowly.

She was aware of this change in her, and if Miss Nutting's remarks made her feel ashamed, she was pleased when the people who visited her mother at the cabin commented on how pretty she had become. As Alice worked on the tablecloth, Rachel lolled at her feet laughing, "Mother, you must work much, much harder if you want to finish it in time for my wedding. I'm growing fast, you know," she said provocatively in Miss Nutting's hearing.

A month passed by, and the Gaons found it a blessing that the cabin next to theirs was empty, and hoped it would remain so all summer. They were disappointed on arriving at the beach one day to find that they had neighbors, and Miss Nutting was particularly shocked by them. The young mother, wearing black stockings rolled down over her garters below her bouncing thighs and dimpled knees, shamelessly suckled her baby in public. Her fat, sleepy-looking daughter was absorbed in picking her nose, and wiped her fingers on her dress. Her young brother, in striped pyjamas, stuck out his tongue at them, and the family was completed by a young Arab maid, in a starched white apron, and a display of jingling jewelry.

The governess settled in her deck chair stolidly, and the two children hovered by, watching from the corner of the eye as the small boy pissed, shaping an arabesque on the sand, looking so disappointed not to be able to complete his pattern that his mother burst out laughing, and exclaimed perfunctorily, "Shame on you!"

Miss Nutting said sharply, "Don't stare, Daniel. Don't even look at those dreadful people. You too, Rachel. Run along, both of you."

The young Gaons shuffled off, but on that day and the following days, Rachel invented all sorts of pretexts to return to the cabin and linger there. She averted her eyes in embarrassment, but try as she might, they turned back to the woman suckling her child. The young mother slipped a breast out of the low neckline of her dress as soon as her baby cried, never denying him, even when he was being merely playful. She held him close, but when one of her other children came to her, she pressed its face in her free hand, saying passionately tender things. There was a sense of abundance about the woman both sweet and violent, so powerful that it could never be harnessed by things like tidiness, decency, and good manners.

Rachel was often jolted out of her contemplation by hearing Miss Nutting cry shrilly, "Yalla, yalla," to a peddler with eyes half-blinded by ophthalmia and running with pus. The peddler aped Miss Nutting and said, "Yalla, yalla." Then, in a monotonous chant, as if he were still praising his goods, he gave vent to a string of curses which took him back to the seventh generation of Miss Nutting's family, and made Rachel blush, although she understood only a part of what was said.

The Moslem woman laughed, and called the peddler to her cabin. Her eyes sparkled with mockery of the Englishwoman, neither young nor old, with the faded bitter face. She and the peddler laughed together, that deep-throated laughter which is prolonged for the sheer pleasure of laughing. The woman pretended disapproval and said, "Oh, rascal, have you no shame?" as the peddler knelt before her, to deposit his basket at her feet. The woman handed the baby over to the little maid, and fingered the nuts and fruit pastes in the basket. "How much?" she asked.

"Do you want one word or two words about the price?"

"Two words, because you'll never start out by telling me the real price anyway." The woman laughed, and when she had done her buying, distributed the sticky candy among her family.

Rachel longed to do something to flaunt Miss Nutting, and yet felt ashamed, after the horrible things the peddler had said about her, when she saw her distracted face and realized how cruel, how unfair they were all being to her.

Still the people in the two adjoining cabins pretended to ignore each other, and all Rachel could do was to brood among her rocks. She watched the sea, remembering Amina, and the many things which had happened when she had been with them. Images linked themselves obscurely in her mind, governesses, British soldiers and policemen, who were the same person, neither man nor woman, but authority, discipline, jails, barracks, all that civilized the life out of people to turn them into joyless, well-behaved automatons. Miss Nutting was the one who wanted to make Rachel ashamed to be like the native woman, hoping to turn her into the same sterile, seedless pod that she was. Sometimes she imagined huge counter-crusades, during which her world invaded Miss Nutting's and utterly destroyed it. After such escapades, she returned to the cabin in a penitent frame of mind, the shame of her secret thoughts stifling her rebellion.

When Alice came to the beach, the Moslem lady greeted her in Arabic, and expressed the wish that they should be good neighbors. Alice replied appropriately, though coldly, and the woman told her how much she admired her children, and hoped that they would be friends with hers. Then she spoke in French, pleased to show that she also was becoming Europeanized and educated. "My daughter, Zeinab, goes to the Sacré Coeur," she said proudly. "She's a good student, and received two prizes this year, one for good behavior, one for application. Did your daughter get prizes at school?"

"Not this year, because she was sick. But last year she had five of them, English, French Composition, Geography, History, and Literature," Alice said mockingly.

"Your daughter is a genius, as I was sure she would be. So I hope she and Zeinab will speak French together," the Moslem lady said placidly.

Rachel was annoyed by her mother's irony. She went toward Zeinab and invited her to play, but did not await her reply. She knelt by the woman and touched the baby's cheek, saying, "You have such a beautiful boy."

"Would you like to hold him?"

"Yes, but I'm afraid he'll cry."

"If he does, I'll take him back," the woman said, beaming as she handed over the child.

Rachel held the baby carefully, pleased that he did not cry. She thought that his mother could not have been much older than she when Zeinab was born and wondered if she had gone to the tree in Matariya.*

At home, during lunch, Alice mimicked the woman's accent and Zeinab's stupid, sleepy face. "Prizes in good behavior and application! You must be as dull as that child to get such prizes!"

"Zeinab's mother could make fun of our bad Arabic, but she didn't," Rachel retorted furiously.

"What's come over you, Rachel? I haven't seen you so angry since the days when you use to defend Amina." Alice, laughing, turned to Miss Nutting. "I had given Amina a girdle, and never having seen one before, she wore it over her petticoat. Rachel was furious because we joked about it."

This was not at all the sort of thing Rachel remembered about Amina. She burst into tears, and ran out of the dining room.

"Adolescent nerves," Alice said philosophically.

After their introduction, the four children played together with formality and only for short periods. Rachel examined Zeinab critically, annoyed to see her so fat and passive, since this spoiled her case. When they were alone together, Daniel asked her, "Do you really like those children? I don't think they're at all nice."

"You're a snob, like Miss Nutting," Rachel reproved him.

In spite of his dislike, Daniel was influenced by the other children, as Miss Nutting soon noted. One day, as they were playing together, she called out, "Daniel! Come here at once." When the boy stood before her, she asked, "Did I see you picking your nose?"

"Did I? I didn't notice, Miss Nutting, really I didn't."

"That only makes matters worse. Give me your spade."

"What hand was it?" she asked, when Daniel handed her the heavy toy.

Daniel held out his right hand, and the governess brought it down two or three times across his knuckles. "Go back and play now," she said.

* According to legend the Holy Family stopped to rest under a tree in the village of Matariya, now part of greater Cairo. The "Virgin's tree" remains a site of pilgrimage for those seeking healing and women wishing to conceive.

"On my life, this is an evil woman to beat a child thus," the Moslem woman exclaimed, glaring at Miss Nutting.

"Did she hurt you?" Rachel asked her brother when he joined them. Miss Nutting had spanked Daniel before, but she had never struck him so viciously.

Daniel rubbed his bruised hand, brushing away his tears. His back carefully turned on Miss Nutting, he screwed up his face mischievously, to calm Rachel's anger. "It didn't hurt so much. I let my hand go down a little each time."

"What did you do that's wrong? I saw nothing. She could have crippled you," Zeinab said.

"Don't talk such nonsense. When my governess punishes me, it's that I've deserved it," Daniel said coldly and marched off with dignity.

"Won't you tell your mother? Won't she see his hand is blue? And what did he do?" Zeinab insisted.

"Of course we won't tell my mother. If she notices we'll say Daniel hurt himself in falling," Rachel said, exasperated that Zeinab's notions of right conduct were at such variance with her own. "And, what he did was to pick his nose."

Understanding crept through Zeinab's sluggish mind.

She laughed, holding her head, swaying back and forth.

"Ya Allah! That's all? If she took care of me, I'd have no hands left. Of course, I hope I'm rid of the habit before I get married."

What most bewildered Rachel was her relief that the incident passed off easily. The peddlers the Moslem woman called to her cabin acted as a constant irritant. Part of Rachel was just as shocked as Miss Nutting was when their neighbors pawed with dirty hands the contents of baskets, but another part of her wanted to eat with them, to have the same fun bargaining, chatting, pretending to quarrel. The Moslem lady was the wife of a renowned judge, but when she joked with a peddler, they were two human beings, while to Miss Nutting, who was only a governess, such people were less than dogs. In Europe, Rachel knew, poor people voted and had a voice in government, but in Egypt, a shamefully backward country, they loved each other better, it seemed to her. The weekends, when her father and Zeinab's father came to the beach, confused and irritated Rachel. They conversed amiably, offered each other's children salted nuts, and although under these circumstances, Rachel knew she could and should accept she invariably refused, just as Miss Nutting would.

Watching the young mother, Rachel vaguely longed for the old order she represented. She suffered to be judging it by Miss Nutting's standards, as she suffered at being excluded from it merely by not eating nuts, or a piece of sweet, sticky nut and sesame paste.

She could not help noticing that they might dislike, distrust, despise Miss Nutting, but dared not challenge her order. The Moslem lady wished to offer her and Daniel the sweets she bought, but dared not do it, nor, Rachel knew, would she dare accept the offer if it were made. Was she a coward, she wondered? Sometimes she drew a fine line in the sand between the two cabins, and truly did not know which side was hers. Perhaps she didn't have a side because she was Jewish.

Day after day on the beach, Rachel looked at the Arab neighbors with longing and envy, because everything was so simple for them. They knew what world they belonged to, without having to ask themselves. And all the time, while Rachel struggled with herself, Miss Nutting's yellow eyes never stopped watching her, and she never stopped watching Miss Nutting. The worst thing of all was that each always guessed what the other was thinking. It had been so from the first day in Paris, but now, it went on without ceasing. They only spoke to exchange the necessary words, but it was frightening, this feeling that came upon Rachel sometimes that she and Miss Nutting were in some way the same person. Then, instead of provoking the final battle, Rachel did all she could to avoid it, and felt disgusted with herself.

One afternoon, when they had friends for tea, including the young Karims and Hakims, and played in the garden, a band of young rioters passed by, shouting, "Egypt for the Egyptians!" In a sudden burst of determination, Rachel ran to the gate, snatching some flowers on her way, and throwing them to the rioters, shouted back, "Egypt for the Egyptians!"

Miss Nutting called out sharply, "Come here at once!" Rachel obeyed, and Miss Nutting snapped, "How dare you do such a thing!" scolding her publicly, a grown girl. Even then Rachel made no retort, did nothing. She saw Daniel turn away, ashamed of her. She was more cowardly, more passive than any native, Rachel reflected bitterly; Miss Nutting had proved it to her.

Miss Nutting, observing Rachel, knew now what had made her stay on. Sometimes with a triumphant, vengeful fury, sometimes with compassion, she saw the conflict in Rachel's face as her eyes turned from Zeinab to her mother, repelled, and attracted, unable to accept or reject them, struggling desperately not so much against her governess as against another part of herself. She sensed that thin line between the two cabins which tore Rachel apart. She knew now why she had waited; she would not leave before she was certain of Rachel's doubt. She knew now why she had pitied; she had sensed in Rachel someone even more dispossessed than she was, another Sheila Nutting, who even if she did not know it yet, had no world of her own. The inner certainty she had perceived in Rachel on the day of her return, if it had even existed, was clearly no longer there.

The Moslem woman, observing her neighbors, could not bear to see the longing on Rachel's face when she distributed the peddler's candy to her children. She did not know whether it was the sweet Rachel wanted, or some gesture of affection, but she could no more deny that hunger. Impulsively, she offered her a piece of the sesame and caramel bar, saying, "Why don't you share with us?" Then, frightened by her boldness, and the difficult situation in which she might be placing Rachel, she added hesitantly, "I mean, if you want to, if you like this kind of candy."

To her surprise, Rachel accepted her offer.

"Throw that filthy thing away immediately," Miss Nutting ordered.

Rachel continued to nibble and Miss Nutting reached over and slapped the candy out of her hand. There was a tense silence between the two cabins, with everyone watching what Rachel would do. She picked up the sticky candy, wiped off the sand, and munched it again. It was so queer, she thought, if the Arab lady had taken a fancy to the clean candy man of old days, this might never be happening. It seemed incredible that so much meaning could be attached to a piece of dirty sugar, that so much of what she would think of herself in the future depended on her eating it. Miss Nutting again flung the candy out of Rachel's hand and this time also slapped her face. Rachel was not angry, but afraid, because she felt she must now retaliate in order to save herself, to be able to live with herself. She made an immense effort to stand up, then, very deliberately, slapped Miss Nutting hard, across both cheeks. Her fingers streaked them, white, then purple; the beach seemed to fade away. Rachel struggled against her faintness.

Miss Nutting said quietly, "We'd better go home," and the three of them hurried to take everything inside the cabin, careful not to glance at their neighbors, who maintained a stricken silence. They remained wordless on the way home, and when they were there, Miss Nutting said, "Daniel, go and play in the garden. I must talk to Rachel."

Miss Nutting had made an effort as great as Rachel's to control her sick nerves and not to indulge in a battle on the beach. She felt exhausted, but also, strangely calm and detached. She sat down, pointed another chair to the girl, and said, "Look at me, Rachel."

The girl lifted her eyes and quickly dropped them.

"Do you really want to be like those natives?"

"No . . . but . . ." Rachel lapsed into silence, wringing her hands.

"Like your mother, then?"

"No . . . But mother never wanted me to be like her anyway. I don't want to be like you either. That was why I had to . . . why I . . ." Rachel blurted out, but did not continue.

"I'm quite aware of that." The governess's face twitched. "You never considered how hard I've tried to teach you manners. Apparently, it can't be done. I see that girl Zeinab picking her nose, and Daniel immediately does it too. It drives me insane."

"If you had only scolded us about those sort of manners, I wouldn't have hated you," Rachel cried out, "but you made everything that belongs to us look stupid and ugly, and then I didn't know what to do."

They looked at one another, each thinking, "She mustn't see me cry."

After a long pause during which both of them regained some composure, Miss Nutting said, "I'll tell your mother I'm going to leave. That is what you want, isn't it, Rachel?"

"I don't know any more," Rachel said dully.

"You mean it no longer matters because the harm is done." Miss Nutting thought of Rachel growing up, and all the turmoil in her concentrated upon one single thought. There must be an act of charity somewhere in her that could save something from this wreckage for

Rachel and for herself. She spoke with infinite weariness. "Perhaps you can't or won't understand what I'm going to say. Don't waste your life chasing after dreams. Some things are lost never to be found again. It would have happened whether or not I came to you. You have lost your world, Rachel, but you still have your life. It's a precious thing, a life, and flees—so fast." Her hands fell emptily, heavily, into her lap.

Rachel, who had crumpled, now straightened up. Her eyes flashed, her fists clenched, and it was through clamped teeth that she spoke: "I don't even know what you're talking about," she said.

"Don't you?" Miss Nutting gave a little laugh. "Why then did you keep putting off and putting off what happened today?" She caught herself up sharply. Even if Rachel threw away the wisdom she could give her, she must not slip back into the old, shabby cruelties. "I'll tell your mother this climate has ruined my health. For the last time we'll pretend nothing has happened."

She smiled ruefully as the back of her hand stroked Rachel's cheek. Then she dismissed her with a jerky little push. "Go now. Tell Daniel."

Her fingers were trembling as she made up her face, to feel collected when she confronted Alice. The moment she heard Alice come in, Miss Nutting went to her room and said, "I must go, Mrs. Gaon. I've become so irritable with the children it's simply not fair to them. I'm not well. I want a rest. Rachel doesn't need me any longer, and Daniel won't really, once he goes to school."

"This is rather sudden," Alice said cautiously. "I noticed you were nervous, and felt a tension between you and Rachel. I wished to speak to you about it, but somehow I couldn't do it as before. It worried me. What has happened, Miss Nutting?"

"Nothing has happened. I only need a rest." For an instant, Sheila Nutting was tempted to sob wildly, to pour out her heart. She did not do it, not only because Alice was Rachel's mother and could not be expected to offer sympathy; she must not break down before she was alone, for she would need some remnant of self-esteem which might help her to live the arid years stretching endlessly before her.

She spoke haltingly. "It's time for me to return home—to England anyway. I'll go to Cook's tomorrow. I'll reserve a passage as soon as I can." She ran from Alice's room.

This time, Alice did not ask her to stay. She guessed some drama had been played out, but almost feared to know what it was. The next morning, when Miss Nutting went into the town to book her passage, Alice took her children to the beach, and noticed the strained aloofness of the neighbors, who had previously been so eagerly friendly. She asked her children, obliquely, "Are you sorry to see Miss Nutting go?"

"Yes, of course," they stated, and said no more.

"Did she make you unhappy? Did you quarrel?"

"Oh, sometimes, naturally. Nothing important," Rachel said.

Alice did not believe her, but chose not to insist. The truth, she guessed, involved her too deeply, and she would rather not know it just yet.

For the last two weeks that Miss Nutting was with the Gaons, everyone in the house was inordinately considerate toward each other. There were too many things that must not be talked about. Miss Nutting behaved as if she had already gone, and Rachel and Daniel, unused to their liberty, hovered around her, but there was nothing they could say. Both were profoundly shocked that she was actually leaving. They had hardly had a life, even in their dream worlds, that did not derive from her existence, and they suffered to think of the vast universe where she was so much alone, of the misery they had caused her. When David came for the weekend, he too was so upset, as he parted from Miss Nutting, that he could not bring himself to say he was sorry to see her go.

Alice and her children accompanied Miss Nutting aboard the ship, a P. and O. liner, filled with civil servants on leave from India. They talked uncomfortably, exchanging advice and promises to write. When the siren blew for the visitors to leave, they kissed goodbye. Miss Nutting realized that, heart-rending as the last two weeks had been, she was still with her children, but in a moment, would have lost them, to be left utterly alone, utterly loveless.

She clasped them to her, and said, "Whatever you think of me, remember—I did love you."

"Yes, Miss Nutting," they said for the last time, wishing that the habit of these words had not been so strong as to blot out all the other things they might have told her.

"Go," the governess said, "go quickly." She fled, without once turning back her head.

Rachel and Daniel wept all the way home, but Alice could sense their relief. They cheered up over tea, and she told them that their father was soon coming home, and mustn't see them look so miserable. When their mother was called to the telephone, they smiled at each other, then in embarrassment, quickly turned their heads. "I'll go out to the garden. I wish I could really paint all the flowers in it," Daniel said.

Rachel quietly slipped out of the house, and for the first time in her life went alone to the beach. She stood on the cliff, looking at the ships on the horizon, she a sentinel protecting her shore and all the world behind it. She had cast out the invader. She had won her battle, whatever Miss Nutting said. It was only Miss Nutting who had made her doubt, but now she and her world were safe. She did have a world, and it couldn't change, not Rachel's world, not ever again.

Everything would be as it was before Miss Nutting had come. No, before Nanny had come. No, before Mamma had gone away to England. No, before Rachel was even born. It would be again the world Grandmother Gaon had lived in. Rachel started at the realization that she had not known that world, and quickly pushed away the thought. She would be, one day, exactly like her Grandmother Hattouna had been. Then Rachel thought irritably, no, after all, even when she was very old, she wouldn't wear a wig, or dress like an Arab, or take snuff. Anyway, now that Miss Nutting had gone, she could ask her father to give her back her snuffbox. She would hold it, hold it, and never let it go. She would never let her world change, even if she had to put it together again every day, stone by stone. That world wasn't like Humpty-Dumpty, who fell and could never be put together again.

She heard her mother's voice calling, "Caline! Caline!" Defiantly she picked up a stone, rubbed smooth by the sea, and flung it at the distant line of ships behind which the other world lay. Then, answering to the old, affectionate name, she turned and ran back toward the house.

*Six*

# Ma'adi

*Upon her death Kahanoff left fragments of an unfinished novel,* Tamra, *a text with which she struggled for many years but never completed. The protagonist, seventeen-year-old Tamra Rashi, recently arrived in Cairo to live with her father, Ezechiel, a wealthy gem merchant. Tamra was born in India and had attended an English boarding school before her father summoned her to join him in Egypt. The text uses Tamra's perspective as an outsider as a device for reflecting upon and critiquing Egyptian society. The novel opens as Tamra begins her first day at a French lycée in 1930s Cairo, where she befriends the intellectual Andrée and the socialite Gina. This chapter also introduces Khadri, an Egyptian Muslim engineer, the object of Tamra's youthful affections. As this chapter depicts, Tamra's new friends help her to integrate into her new environs. The chapter's title refers to a leafy suburb of Cairo. This chapter has never before been published in any language.*

Tamra felt that life was starting at last, full, exciting, all of it new. A new school, a new country, new friends, new clothes, a new year, and perhaps—perhaps—the newness of loving. It was almost too much; caught in the swirl of the holiday season, so different from any she had known before, she could hardly sort out the wealth of impressions that assailed her, but surrendered to them.



Happily discarding her schoolgirl tweeds and plaids, she hastily assembled the wardrobe of a young girl going to the theater, the opera, parties. In Egypt, it wasn't considered proper to buy ready-made clothes, so she rushed around, usually with Mrs. Ptesh, to get samples of materials she showed to Andrée, whose taste for clothes was exquisite, yet strict. Wasn't this pale green woolen a little fancy for a suit? Could she recommend a good tailor? And what about her afternoon dresses? Mrs. Viterbo had offered that the Greek dressmaker who worked for them at home make them; and since there was little time, Gina and the maid would help with the actual sewing. Anything looked nice on young girls, she had said; girls didn't need to go to expensive dressmakers for little party dresses, Andrée had sniffed, making little disapproving throat noises. Mrs. Viterbo was a sweet woman, but no authority on fashion, and Gina, poor dear, had no "chic," going in for overly bright colors and complicated models. Tamra should at least make sure her dresses were very simple, particularly since, although endowed with a nice figure, she was so "petite." Feverishly, they looked through fashion journals, selecting models to match them to the samples of materials.

Coaching and homework were almost set aside. Andrée, the intellectual, seemed to enjoy by proxy that Tamra would be out, and was determined that her first encounter with Cairo society be off to a good start. It touched and puzzled Tamra that Andrée, who despised Cairo society, should be so concerned about her success. Andrée, controlling the shrillness of her voice, remarked that it was far better to choose to turn one's back on society because one could, rather than to have it turn its back on you. In her case, she candidly admitted, it was different; she would have nothing to do with those awful, vain, vulgar young men of Cairo's so-called high society. She knew very well they made fun of her behind her back because she was ugly and intellectual, while trying to seduce her because she was rich, thinking she'd be fool enough to fall for any young man who'd court her. She wasn't going to live in Egypt anyway, but in the intellectual milieu of France. She didn't think she'd go to Gina's party. Her parents weren't too keen on it, and she was invited to another party she wouldn't go to either. She could always give as a pretext that she was in mourning.

"But you have invited us to the opera," Tamra protested. "So how can you say you are in mourning? You'll hurt Gina's feelings terribly.

"Well, I'll see. Don't tell her a word about it anyway. Promise?"

Tamra promised, rather unhappily. But she was too absorbed to give much thought to the matter—she simply felt elated and subtly ill at ease. It was astounding how much time could be used running from one fitting to the other, getting the proper accessories, a couple of hats, and shoes made to measure by a dour Armenian craftsman who received models from Italy. The shoes pinched dreadfully, to make the feet appear as small, narrow, and dainty as possible.

Still, Tamra was determined to suffer as much as Cinderella, if that was the condition for meeting Prince Charming. It was fun—but also disturbing—to spend money so freely. Now, when her father asked her if she needed anything, she no longer said, "No thank you Father, I have everything I need." She shamefacedly confessed that she needed money. He gave it to her, telling her she could also open charge accounts, but to remember elegance was one thing, extravagance another. He predicted daily, reading the Arab-language paper *al-Ahram*, that extravagance would be the undoing of the Egyptian Jewish community, flaunting its wealth, forgetting that while the poor excused, even enjoyed, their own aristocracy basking in wasteful luxury, they did not forgive it in the case of minorities. Foreigners—Jews in particular—should be more cautious, taking as an example the Parsis of India, immensely rich, but disciplined enough not to show it. Tamra hardly paid attention to these warnings, nor argued. What was the point of hoarding wealth without anyone enjoying it, either the profligate or the poor? Giddily spending—by her standards—not bothering to add up what it amounted to, it still nevertheless nagged at her conscience that she was spending so much and found it intoxicating. There was something rather perverse in feeling compassion for someone like Marika, the Greek dressmaker, with her bad breath, her stooped shoulders, and her black dress that smelled of perspiration, while feeling elated at being able to afford pretty, useless things. Up to now, she had gone along reluctantly when her aunt chose her clothes for her. Now she enjoyed choosing her own, surprised to discover she enjoyed luxury more than she knew.

She wanted to enjoy life, her life, and the brilliant winter sunshine, so different from the icy British fog, gave a special sparkle to this enjoyment. The air, outside, was like champagne, while the houses were rather chill. Gina said that in Egypt, people hibernated in summer, crushed by the heat; everything was tan, dusty, bleached white by the sun; nor was there much to do except go to the movies. But when the Nile flood had receded, leaving behind it its vivifying silt, everything came back to life. The fields sprouted, a bright tender green, and the winter season was marvelously exciting, particularly if the cotton crop had fetched good prices.

In winter, all kinds of foreign troupes came to perform—the Comédie Française, the Italian Opera, the Old Vic, ballet troupes, Indian and Spanish dancers, and even the Palestinian Philharmonic Orchestra with Toscanini conducting. Gina was insatiable, attending every matinee performance. Sometimes they went together, with other young people from Maʿadi, sometimes with Andrée, inevitably accompanied by Trude, who sat stolidly through the performances.

The public intrigued Tamra; it was so uninhibited, and so diverse. Up in the gallery, girls chatted volubly, and Gina, who as a child had attended first a Catholic girl's school then a lay Italian one, seemed to know and be liked by everyone. Boys folded their programs into darts which they sent flying across the hall with ear-splitting whistles, but when the lights were dimmed and the curtain went up, an almost religious silence descended upon the rowdy crowd.

What puzzled Tamra most was that the distinction between native and foreigner, so clear in Great Britain, was here blurred—even the word *native* was a tricky one to use. Students from many schools attended these matinee performances, each program drawing a special public; thus the Italian pantomime troupe, the Piccolini, attracted a predominantly Italian public. But it surprised her that many schools and school systems coexisted side by side in Egypt—religious schools and lay schools; French, British, Italian, and Greek schools; and those of the Egyptian government. There didn't seem to be any unifying factor, not even that imposed by the occupying power. Many languages were heard during the intermissions, but almost no Arabic, and the public seemed composed almost exclusively of members of the minorities, with Jews predominating, and apparently studying in most of the schools. Nor for that matter were "real" Europeans much in evidence. Her own bizarre education, her non-belonging, so painful in Europe, seemed here a kind of normal anomaly.

"But why don't students from the Egyptian government schools attend these performances?" Tamra asked Gina one afternoon as they sat with Lucien up in the gallery. "I suppose they don't know French well enough to follow a play in French. But what about the Italian pantomimes? There's no language barrier there."

"They come only when an English company presents a play that's included in their school program. Why should they be interested in ballet, opera, or music? It's foreign to them. We are Europeans, de culture française," Gina explained, with obvious pride. "We care about French culture even more than the French do themselves. They take it for granted, but for us, it is our most precious acquisition, more precious than the air we breathe."

"But isn't there a native Egyptian culture?" Tamra asked.

Lucien shrugged. "Belly dancing. That's all Moslems are interested in. Ils sont abrutis."

Gina conceded that there were some Egyptian writers. Taha Husayn, for instance, who was blind, a village boy so bright he had been sent to study in France, where he had married a French woman. He was said to have created modern Egyptian literature, by writing in an easy, simple colloquial language rather than in the flowery classical *nahw*.* Did Tamra see that slim, distinguished-looking boy whose face was so much like those seen on the bas-reliefs of ancient Egypt. That was Taha Husayn's son. No, she didn't know if there were any other Arab writers, probably not any of a worth comparable to that of the French moderns.

"But they write about their world, the country you live in, and you aren't interested?"

"One story of fellahin is much like the other," Lucien sneered. "What do you expect them to write about?"

Even Andrée, with whom Tamra discussed the question, seemed very little interested. She seemed to think that while at present a European culture was the exclusive privilege of a snobbish, moneyed class, the revolution would make its finest works available to all. But was a

* *Nahw* [Arabic] is the formal grammar and syntax of literary Arabic. Kahanoff is mistaken in her assertion. Husayn wrote in literary Arabic; however, his accessible style helped shape the development of modern literary Arabic prose.

revolution needed, Tamra wondered, for youngsters who all went to school to share at least some elements of a common culture? The chasm separating minority and majority seemed serious indeed; it wasn't only a matter of poor and rich, or of generations, but of people of the same generation who had the same level of education. Gina felt offended if she was told she was native, insisting that she was European and that *native* was used only by the British in reference to the "locals," with a pejorative connotation. She warned Tamra not to use that word as she might in England. But when Tamra asked her if she considered herself a foreigner, Gina protested, "Of course not!" At least on her father's side of the family, they had lived in Egypt for many generations. Tamra did not pursue the matter. It was an odd world where people both belonged and didn't belong, mixed and didn't mix. Had it always been that way, she wondered, or had it happened at a fairly late date, that of, say, her father's generation? This Egypt, which enchanted and fascinated her, and repelled her, too, at times, was not one, but two—the dim unknown Egypt of the majority, and the semi-European Egypt of the minorities, to which she supposed she belonged. She had hoped, coming East, to come closer to her own roots, to understanding her own being, which she had always felt was rooted in the East. But most of those she knew, Andrée, Gina, and in his own way Lucien, felt the attraction of the West. They and their parents were born in Egypt, and yet they, too, were rootless, although in most cases, they didn't seem to know it yet. And Khadri, where did he belong, or the son of Taha Husayn, who spoke such beautiful French—with a Parisian accent. Were these crossbreeds just freaks in regards to the norm, or something new, a valuable part of a new kind of world in the making? There was no way of knowing, but in this peculiar patchwork of people, cultures, religions, she didn't feel as strange, as cut off as she did elsewhere, and for the time being that was enough.

The streets of Cairo, fleetingly glimpsed, most often from inside the car her father always sent for her, offered Tamra her only point of contact with that other Egypt, that of the majority—a fascinating yet at times disquieting spectacle. Women, shrouded in black, glided by; innumerable street vendors and shoeshine boys assailed the passersby; beggars in tattered rags exposed their stumps or pounced on cigarette butts, chased by the policemen—one knew not why. Many had eyes ruined by some infection and did not even bother to chase the flies which clustered there, feeding on the pus when the sun was hot. No one seemed to care. She knew, of course, of the poverty of India, but hadn't expected that Egypt would be so poor. Once, when they left the theater and were caught by the rain, one of those rare winter downpours, the street urchins turned their torn, soiled robes up over their heads—they were quite naked underneath, the girls as well as the boys.

"Where do they sleep at night?" Tamra asked.

Gina said she didn't know, adding that many curled up at the entrance of department stores to protect themselves from the wind.

"But that's terrible—and nobody cares?"

Lucien shrugged. "Their own leaders don't care. Why should we? Besides, they are used to it. I suppose their own dirt keeps them warm."

"That's a nasty thing to say," Gina reprimanded.

"Would saying it in a nice way change the facts? You girls with your sentimental hearts!" Lucien scoffed, and Tamra could not quite blame him. Giving alms did not assuage the prickings of her conscience, and Lucien, who planned to settle in a kibbutz in Palestine, was more of an idealist than either she or Gina in his own, rather grim way. "In Palestine, we can at least work at solving our own problems," he'd explain. "Here, we Jews are the fleshpots of Egypt, too blinded by the pleasures of this soft, corrupt life to see the dangers ahead. Here, a nationalist explosion will blow us all away. And we don't even really bother to see what Hitler means. It's going to do a lot of good if Jewish schoolchildren boycott Faber pencils! It will ruin German industry. No, I'm not wasting time on compassion. Who has felt compassion for the Jews? In Palestine, at least, we'll fight, our backs to the wall, to have a country of our own."

Gina argued that Egypt was the most hospitable of countries—their father always said so. Lucien answered with a shrug, "The British are hospitable at the Egyptians' expense, because they still need us. If ever they leave . . ."

"Lucien has always been rather fanatical about Palestine," Gina remarked lightly, as if to reassure Tamra.

"A fanatic? We'll see ten years from now. You hide your head like an ostrich. But the good life in Egypt, it won't last forever. Hitler will see to that. Father thinks that because he has pashas for clients we're safe. He prefers to ignore how treacherous they are."

Tamra didn't like Lucien. He made her feel life in Egypt was so precarious that, with a little shame, she felt rather glad she had a British passport. Yet she wondered about Palestine. She knew Hebrew fairly well—her father had always seen to it she had Hebrew lessons. Indeed, in their wandering, she was glad for it, feeling that through their nomadic existence, there was at least this bond with the only people she could call her own. She did not know what else she was, but about her being Jewish, there was no doubt. Palestine had represented a kind of far-off ideal, but the Zionists she met in Egypt—Lucien, the girls at school—seemed somehow simple minded in a dour way, reducing everything to an obsession about Jewish fate to the exclusion of anything else that was happening in the world. Perhaps they felt at once fearful and guilty, and that the Zionists who were actually in Palestine were different.

Most of the time, she managed to push aside these disturbing thoughts, giving in to the enchantment of Egypt, the delight of a balmy winter sunshine. The air itself was fragrant, and sometimes she'd stop to sniff the indefinable, fruity odor of Cairo: rotting fruit, fresh flowers, vegetable debris, dung from the droppings of camels and donkeys which tangled up the cars, bicycles, and throngs of people even in the main streets. Early in the morning long-toothed camels, looking rather like disgruntled British old maids chewing their cud, brought in produce from the country in rope bags slung over their humps. It was still a primitive world where much of life's drama took place in the street. Once, Abdu slowed down the car to give passage to a Moslem funeral procession. The men carried the coffin on their shoulders, followed by women piled up on brightly painted carts drawn by donkeys with blue beads on their foreheads. They howled and shrieked, and tore at the blue tattoos on their cheeks. The front end of the coffin carried a sort of truncated column on which was perched the dead man's headgear. Tamra thought, irreverently, how funny it would be if in England a gentleman's coffin was thus decorated by his top hat perched on his umbrella, and English ladies, instead of looking so pinched, piled on carts and just let themselves cry out loud. And then of course there was the Nile, the oldest of

Old Man Rivers, just rolling, rolling along from the heart of Africa to the Mediterranean, the green valley enclosing its brown majestic waters. Sometimes, when she crossed the Qasr al-Nil bridge to go to Andrée, she'd see the feluccas with their huge white sails slowly move downriver, at once heavy and graceful. Some lowered and rolled up their sails to pass under the bridge; others waited for the hour when the bridge split open, its two halves lifting up in the air to let them through. Such river boats, bringing the produce from Upper Egypt—perhaps even precious woods and elephant tusks from Africa—had probably existed in the days of Pharaoh, whose presence subtly pervaded the still melancholy of Egypt. The three triangles of the pyramids, outlined against the sky, or dimly perceived through a veil of haze, reminded the busy modern world how very ancient Egypt was, and somehow, just because at the dawn of history her own Hebrew ancestors had been so dramatically involved in Egypt, she felt this world closer to her than any in which she had lived in so transient a manner. She longed, rather than go to a French school, to come to know this Egypt, its countryside and villages, to walk the streets of Cairo on her own, get lost in the mysterious Arab quarters. But she held back the wild wandering impulse; she was enjoying more freedom and having a better time than ever before in her life, so it would be foolish to jeopardize this pleasant state of affairs. Later, she would contrive to see the city, and Egypt, in their own way. Now, she must bide her time, with plenty enough to occupy her.

Tamra felt the dreamy, almost hypnotic charm of Egypt envelope her, as if the land itself watched, patiently, the agitated world of foreign cars and their passengers rushing to and fro, but then a street scene of incredible brutality shattered this illusion of a stillness akin to eternity.

Nationalist manifestations occurred almost every year, Tamra learned. She found it quite understandable that the Egyptians should want the British to leave. She had no idea what had provoked the present flare-up, or why young men wearing tarbushes, waving the Egyptian flag, milled about the streets, shouting slogans. Traffic was stopped, the car caught in the eddies of the swirling crowd, and she watched hundreds of street urchins climb atop the streetcars, dancing, gesticulating, shouting, hanging all over it like clusters of ants. Then there was a long scream, a blood-curdling scream, and a clamor rose from the crowed.

She couldn't believe she had really seen a little boy fall off, the crowd surging around him. Had he been electrocuted? Caught between the wheels by the crowd as he fell?

"Close the window, Miss Tamra. It's dangerous now. Don't look." Slowly, but relentlessly, Abdu pushed her car through the crowd.

"Shouldn't we stop? This boy . . . we should take him to the hospital."

"The police will take care of it, Miss. Europeans, they no meddle. Too dangerous. Them only street Arabs. Ladies no mix. Anyway, the boy he dead now. He go under wheel."

Abdu, who was proud to have worked many years for an English family, seemed to think it was of no consequence that a boy was trampled to death; this kind of thing took place in a world where she—a European!—had no need to concern herself. She felt quite sick, and yet realized she had better not get out of the car with those ogling, grimacing faces pressing against the glass leering at her. Abdu managed to extricate the car, and taking a roundabout way, deposited her at Madame Rayme's, where she was due for a final fitting of her evening dress.

The cloying scent of warm, perfumed flesh nauseated her.

"What is the matter, you look not quite yourself. Were you caught in the riot? How dreadful!"

The news that a boy had fallen off the tramway and been crushed to death had spread like wildfire, Tamra gathered.

"Ya Allah, what is the world coming to!" exclaimed a gorgeous sleek woman with very white skin and very dark hair, bringing her long bejeweled hands to her cheeks, then to her powdered throat where she fingered her three-strand pearl necklace. "It's terrible!" she wailed. "If the riots spread we might be blocked tonight. It's the premiere at the opera! Quelle catastrophe!"

"Voyons! Voyons! Calmez-vous ma chère! Ne dramatisons pas!" Madame Rayme soothed her clients, waving her long cigarette holder at the end of her long red nails, all her costume jewelry jingling. "At sundown quiet returns! The police have the situation under control."

Tamra went into the booth. Mechanically, she undressed, slipped on her shimmering evening dress, helped by a little girl of fourteen. She came out into the salon, her eyes downcast, not wanting to look at herself in the mirror.

Madame Rayme was talking very fast in her brittle, tough voice. "It's perfect! Ravissant! Turn around please, Miss Tamra. Straighten up, otherwise the dress does not fall as it should. I'm sure you'll enjoy wearing it. May it be on many happy occasions."

"Yes, thank you," Tamra answered, as if voices reached her from a great distance. Her face was suddenly beaded with drops of sweat. She had glanced at the mirror; not really looking at the image there, or rather, overlaying it, she saw the demented street scene, a small mangled brown body.

"Quickly! A glass of water," Madame Rayme called to the petite man. "Did you actually see? Pauvre enfant!"

The *pauvre enfant*, Tamra realized, applied to her, not to the child who had been trampled to death. In a frenzy, she changed back into her skirt and sweater, wanting to be out in the street, to get some fresh air.

"The dress will be delivered this afternoon," Madame Rayme was saying. "Best wishes for a happy new year, and may you come for many more exquisite dresses. J'aimerais beaucoup vous habiller . . ."

"Oui, oui merci beaucoup Madame," Tamra stammered.

People died in automobile accidents, in wars. Life went on. A little boy fell off a streetcar and died. One turned one's head the other way. Life went on. It wouldn't change anything not to wear that dress, not to go to the opera or to Gina's party, even if that scene could never be erased from her memory. She was, after all, a European. What business of hers was it that life, that of street urchins anyway, counted for so little that the policemen did not trouble to prevent them from climbing on tramways? Indeed, who was his brother's keeper? What did she have to complain about? Her father was a dealer in precious stones. It couldn't be helped. One was born in a gutter and died there, and the other could afford evening dresses that cost a small fortune—and the added luxury of the proper humanitarian feelings. There was no sense to the world; it was just like a film turned too fast—beautiful women, venomous flower beggars like gutter cats scrounging in garbage cans for food, rose gardens fed with the blood of slaughtered animals, Nietzsche, Proust, the Princesse de Clèves. It made no sense, no sense at all, except to God above; perhaps to him each life was no more than a particle of sand lifted in the swirling wind, falling with the wind, of no more consequence. If one wanted to live, one must have eyes not to see, ears not to hear.

Angela opened the door for her. La Signorina Gina had dropped in, deposited a parcel, and asked Signorina Tamra to call her back. "I'll call back later," Tamra said. "I just want to lie down a little while." She wanted to be left alone, crawl into a dark corner and be left alone.

Tamra flung off her clothes. She just wanted a bath. But Angela knocked at the door, bringing in a second parcel, with a note from Andrée. Both parcels came from the French Library. She opened the parcels and laughed out loud. Both Andrée and Gina had sent her Proust's *À la recherche du temps perdu*, Gina in a current *poche* edition, requiring the pages to be cut, maddeningly, from the top and sides, and Andrée in a beautifully bound luxury edition. She first read Andrée's note: "You will discover an Andrée in the pages of this work. By the time you find the Andrée who is at present guiding you through the shoals of French literature, she will no longer be needed, but her love and friendship will endure forever and ever."

So she would have to discover Andrée in the pages of a book? Gina had written a letter rather than a note, in her bold handwriting: "Before we go to the opera, I thought you might enjoy reading Proust's description of an evening at the opera in Paris. It is a marvelous passage, difficult, but marvelous. The Egypt we live in is a reduced model, an orientalized version of Proust's world, something precious which survives from the nineteenth century. It describes a world that is snobbish, corrupt, refined, cruel but enchanted. Our generation has been fed Proust, grown up on Proust, lived on Proust, and this world, too, like Proust's, is one whose ephemeral beauty can be remembered only when transfigured by the greatest of all geniuses who knows that only through the magic of art can 'le temps perdu être retrouvé.' Long after the grand spectacle is over and the actors forgotten, gone, something is remembered, lives on. So will it be with us, Tamra, later in our lives, when we shall remember this year when our friendship was born." It went on, disordered and romantic, for seven pages.

"They are crazy," Tamra muttered. It would be embarrassing to tell them both they had sent the same present. Perhaps she needn't tell the one about the other's present. She had sent them quite different presents: to Andrée, who hated anything "exotic," a big square vase of a beautiful blue that would go very well in her room, and to Gina, who loved the exotic, a sari, dark blue, threaded with gold so that for once, she would have to abstain from the strong colors she was so fond of.

Since her father wasn't coming home, Tamra had a hot bath, and instead of lunch, she had her favorite meal—nuts, dried fruit, and fresh fruit—and curled up on her sofa bed with Proust. She did not grasp the meaning of his long, intricate sentences; Proust was way beyond her, and anyway, she preferred biology to literature, but she did try to read the passage Gina had indicated, about the opera, thoughtfully noting down the volume and the page numbers, but that, too, was beyond her, although in spite of herself she was caught in the shimmering net of words. The titles of the books piqued her curiosity, especially "À l'obre des jeunes filles en fleur." That was where she found Andrée, who seemed somewhat of a libertine, although she wasn't very clear about her relationship to Proust.

She dressed carefully that evening, put on a little lipstick, hesitated about wearing some jewelry in spite of Andrée's advice, and decided against it. She told herself she was silly; nevertheless, Tamra felt intimidated as she and Andrée climbed the marble staircase of the Opera House, where they were joined by Gina, who arrived breathlessly in blue taffeta and tulle that Andrée surveyed rather disapprovingly. She wore a pale, pearly ivory brocade with just a hint of pink. Cairo's Opera House, built by the Khedive Isma'il,* was indeed a reduced copy of the Paris Opera, in a slightly orientalized version. Extraordinarily beautiful women—wrapped in satins, velvets, and furs, scintillating with jewelry, diamonds—strutted like peacocks. The three girls sat down in the box, Andrée placing Gina and Tamra in front, while she sat behind, in the shadow with Trude, but leaning forward to tell Tamra who were the people coming in and greeting one another. The one with the bicorn and the plumes was the French ambassador . . . that one the British high commissioner . . . the woman in the white satin dress was Mrs. Diacomides, the celebrated beauty . . . the rotund little man was the director of the Compagnie du Canal Suez . . . the tall handsome young man with the tarbush

* Isma'il Pasha was the Ottoman khedive (viceroy) of Egypt from 1863 to 1879.

was Prince Hassan Tousson, the love of the French actress Solange Dufy . . . and did Tamra see those boxes, the biggest, closest to the stage? The one covered with black gauze and embroidered with a floral motif was the box of the queen and royal princess, who thus could see but not be seen. One could guess when the ladies of the Turkish aristocracy were in their boxes, because unlike Arab women, they did not wear black veiling, but white, just a little bit of it wrapped gracefully around their chins. And that very tall man in the black uniform with the gold buttons, he was the chief of police. It was an extraordinary spectacle, with men in brilliant uniforms, their chests covered with medals, others in tarbushes, and the women, some dark, some blond, all dressed sumptuously, extravagantly, as in a fairy tale, as if in the cavernous depths of the Opera House the treasures in Ali Baba's cave had been flung with open hands to fall on the diplomats and princes and the beautiful women, whose names—Greek, British, French, Italian, Armenian, Arabic—Tamra could not distinguish.

"Look!" Gina cried out excitedly, "the Agha Khan and the Begum!* They always spend their winters in Egypt." The Agha Khan, portly, indeed enormously fat, reminded Tamra of her father because he was dark and had a peppery walrus moustache. As to the Begum, who was French, she was like a giantess—beautiful, but so tall and so large that everyone around her looked as though they belonged to a race of dwarves. The spectacle on the stage, splendid as it was, was only a part of, almost a pretext to, the grander spectacle in the cavern where the jewels glittered in the dark.

During the intermission, gentlemen kissed ladies' hands, the ladies bowed to one another, people visited one another in their boxes. To Gina's disappointment, Andrée wouldn't go out to the foyer, but Tamra was entranced by the display in the gaudy red velvet hall trimmed with gold. *Aïda*, with its Egyptian setting, was just right for this public; it had first been performed in this very Opera House for its opening,

* Agha Khan is the title bestowed upon the imam of Naziri Isma'ili Muslims. Sultan Mohammad Shah, Agha Khan III, bore the title from 1885 until his death in 1957. He was also a diplomat and served as the president of the League of Nations from 1937 to 1938. Begum is an honorific title granted to the Agha Khan's wife.

which had been attended by Empress Eugénie.* Andrée pointed to some members of her family, descendants of the famous beauty Céline, the lady in waiting of the khediva, who had received Eugénie. The tall, very ugly woman in the dark red velvet dress trimmed with black beads, which she dragged out for all great occasions, was her Aunt Caroline. To Tamra, it was as if the world of those days had been briefly resurrected in this pantomime which was being acted down in the parterre, in the boxes where people visited one another. A few young men of Andrée's family came to Andrée's box. They knew Gina, whom they greeted with standoffish formality. Andrée introduced Tamra, whom they examined with a barely disguised curiosity. Although she did not know it, and hardly noticed the young men, her sudden friendship with Andrée was much discussed, a matter of rumor and speculation, particularly since nobody had seen this young girl, reputed to be very dark, very rich—and a little strange. Aunt Caroline herself came to the box, ostensibly to kiss her niece, and deplored the fact that "le pauvre Juliette" simply refused to pull herself together and lived as a "malade imaginaire." Of course, every one was chagrined about the passing away of poor dear Jojo. Foie gras had really finished him off, but at least he had enjoyed his life. As she rattled on, Aunt Caroline examined Tamra through her bejeweled *face à main*, but this time it did not disconcert her, as when Andrée's mother had done so. Tamra stood up and bowed to the lady, the confidante of so many Turkish princesses. She was not intimidated or put off because Aunt Caroline was somehow not quite real, something between a ghost and a caricature of bygone days. "Mais je dois te gronder présente moi ta charmante amie . . ."

Aunt Caroline peered closely at Tamra, who wondered if anything was amiss with her dress or her hairdo, but managed to keep her hands at her side. In her screechy voice, the lady launched into a complicated story about two sisters who were "brouillées à mort," concluding, "Alors j'ai dit à la pauvre Marie, que voulez-vous ma chère, il en va de même pour la parenté et la torture: elles existent à tous les degrés." Obviously pleased with her latest bon mot, she cackled her laughter, and

* Although Verdi's *Aïda* did premier in Cairo in 1871, it was his *Rigoletto* that was performed at the Opera House's 1869 inauguration.

straightened up abruptly, to pass judgment. "Elle est charmante, ton amie, Andrée, c'est donc vrai quelle ne porte absolument aucun bijou! Quelle idée ravissante de ne porter que des fleurs—surtout quand on est la fille d'Ezechiel Rashi." Then speaking directly to Tamra, as she touched her arm with her *face à main*, "Il faudra venir me voir un jour avec Andrée!"

Switching to Italian as she spoke to one of her nephews, who Tamra learned had only just returned from Cambridge, she swept out of the box, a frumpish, aged fairy.

The lights were dimmed for the second part of the program, and Andrée, leaning toward Tamra, whispered, exultantly, "You see how right I was about your wearing no jewelry whatsoever? Aunt Caroline and her crowd were prepared to dismiss you as ostentatiously nouveau riche if you wore a great deal of it—tellement déplacé pour une petite jeune fille!—and skimpily put together if you wore just a little. They didn't expect none. That won over Aunt Caroline. C'est un chameau, but she appreciated a certain type of insolence. With her approval, you've made it."

Tamra found the incident rather funny—not properly evaluating the importance of being launched into Cairo society by no less than Caroline de Soria, the intimate friend and confidante of so many Turkish princesses. She asked Andrée why Aunt Caroline had spoken to her in French and to her nephew in Italian. "It is a principle with her to speak to people in the language they are least familiar with," Andrée whispered. "It cuts their repartee. It is only with the British high commissioner she deigns to speak English, and the French ambassador that she'll speak French."

The curtain was raised, Verdi's music reverberated through the hall, and Aïda let loose her tremendous voice. Everything seemed to happen through some kind of enchantment, Tamra felt. The real world and a fairy tale world of illusion could not really be told apart. The conductor's baton animated the figures on the stage, and apparently the touch of Caroline de Soria's *face à main* was enough to transform an obscure, dusky girl from India into a social success. The real and unreal overlapped, the result of unpredictable, arbitrary, magic transformations.

A thunder of applause followed upon the prima donna's last passionate outburst. As the girls left, Andrée met a number of people she knew, to whom she introduced her friends. The Swiss, French, and Belgian girls with whom Andrée played tennis at the Sporting Club were more friendly toward Tamra than toward Gina; the rumor had already spread that Caroline de Soria had described her as "délicieuse—une petite fée très brune sortie tout droit des mille et une nuits."

Outside, under the cold starry night, Rolls-Royces swished by to pick up their precious cargos of plumed ambassadors and scintillating ladies, while police kept the crowd of street Arabs at a respectable distance. Perhaps some of them had participated in the riot that very morning, when a little boy had died. It was all unreal, the touch of a magician enough to change princes into beggars, beggars into princes. Inside the Opera House, the stage was already dark, and the beggar on the brightly lit staircase of the building would also be gone in a moment. The beggars on the outer rim were merely those who had not been touched by the magic wand which allowed some to corner the sugar market or a good part of the cotton crop, or provided the gems that sprinkled these people as stars were strewn over the dark velvet of night. Simply tonight, the magic wand had touched Tamra, too, and the dark little clod of earth was transformed into something that shone and glowed for a little while in the eyes of others; one in a myriad of ephemeral stars. The same particles were bathed now in light, now in darkness, neither being of their choosing, and the particle of consciousness could enjoy the transient happiness, knowing it would not last, just as pain also passed, neither having more reality than the play of light and shadow. Then one could accept the world, even enjoy it, because one didn't believe in its existence—or one's own.

When home, Tamra saw the light in her father's room—he had left his door very slightly ajar. She hesitated, then knocked.

"Come in!" Her father in his dressing gown was playing a game of solitaire. She wondered if he had waited for her.

"It was . . . beautiful." She began excitedly, but ended lamely; her shyness toward him made her tongue-tied. But he knew that as well as she did. And how could she tell him about the evening? He wouldn't understand—or approve.

"You aren't sleepy? No? Then sit down for a little while."

Slowly, he sifted cards, set a red one on a black one. "So that's your new dress. Hmm. I don't know about such things. But of all the women who were there tonight at the opera, it had to be my daughter who didn't wear any jewelry. Sometimes, I think you have a sense of humor all your own." He sounded annoyed, a little hurt, yet amused.

Tamra followed the movement of his hands on the cards. "I think I see a better place for that diamond," she said.

"What? Ah, you mean the cards." He glanced at the cards, moved the one she had indicated, glanced at her and caught a glint of mischief in her eyes before she demurely lowered her eyelids.

"Those women, they were just glittering with diamonds . . . I mean the women at the opera, of course." Tamra fidgeted on her chair. She couldn't tell him about Andrée's advice, or Aunt Caroline. Still, she tried to explain something. "It's not that I don't like jewelry. I'm . . . a little afraid of it, afraid of liking it too much. It represents such unjust power. I don't like to own it or wear it."

"Our prophets railed against the daughters of Israel who adorned themselves. But when all is said and done, it is better to have than not have. Abdu told me about what you saw today in the streets of Cairo. You saw how worthless the lives are of those who own nothing—even to each other. And in countries like Egypt, or India, it would be worse, much worse if the British ever left. They manage to maintain order, even justice of a kind. They represent a standard people respect. Should the British go, it would be a massacre. We Jews, everywhere, must always be their staunchly loyal friends."

Tamra pressed her lips together, not to get into an argument. Her father was proud of his British citizenship, a steadfast supporter of the British Empire who felt only disdain for the natives over which it ruled. Perhaps because she had seen so much of the pettiness of British schoolgirls and schoolteachers, she felt or would like to feel closer to the natives. "They don't exactly like Jews," she couldn't help saying.

"No. I guess not. But at least they respect laws and apply them fairly, in the same ways to all. And that's more than most people have done. They aren't as clever as the French, but are more trustworthy."

He turned a few more cards and then said, hesitantly, looking at his ugly duckling which had suddenly become an attractive young girl.

"There are things a mother should rightly tell her daughter. You were a child and now—you're a young woman. How can I say it? It's not the same with boys, but with girls their reputation is their most important possession. If you had an older woman or friend to whom to confide . . . I wouldn't like you to be hurt."

"I don't think you have to worry, Father." She felt strongly that it was a woman's right to dispose of herself, but there was no point in saying it, and somehow, her father's concern touched her.

"I also wanted to say," he continued, "I've just about made up my mind to buy the house in Maʿadi. That is, if you really like it."

"If I like it!" She clapped her hands. "Oh Father, I'm so happy! Thank you! Thank you so much."

"May you be happy with it child. Well, it's getting late."

"Yes. Good night, Father."

"Good night, Tamra." She lightly touched his cheek.

But she was too excited to sleep. She undressed in front of the mirror, smiling at the image that smiled at her. She danced by herself in her nightgown, opened the window to look at those brilliant stars in the sky. She thought of Khadri, with whom she would dance at Gina's party, and a warm glow flowed inside of her just at the thought of it. She and Khadri must not fall in love, never, on no account. But was it forbidden to feel this tingling of flesh, that something that hurt, below her tongue, inside her nostrils, all over her? Not just a vague longing but a longing for him. And it suddenly occurred to her that her father knew of this attraction, and probably bought the house in Maʿadi trusting her, wanting to show her he trusted her.

In bed, because she couldn't sleep, she took out her new books, *La princesse de Clèves*, *War and Peace*, and *À la recherche du temps perdu*—three worlds, aristocratic and tragic, which had fallen, fallen like leaves from the tree of life. And one day much later, she would remember all that was now: the night at the opera, Andrée's huge silent house by the Nile, this Egypt, which was a little like Proust's world transferred to the East, and something like Tolstoy's feudal world, with its princes and princesses, open, hospitable. Those who had lived in the worlds described did not see the cracks in them, how fragile they were—one to perish in the French Revolution, one in the First World War, and one in the Russian Revolution. And in Egypt, they did not see that their world was cracked and fragile, that it too would become a leaf falling from the tree of life. But alongside that tree, the real one, there was the imaginary one on which the artists stitched the likeness of the leaves fallen from the tree of life. Andrée, Gina, Tamra, Khadri, Ariel, Aunt Caroline, Ezechiel Rashi. As she dozed off, not turning off the light, she half visualized a future time when they would meet in Egypt again, having lived unexpected lives in unexpected places, and they would meet in an Egypt that would be, then, breaking apart like splintered glass, and remember the days of their youth. . . . It was as if she were there, in that future time, when she'd come back to Egypt, to the house in Maʿadi, and her father would no longer be there, but in his room between his two silver peacocks there would stand that picture of her as she had been at seventeen . . . and she'd want to die, to let herself sink in the whirlpool of darkness, and die . . .

Tamra shook herself out of the nightmare. She had been dreaming awake, had lost consciousness of time. It was already two o'clock in the morning. Shivering, she huddled under the warmth of the blanket. Why did she sometimes have these visions of something that was to come as if it had already happened? It was strange; she would forget these scenes, and then something would happen and she'd recognize it as if she had already seen it, lived it. Was this something abnormal? It didn't frighten her when it happened, as did her fits of black despair, when the world seemed to draw into darkness. But she would have liked to talk to somebody about these things—the queer feeling of living in another world, knowing that she was this person here, now, but also another person, not even a person, somewhere else, in another world.

*Seven*

# Alexandria

*Like the previous selection, this chapter is from Kahanoff's unfinished novel* Tamra. *The story related here is unique in Kahanoff's work because it depicts a forbidden love between a Jewish girl and a Muslim boy in Egypt.*

The Viterbos' house in Ma'adi was made ready to withstand the long siege of summer before the family moved to Alexandria. Velvet-upholstered armchairs and sofas were covered with cool cotton slips, and the heavy curtains were removed to be replaced by light cotton ones. Men were hired to clean the rugs, which they rubbed with slightly damp tea leaves, using their feet, progressing in twisting, jerky motions, sweat streaming down their faces. This treatment, Tamra learned, not only cleaned the rugs but restored and preserved the freshness of their colors. The rugs were then rolled up with pepper, camphor, and naphthalene, sewed up in jute bags, and stored away. The knickknacks were removed, the lamps and chandeliers shrouded in stiff gauze to protect them from the myriad of insects which came in spite of the netting fixed to the windows. In the evening the very air vibrated with the faint stridency of their wings, and in the morning every flat surface was covered with the green dust of their dead bodies. In the course of just one night, the tiny insects were hatched, danced tirelessly their love and death dance, laid their eggs, and terminated their brief existence. Mrs. Viterbo found them an awful nuisance, but Tamra could not help wondering at nature, which, however short the lifespan of a species, ensured its survival.

The house, thus stripped, was much cooler, but looked ghostly and sounded hollow, and Tamra now understood what Gina had meant when she had said that in Cairo one hibernated in summer. She thought it would be sad for Mr. Viterbo to live in this deserted house, as he would be coming to Alexandria only for the weekends, but perhaps his concentration on work was such that he was indifferent to his surroundings.

Tamra did her best to follow the Viterbo example. In spite of her inexperience, she enjoyed bustling about, putting things away with Maria and Hassan, who pretended to obey her instructions but knew what had to be done without her telling them. Still, it gave her a good feeling to be the mistress in charge of a house, and she was disappointed that her father simply had the rugs put away in storage with a carpet dealer rather than give them the tea treatment.

As the date of their departure approached, the Viterbos seemed seized with a fever. The house they had rented for the summer was furnished; nevertheless, they were taking household linens and, as Mr. Viterbo put it, "a million and one other things." Nona, in the kitchen, presided over the packing of the cooking utensils and the tableware.

"Aren't those English people leaving any pots and pans?" Tamra innocently inquired.

Nona sniffed. "First, we aren't going to eat in other people's dishes or cook in their pots and pans. They aren't kosher. And besides, what do the English know about cooking? I need my *hamin* for Saturday *dafina*, and all the proper utensils for our oriental dishes." She even packed her spices and herbs, her cases of homemade jams, syrups, and preserves, and her bottles of rose water and orange blossom water for the pastries. The old lady bustled about, the key to the pantry attached to her waist. Tamra loved to see Nona's big jars of jams shining in the pantry—the dark, sensuous red of dates, the orange-rose of quinces; indeed, they were the color of precious stones.

Mrs. Viterbo spent the best part of a day packing medicines, carefully wrapping up mysterious bottles, tubes, and boxes in tissue paper and fitting them tightly in a chest reserved for this purpose.

"Mamie, do you expect us all to be sick all summer?" Gina teased as she helped her mother screw the corks tight and wrap up the breakable containers.

"I've never seen a summer when children don't get sunburns—starting with you, Miss Gina—bruises, cuts, colds, tummy aches, infected mosquito bites. I like to have all I may need on hand," Mrs. Viterbo defended herself.

"And let's not forget your old pieces of linen for compresses, linseed poultices, for dry coughs, hot cups for wet coughs . . . they might run out of supplies at the local pharmacy," Gina laughed and kissed her mother. "I'll never be as good a mother as you."

"I know about physical aches. But perhaps I'm too ignorant a woman to understand your soul," Mrs. Viterbo said, with a sigh.

"Oh, but that's not true," Tamra exclaimed, flinging her arms around her. "I feel so happy here, with you." Then she felt embarrassed by this display of feeling—all the more so because she was not Mrs. Viterbo's daughter. Here she had never felt excluded and was grateful to be accepted in the intimacy of this feminine world of remedies and recipes. Mrs. Viterbo kissed her back. "That was a sweet thing to say. I'm glad you are fond of us, as we are of you."

So this was what it was like to have a family, to be a family, Tamra thought. A home long lived in, with its hidden corners, the particular smell of the pantry, of the medicine chest, of the linen closet where jasmine dried between the sheets; a house with its weak spots—the door that creaked, the drawer that was a little stiff. She tried to help, wondering whether she wanted or could have such a home and family one day. She had known the Viterbos' home for its hospitality, but now she knew it from the inside, with its secrets. This feminine world was the real life of a house, something men knew nothing about. Mrs. Viterbo, she thought, was not an ignorant woman, but her knowledge was a kind of experience handed down from generation to generation. When people spoke pompously of "civilization," they meant big, formal things, such as art, books, museums, paintings, but beneath all this, as its invisible foundation, there were the modest skills and crafts used in households, each of which had a slightly different character. Women used this lore much as people use language, making their own particular mode of expression of the vast fund called experience. Tamra knew she would never run such a household—she did not have the patience for it, and its very economy was too time-consuming. Yet she was glad to have known this world, to learn to love and respect it while it still existed, and remember it when it would be no more. Through all this packing period, Gina hardly touched her piano, and then mostly in the evenings, to play the brilliant romantic pieces she loved, hardly practicing the difficult technical exercises needed to become an accomplished performer. But then, Gina was more balanced, and happier than other girls she knew. She even found it natural to prepare an *ouvrage de dames* she would take along with her to Alexandria—a fine piece of *dentelle bretonne* embroidered on tulle, to adorn the bodice of a slip. Once, she spilled out before Tamra a drawer full of fabric remnants. "Mother keeps the remnants of everything we have ever had. How I loved to rummage through these drawers when I was a child!" Gina told her. "We used to dress up in fancy costumes, or I made clothes for my dolls."

Tamra for her part was discovering the many strands that made up a person's roots, what she had missed but what her grandmother had surely possessed, a life encompassed by family and home, something much older than her generation's aspiration to freedom. But roots were a complex matter.

The great day of their departure arrived. The Viterbos still had plenty of luggage, although a truck had taken their cases to the house in Alexandria, where a servant awaited it. The porters at the station fought fiercely to get the luggage, while Mr. Viterbo, Nona, and Gina, afraid that any would be missing, counted the pieces over and over again as they were squeezed into their first-class compartment. Seated by the window, Tamra watched the flat landscape of Egypt run by. Green fields cut by canals. Mud-hut villages huddled under the shade of the banyan tree, bits of branches plunging into the brown water to take root, the life of the small villages concentrated in this pool of dense shades. A donkey tied to a tree, children playing in the mud, women cooking and washing, people going to the big water jar for a drink of cooler water. Nearby in the blinding sun the buffalos turning round and round, chaffing the grain. How poor Egypt was, and yet with a gaunt beauty and dignity that reminded her of India. There, too, sacred rivers flowed from their distant mysterious sources, gathering so much of life along their banks, rivers flowing from some mythical past, at the beginning of time into the present. After all, the Nile and the Brahmaputra were of a different nature from the Thames or the Seine, not only because they were much longer rivers, but they were rivers connected with the mysterious birth of a people, and with divine intervention. To see the fellahin in the fields, brown and lean, their women carrying jars on their heads, the very quality and grace of their slow movements, moved Tamra, as did the sight of small children with bloated bellies above their matchstick thin legs. To see them made one feel ashamed of one's comfort, one's possessions. And those who left the village, like the porters competing savagely for their pittance around modern ships and trains, were they still rooted to these tiny villages strung along the banks of the Nile?

Why did the children have such swollen tummies? Tamra wanted to know. Well, Gina said, it was because of bilharzia, caused by a worm that laid its eggs in the river's mud. These entered the bloodstream, proliferated, and so debilitated people that many died of it. One must never drink unfiltered Nile water, or bathe in the river, or even dip one's feet in it. The poverty that crushed Egypt's fellahin appeared to Gina so inescapable that she accepted it as a condition of their lives. These people, Tamra thought, lived in and from the river, as if molded from its mud. What did it matter to them that the cause of the disease was known, if the cure for it was so far beyond their reach?

They saw men tending the cotton fields, the fluffy white balls emerging from their brown pods; they looked like roses in the distance, but the train went too fast for them to see exactly what they looked like.

These humble little mud villages had hardly changed since Pharaoh's time—as Egyptians said when wanting to stress the antiquity and continuity of Egypt—except for the cotton, the beautiful, long-fibered cotton of Egypt, its export crop which fed the textile factories of Great Britain. Gina was telling Tamra about the Greek cotton kings in Alexandria, who bought the cotton crop from the landowners, selling it abroad, making huge profits in the good years.

Tamra felt the uneasy stirrings of guilt and shame that she, even if uprooted, did belong to the city, to the people who traded, brought about change and progress, which seemed to make the rich richer and the poor poorer. After all, before the cotton crop was introduced, the fellahin had surely grown more food for themselves. She would never know the life of these villages, briefly glimpsed as the train rushed by.

She wished she could lift them tenderly in her cupped hands, but at least she would remember, always, that whatever was to happen as progress overtook them, it had been given to her to see the world that had existed before machines had been invented, before the cold steel gray of Europe would change it beyond recognition.

Gina was saying, "The smell of Cairo is dry. The desert wind blows in the scent of flowers, dung, fruit. But Alexandria . . ." She closed her eyes. "Alexandria smells of the salt marshes that surround it, a salty, slightly putrescent smell. Cairo is an Arab city, Alexandria, in many ways Greek, a Mediterranean one. Where else in the world would the street of the Ptolemys intersect with Nebi Daniel, the Prophet Daniel? And there stands the great synagogue. From the center of town, all along the Corniche, a string of Greek casinos and cafés. I love Alexandria. The railroad station in Sidi Gaber. I sniff the brackish smell of Alexandria, the whiff of sea breeze stirring its indolence. Alexandria is Cleopatra. The tramline links all the stations of Raml, along the coast, all the way to Montazah, where the king has his summer residence. Alexandria is the most European of Egypt's cities, but a Europe that was always part of the Mediterranean world. It has its Greeks living here since antiquity, its Italian colony and its Italian Jewish community. It is really a city of the Levant." Her voice dropped. "In high society, Greek men are supposed to have Jewish mistresses, and Jewish men have Greek mistresses. It is whispered that the mothers themselves do not always know who fathered what child. They are almost a race apart, Greco-Jewish. We are so ignorant of the past, but Alexandria is so much older than the Arab-Moslem conquest. It is still a Greco-Jewish city."

What an extraordinary country Egypt was! Tamra recalled their arrival at night in Port Said on a Peninsular and Orient liner full of English people on their way to India. Across the canal, the wilderness of Sinai, and at the Suez end, the Red Sea and India. Port Said turned toward the East much as Alexandria turned toward Europe, and farther up the Nile, the Sudan was already African. But Cairo was at the center. In Europe, she had felt rootless, but perhaps her roots were in this land, half mythical, half real, where Europe, Asia, and Africa confronted one another. Roots which, unlike those of the fellahin who were molded from the very loam of the Nile, ran invisibly below the surface, far, deep.

Were there not desert plants that bloomed briefly, seemingly out of nothing, out of nowhere?

The train came to a stop in Sidi Gaber. Yes, the smell of Alexandria was as Gina had described it, sultry, languid, slightly putrescent, shaken now and then by gusts of vivifying breeze. The house in Bulkeley shaded by flame trees was pleasant in a British colonial style—Chippendale furniture, sofas and armchairs in bright blue covers, punctured by daffodil-yellow cushions, with here and there the bright touches of oriental brass. The bedrooms opened on a veranda facing the inner courtyard strung with clotheslines, scented with jasmine, filled with the color of bougainvillea. The living room and dining room faced the narrow strip of garden sloping down to a small pond surrounded by tiger lilies, their orange petals spotted with brown. They looked like flaming swords reflected in the water. Tamra leaned over to see her reflection in the pond, and as her dress brushed against the flowers it was streaked with stains the color of dried blood—the tiger lilies' pollen. A hammock tied to the trunks of palm trees swayed above the tiger lilies. She climbed into it, to be carried above the liquid fire of the pond streaked with the reflected deep blue of the sky. It was a magic corner, peaceful, remote, and yet one felt, the passionate violence in the flower could at any moment explode into real flames. Gina was calling her. "Tamra, in heaven's name, where are you hiding? Lunch is ready."

In no time, the atmosphere of the house became the Viterbos', warm, noisy, hospitable. The very first night, relatives and friends dropped in. Nona treated them to pastries she had made the day before in Ma'adi—some stuffed with cheese, others with almond paste. These were served with iced fruit and Turkish coffee. Life acquired a certain rhythm, if not exactly a routine. In the morning, they usually went to the beach in Sidi Bishr, where the Viterbos had rented a cabin. It was a marvelous beach of glistening white and extending indefinitely, with the king's summer residence in Montazah visible in the distance, still a half wild beach, with the cabins straddling it at a distance from one another. Of course, the young Viterbos were sick the first few days, exactly as their mother had predicted. Instead of taking a short dip, they spent the first morning splashing in the water, then sunning themselves on the hot sand. They returned home with headaches; Jojo was feverish, and Gina's shoulders were so blistered she could hardly move. Mrs. Viterbo, scolding her, swathed her in compresses soaked in a starch and yoghurt mixture, while Jojo's tummy was rubbed with heated camphor oil and wrapped up in a woolen blanket. He had eaten shellfish he had found. "You see, I've not even had time to unpack the medicine case, and we already need all sorts of things. Only Tamra was reasonable."

"I could hardly get much darker, could I?" Tamra remarked, but she had been perfectly content just to contemplate the sea, her arms around her knees, trying to imagine the beaches of Sinai, the bitter lakes, the oases, and whether, perhaps, Khadri would come.

In the afternoons, they sometimes went to the club for a game of tennis, but often they stayed home. Gina practiced her piano, then played something brilliant, wildly romantic. Mrs. Viterbo had friends in for a game of cards in the front terrace, while Gina held court in the back one. The house was full of young people, Gina being as popular in Alexandria as she was in Ma'adi. When her friends came, Gina was usually at the piano. "Am I disturbing you?" one or the other would say. They would discuss music, literature, philosophy, politics, their plans for the future, their torments and anguish, terribly French and sophisticated. The girls came too, in part to meet the boys, in part because they were genuinely fond of Gina. Mrs. Viterbo thought Jean Diacomides, a Greek boy, came rather too often, and she scolded Gina for being flirtatious. Tamra thought Mrs. Viterbo misjudged her daughter. Gina was not a flirt. She was short, so she threw back her head provocatively when speaking to taller men, her chin jutting at a cocky angle. How could she help it that her voice was caressing or that her liquid brown eyes shone as she seemed to swoon listening to young men? Tamra defended her: "All the girls like Gina, Mrs. Viterbo. They know she'll never go after their boyfriends. A girl other girls trust is not really a flirt."

"But people think she is and that's what matters. And you, Tamra, why don't you stay more with them, instead of running off alone to the pond like a little savage? You should be more interested in boys. Is anything bothering you?"

"No. I'm perfectly happy here with you. Perfectly content."

The Alexandrines were too sophisticated for her. Most of the time she did not know what they were talking about, and she preferred to read by the pond—all those books they were familiar with already.

The Alexandrines, proud of their sophistication, claimed that the Cairenes were provincial, the Cairo girls somewhat dowdy; their petticoats showed below their dresses, and they boasted that the really beautiful Cairo girls all married in Alexandria. To prove their point, Alexandrines invariably mentioned the celebrated *Quatour Fleuri*, four beautiful young brides, all Cairo born, who had all married Alexandrian men—and were supposed to have acquired that extra chic in Alexandria. The foursome, Rose, Lily, Iris, and Violette, always had tea together after the races at the Sporting Club, dressed to kill, their pretty faces shaded by their flowered hats, their husbands hovering around them like bees over flowers. Cairenes, for their part, were critical of the lax morals of the Alexandrines, who lived only for show, way beyond their means. But, in spite of this rivalry, Cairenes and Alexandrines were obviously eager to have their children meet. "I see your son Fabio is now back from Europe after his studies," a mother would say, or "Your daughter Marise has become such an attractive young girl." The families then began visiting one another's seashore cabins, and if Fabio and Marise hit it off, the parents' visits were prolonged. When a family was invited to stay for lunch, *sans façons, en famille*, it was almost certain that an engagement would soon follow.

Greeks, Italians, Jews, Copts, now and then a few Moslems also dropped in on one another. But the pattern was different: men met for coffee at the beach restaurant, and women, taking their walk on the beach, would nod to acquaintances or stop by to say hello. Unless they were on intimate terms, they did not accept the invitation to join the group on the veranda, pretending that they were awaited at some other cabin. It was rare that men and women belonging to different communities—that is, whose children could not marry—would sit together on a veranda, and rarer indeed that they would share a meal. These subtle, invisible barriers were what prevented intermarriage between children of people who did business together, or went to the same places. Even if one was invited, one did not linger too long.

Parents chaperoned the young girls at the fashionable dancing places. For a young man to ask a girl of another religion to dance was considered bad manners, except among very upper-class people. But there were always exceptions, usually among families who were neighbors, whose children had played together when they were growing up.

Mrs. Viterbo had warned Gina and Tamra that now that they were young girls, she would take them to dances, but never, under any circumstances, should they accept a dance with young Moslems. All *they* wanted to do was to seduce young Jewish girls, and Jewish girls couldn't and shouldn't marry Moslems. Of course, it wasn't only a question of religion. Moslems were notoriously bad husbands, and they were bigamous, had mistresses, never came home to dinner, beat their wives, and didn't give them money. The European women who had fallen for wealthy young Moslems learned this all too soon.

Gina laughed at these dire warnings, which made her mother angry. "Just look at la grande Caroline, with her Moslem prince. She's been in love with him since she was sixteen, she is now twenty-five, and everybody knows she's his mistress. What decent Jewish man would have her? God save us from such a fate!"

"What about Khadri? Are we to refuse to dance with him?" Gina asked.

Mrs. Viterbo floundered. "Well, no . . . you've known him since childhood. And Khadri is too well brought up to ask either of you to dance with him too often. He knows how careful girls have to be about their reputation."

Mrs. Viterbo had glanced at Tamra, who was taken aback. Even if Khadri came, they would not dance together.

Saturdays and Sundays were torture; Tamra hardly dared to go out swimming in case Khadri would come, hoping, hoping he would come. Sometimes she wondered whether she would recognize him if he did come and felt angry with herself for this waiting that filled her. Men were free to lead active lives, but women only waited. Oh, but she would be free one day, as free as any man, freed from the waiting. She could not speak to Gina about Khadri, but she knew Gina knew, and she was grateful for her affection. She greeted Mondays with relief, certain that Khadri would not come.

Then one day, a Monday, Khadri was suddenly there. Tamra had not even noticed his coming. She was reading under the parasol, saw a shadow fall across the page, she looked up at a pair of long brown legs. Could it be? She looked up. It was Khadri. She scrambled up as he dropped at her side, on his knees, slender with his broad shoulders and narrow hips, his eyes ablaze.

"I thought . . . you would come for a weekend."

"And run into all the Viterbo guests? No. I took a week off, a whole week. You are prettier than ever, Tam. Come, let's go swimming." He caught her by the hand and they ran into the sea. Balzac's *La femme de trente ans* lay forgotten on the sand.

It was bliss to feel the cool water with its tiny eddies move caressingly around their bodies. Bliss to feel him so near, to swim at his side, place a hand on his shoulder. He swam out with a powerful crawl, returned, dived, swam under the water, brushing against her legs, then he emerged, and she swam under the water toward him, through the bridge of his legs, up again. A kind of ballet, their hands and heads and legs touched in the clear transparency of the water. They emerged to get back their breath, laughed, dived in again. Then they swam out far, to the line of floating life buoys, where they rested. They hardly spoke: their bodies spoke for them. Then they heard shouts. Gina and her brothers were approaching on a flat boat. Their bodies moved apart. "Khadri, let's ride in on the waves," cried Gina. He climbed on the boat, and standing, caught the breaking wave that carried him clear to the shore, like a young god. The moment of bliss was over. Tamra and Gina swam back.

Later, as they sat under the parasol, Gina and the boys were full of questions about Sinai, and Khadri told them about the Texas oil drillers, the geographers making surveys, the infinities of sand, the palm oases, the fantastic fish and shellfish in Atur. In fact he had brought them some, and he opened his bag and spread them at their feet. Each picked those they liked best. Tamra chose some tiny ones that looked like mermaids, or seahorses.

Gina invited Khadri for lunch. He accepted. Throughout lunch, the boys listened, entranced by his stories about lost trails, and the time when they ran out of water and fell upon some brackish water, drank and were sick.

Tamra listened raptly, and yet was intensely jealous. He was an independent man now, living a great adventure in the desert while she was just a girl, sitting at home, waiting. She didn't even have anything interesting to tell him about how she spent her time. It was unfair!

They escorted him to the gate, and he drove off noisily in his rented car, not saying anything about when he would be coming back. Tamra realized the waiting would be even worse now, knowing he was in Alexandria and could come if he wanted to. She almost wished the week was over so she would know she need not wait for him for at least another month, until he had money again. Gina squeezed Tamra's hands, whispering, "It's because of you that he came. But he has to cover it up, because of mother. You'll see, tomorrow he'll come to the beach." Gina had this way of guessing things.

And indeed, Khadri did come to the beach, the next day and every following day, although not on Saturday and Sunday.

He usually stayed close to Gina and the boys. But one day, when the sea was unusually calm, they all swam out to the rocks that barred the bay. The boys were busy catching the tiny crabs that hid in the little pools that the sea left behind. Khadri, Gina, and Tamra climbed to the top and sauntered down to the side facing the open sea. Khadri held out his hand to Tamra as if to help her down, and kept her hand in his. They sat on the ledge of rocks, listening to the rhythmic rumbling of the sea, the crash of waves, tickled by feathery sprays. Gina had vanished, they had not noticed at what moment. Bliss to be so close together. Bliss and exquisite torture too. Khadri's large, roughened palm brushed against Tamra's thigh. "I thought of you often, in Atur—a mermaid emerging from a seashell with pearls in her long hair." She did not tell him of her waiting, having forgotten it now that he was here, the warmth of his hand making her flesh tingle. She leaned her head against his shoulder, her body aching toward him, arching, straining, her lips reaching for his, wanting to be dissolved, to melt in his being.

His hands were on her shoulders, big brother fashion, and he kept her at a distance. "No, Tamra, no. We mustn't. You are just an innocent young girl. We just mustn't."

The surging wave in her body slammed somewhere inside. She pushed off his hands, stood up panting, and fled, lumbering up the rocks, then down, throwing herself into the sea and swimming with all the rage and frustration in her body. She flung herself against the hot sand, her hands opening and closing. Soon he was at her side. "Tamra, I didn't mean to hurt you. It's just that . . ."

She sat upright. "I'm a pure innocent girl," she gazed at him, her green eyes steady, holding his. Why did he keep coming to see her in Alexandria if his intentions were all that pure?

"Won't you even say goodbye?"

"Goodbye Khadri."

Gina came toward them, sensing something was wrong.

"I'll be pushing off," he said. "So long, Gina."

She said quickly, "Don't forget we're having a party this Saturday. I hope you'll come."

"I'm not sure I'd be welcome."

"I welcome you," Gina said. "Come for my sake."

Tamra had withdrawn into her shell. Clamped it shut. Still, Gina tried to reach her. "It isn't much fun to be a girl. The body aches for love, and one mustn't have it. But Khadri does care about you, Tammy, I'm sure of that. But he can't be your lover. It would lead to the most awful mess. Can't you see that? Try to accept this first love as something sweet and poignant that you'll remember much later in life, fondly. After all, perhaps loves, like stories, have first drafts, different from the works of one's maturity but cherished for all their incompleteness. I'm not expressing it well. But perhaps this is just preparation for a great love that will come later, for the first person at some other time. Or perhaps it is an apprenticeship for learning that so many things in life give joy and hurt, mixed together. Think of the beautiful poetry de Musset wrote when Georges Sand took up with Chopin." Gina, as was her wont, was carried away by literary references.

And because the literary references annoyed Tamra she retorted, "Oh, sure. But I don't want the dust of love, the memory of love twenty years from now. I want love *now*. What do I care if a few men write fine poetry about love? Women don't. For them it's just wanting and waiting and not getting what they want or wait for."

"I didn't mean to hurt your feelings," said Gina, her feelings hurt.

Khadri did not come to Gina's party that Saturday—he called to say that some unexpected occurrences prevented him from doing so. Tamra danced with the young men present, even seemed to take some interest in them. They saw Khadri at the races the next day. Tamra noticed him first, leaning over a ravishing blond English girl whom he was holding by the elbow. Gina felt Tamra stiffen and turned toward the direction in which she was looking. Khadri then noticed them, and came toward them, to introduce Miss Crawford Price. Miss? So she wasn't even the wife of one of those drunken Shell company engineers. The daughter of an English colonel. Tamra, looking at the girl's radiant cream and peach complexion, thought bitterly that she was as dark as a beetle. Why indeed should he bother about her, when this luminous creature was so obviously attracted to him—as most women could be—indeed were?

How strange, she thought, I feel nothing, nothing at all. The races, the crowds of people, seemed to be at a great distance, and she was not part of it. She knew though from experience that she felt so numb when something had hurt deeply, making it difficult for her to move. She only wanted to be back in the garden, to stretch out in the hammock, under the stars, until the unbearable tension between her shoulder blades, the steel fingers tightening around her heart, loosened.

That night, Gina was worried, almost frightened by Tamra's refusal to speak. They lay in the darkness, and when she thought Gina was asleep, at last, in the quiet house, Tamra stealthily slipped out into the garden. Gina, knowing that she had run away before, followed her, and saw her wander in the garden and make for the hammock near the pond.

She just needs to be alone, she thought, but kept watch anyway. After some time had passed she called out, "Tammy! You gave me such a fright. I woke up and didn't find you. What on earth are you doing out here at this time of night? It's so damp and chilly. Come." Gina pulled her inside. They tiptoed through the garden and climbed back into the room through the open windows. Tamra was trembling.

Khadri did not return to Alexandria, or if he did, neither the Viterbos nor Tamra knew about it. But he was very much talked about one Sunday on the veranda of the Viterbos' cabin. He had become the lover of the famous belly dancer Farida, who was mad about him, and when he was in Cairo, he spent his nights at the casino where Farida performed.

Tamra felt a dagger go through her heart, and then a stillness, as if she had stopped living. I feel nothing, nothing at all, she thought, surprised, not yet aware that the shock had made her numb. She would have liked to be alone, finding it unbearable to feel the watchful eyes upon her face. To hide, to flee, to drown, to sleep, to be gone. She was such a fool, to have thrust herself upon Khadri. To her, the pain, the humiliation; and to him, the freedom. She had visions of their making love, passionate, in utter abandon.

She heard Gina say something about Khadri loving her, respecting her, and so, to keep away from her, was having this affair. She thought to herself that actually it wasn't her, Tamra, whom Khadri respected, but the property rights of her future husband. Actually, he was upholding the system to his own advantage. He, too, would one day marry a "pure" girl, not a belly dancer or some other such "unpure" woman. Few men married the women from the other side of the respectability line.

Why was this so? The only answer that came to mind was that a man wanted to be sure his children were his own—particularly the firstborn son who would inherit the family name and property to perpetuate it. The woman was merely a means to this end, the vessel of his progeny. Suddenly, the thought of her mother came to Tamra. For the first time, she thought of her as another woman, who had wanted to be a free person, a person in her own right. To her surprise, she felt a curious sympathy toward her, even though she had abandoned her as a child. What was she like, where was she, what had become of her? If they ever met, would they have anything to say to one another?

For her part, she must become strong, do away with her girlish sentimentality about love—she must study, become independent, like a man. No man ever would seduce her, which didn't mean that she would not have a lover. Part of her would remain cool and control the foolish girl who longed for love. Perhaps a woman could not separate love from desire as a man could. But she would try to separate the two. In fact, she loved Gina and Andrée, as she would never love a man, as she did not, had not loved Khadri, as she loved her friends.

*Eight*

# Cairo Wedding

*This short story, Kahanoff's first known publication in the United States, appeared in the literary and cultural journal* Tomorrow *in July 1945. The story depicts the pressure to conform that female intellectuals like Kahanoff felt in 1930s Egypt. The bleak depiction of the protagonist's options offers a scathing critique of women's status in Egyptian-Levantine society of the era. Interestingly, although the story bears many specifically Egyptian-Levantine cultural markers, it never identifies the religion of the bride and groom.*

Baheya, in last year's best silk dress scaled down to morning use, rang her wealthy Hakim sister's bell. Fatma, the little Arab maid, ran to the door on her bare feet and tinkled, "Ya Allah, Sitt Baheya, such a row your niece Suzanne is having with the elder lady. She refuses to marry."

"Mind your business, you little bitch. I don't need you to know what's going on in my own sister's house."

Baheya waddled down the Hakim's long corridor cluttered with Moresque ebony and ivory tables and Louis XVI armchairs, their gold legs scrawny in the thick oriental rugs.

When she entered her sister's bedroom, Suzanne was shouting, "No use insisting Mother, I won't marry Selim Basri."

Mrs. Hakim turned to her sister and wailed in a Levantine squall of French and Arabic, "Speak to Suzanne, Baheya, for the love of God, speak to her. Make her understand she has to get married. I'm too ill to try any more."

Baheya dropped into a blue velvet armchair facing her niece. "Suzanne, you stubborn girl, do you want to kill your mother with grief?"

"I don't want to kill my mother, I just don't want to marry that fool."

Such was the prelude to a marriage in Cairo's Levantine society when a girl refused to marry the man her parents had selected for her. The older women of a family worked in concert until they had extracted the girl's consent.

Baheya was there to help her sister break down Suzanne's resistance. She said, "Suzanne, you're twenty-three. And you've not been able to find yourself a husband. Then why make such a fuss when your father gives you a big dowry and finds one for you? You should be grateful he's rich enough to do it."

"But how can I marry someone I dislike?"

"Look at yourself in the mirror there. No figure, no chic, yellow as a quince, no beauty, but such pretensions. Oh là là, ma chère, such pretensions! Ugly as you are, who do you think you can marry, a prince?"

The girl turned away from the mirror, trembling.

Her aunt continued, "You see yourself how right I am. Selim Basri isn't very bright, but he's not a bad boy. And you have two young sisters behind you who can't marry before you do. So you have to marry. With your face, you can't be too choosy."

Suzanne went to her mother, begging for a little tenderness, a little understanding. She knelt, rubbing her cheek on her mother's hand. She asked, "Mamma, do you love me, really love me?"

Mrs. Hakim quoted an old Arabic saying: "I would give you my blood, I would give you my soul, my beloved."

Suzanne smiled. Whenever her mother wanted to show emotion, she spoke Arabic. Gently she asked, "Mamma, how can you want me to marry without love? I've dreaded it from childhood. We've gone through all this before, but please try to understand this time, please try."

Mrs. Hakim cried, "But habibi, ma chérie, in my time girls got married that way. Baheya and I didn't even see our husbands before our wedding day. What's different with you?"

"We weren't brought up that way, that's the difference."

Mrs. Hakim became angry. "God curse those French schools! We send our children there to be educated, and they come back with the crazy modern ideas and turn against us, their parents, who have sacrificed everything for them! You know yourself, Suzanne, how much your education has cost us! I should have kept you at home working like a kitchen maid!"

"It might have been easier that way. As it is, I'm caught between two social codes and belong to neither."

Baheya felt it was time to intervene. "Suzanne, stop this nonsense about social codes. You are in Egypt, where there is no life for a woman except marriage. You know a girl who works is a disgrace to her family, and you don't want to be one of those useless old maids everybody laughs at."

"I think I'd even prefer that."

Mrs. Hakim lamented, "What did I do to God for Him to punish me with such a rebellious child?" She sobbed hysterically, while her sister patted her shoulder, saying, "Calm yourself, Zaffira for the love of God, calm yourself."

But Suzanne's mother kept repeating, "My own daughter is killing me. My own flesh and blood has turned against me. My own child is killing me . . ."

She closed her eyes and fell back in her chair. Baheya screamed, "My sister, my poor sister! She's fainted! She's dying!"

Suzanne, badly frightened, rushed out of the room and returned with smelling salts and cold towels, Fatma trotting in behind her. The three women lifted Mrs. Hakim to her big brass bed with its shiny globes standing guard at each corner, and busied themselves reviving her.

As Mrs. Hakim groaned and moaned, Suzanne looked at the tired old woman, her disheveled wisps of thin gray hair, her breasts drooping out of her open housecoat like half-filled water bags. She pitied this woman who had borne eight children and had tried so hard to polish her own coarseness off them. But her mother had only wanted them to have French names, wear European dress better than she did, and speak French and English pure of her own Arab colloquialisms. She could not desire more for her children because this was the best she knew. Understanding this, it seemed now to the girl that loyalty to her mother was more important than her own happiness. "All right, Mother darling," she said. "Forgive me for hurting you. I'll marry Selim Basri."

Mrs. Hakim was immediately on her feet. She and Baheya kissed and congratulated Suzanne. Little Fatma jumped around the room, bracelets jingling on her bare ankles, clapping her hands and shouting, "God blesses the house in which there is a bride! May Allah bless the *'arousa* and give her plenty of children!"

The two older women ran out of the room to announce to family and servants the news of Suzanne's engagement. Neither stopped to notice the lucky girl, crying all by herself.

*

Suzanne Hakim sobbed, her head in the pillow. Through the closed door she could hear her mother shrilling over the telephone, now in French, now in Arabic. For the last hour Mrs. Hakim had triumphantly repeated, "I have good news to announce, ma chère. A big surprise. Suzanne is engaged to Selim Basri! They're madly in love, le vrai coup de foudre, ya habibi. What could we parents do but give our consent? You know how headstrong children are nowadays! Yes, Suzanne is madly happy. No, you can't speak to her, she's crying. You know how emotional my Suzanne is."

The doorbell rang. Fatma slipped a starched white apron over her torn dress and flew to the door. A girl stood there with a huge bunch of roses. Fatma whispered, her brown hands cupped on her mouth, "Ya Allah, Sitt Marcelle, your friend Suzanne has cried for so long. The elder lady is on the telephone, but . . ."

"Sh, sh, I know," Marcelle silenced her. Putting on a bright smile, she walked down the corridor to Mrs. Hakim and kissed her. "Congratulations, Mrs. Hakim. I wanted to be the first to tell both of you how happy I am to hear the good news. I came as soon as I knew."

"Thank you, Marcelle, habibi, thank you. You're Suzanne's best friend, and I knew you'd be here right away. Well, when will it be your turn to be a bride? Soon, I hope?"

Mrs. Hakim did not wait for an answer. A worried expression came over her face. "Suzanne is being fussy. She's in her room, if you want to see her," she said hesitantly.

"Thank you, I will."

Marcelle gave the flowers to Fatma. She felt she could not go to her friend carrying roses. She knew Suzanne had been forced to accept Selim Basri, and Mrs. Hakim knew Marcelle knew it. Marcelle, in her role of *amie intime*, had come with the first bouquet, as she was expected to do. But she could not enter Suzanne's room exclaiming, "Darling, I'm so happy!"

Softly she opened Suzanne's door and sat down by her friend, murmuring, "Chérie, ma chérie."

Suzanne sniffled and tried to smile.

"No . . . life is that way."

"Maybe I'm a coward. I shouldn't have given way. But mother fainted and I said I'd marry him. I couldn't stand seeing her like that, though she might have done it on purpose to make me say yes. I know it's horrible to think such things, but sometimes I wish I didn't have a mother."

"Let's have a cigarette and talk things over calmly . . . that is, if you want to."

The girls smoked in silence. Finally Suzanne said, "Can you imagine what a life it's going to be?"

"Perhaps it won't be so terrible as all that. After all, look at the life you'd have at home if you didn't marry him. The family would be at you all the time. You'd have no peace at all. This way, you'll have your own house and can fix it up as you like. You know, very modern furniture and lots of American gadgets. You'll have parties and see the foreign set, not our kind of people. All day long you can do as you please, and when you go out with your husband in the evening, you needn't play bridge at the same table. Besides, Suzanne, you're an intellectual, and that'll help. You've always lived in a dream world of your own, with your books. You can go right on doing it."

"How nice," Suzanne bitterly, "to be in bed with Selim Basri and say, 'But it doesn't really matter, because what really matters is my cozy private little dream world, where I'm so happy.'"

"But what else can you do?"

"I'm out of luck, I guess. I'm homely and intelligent in a society where a woman's only salvation is to be pretty and stupid."

Marcelle smiled. "You see, you can already rationalize the whole thing. It's a very hopeful sign."

Both girls laughed, as they always laughed when life seemed unbearable. Suzanne said, "You know, I can always patronize and be condescending with the girls who haven't yet found husbands. That's something, isn't it?" At this they laughed even louder.

*

Suzanne started her life as a fiancée with a tea attended by her girlfriends who came to congratulate her. The unused grand salon was thrown open for the event. The monumental bronze and crystal chandelier swayed as it came out of the blue tarlatan wrapping which had protected it from dust. The gold-fringed red brocade armchairs—matched to the heavy brocade curtains—were stripped of their white cotton slipcovers. Fatma gave a new sheen to the white porcelain statue of a naked woman holding an ashtray between outstretched arms, by spitting on it and rubbing it with deerskin. On the wall, the French peasant girl filling her jug in a brook full of pink sunset peered demurely out of an embossed gold frame at the blanket which had covered her for so long. The Bokhara rug was massaged with damp tea leaves to restore the lushness of its colors. The grand salon, now ready for the reception, overflowed with flowers sent by friends.

Suzanne sat in one of the obese armchairs that circled the room. Her friends came in wearing the suitable in-between dresses—not too formal, as for a cocktail party, but not too informal as for *un petit bridge entre amies*. Each girl kissed Suzanne and said, "Darling, I'm so happy!"

Suzanne invariably replied, "Darling, I'm so happy *you* are."

An embarrassed silence spread among the girls. Somehow, the usual comedy seemed out of place.

"Mon Dieu," Marcelle exclaimed, "this is worse than a funeral."

"It is rather worse," Suzanne agreed. "You see, I'm not really dead . . . I'm only buried alive, that's all."

The girls were shocked at Suzanne's bluntness. As they ate too many sandwiches and cakes some of them said she was taking the affair far too seriously. Others said that since she was going through with the business anyhow, she might as well do it gracefully and *garder les apparences*. Suzanne retorted that she saw no use in playing such a farce *entre amies*.

It was her life which was being ruined. She might as well enjoy it, after a fashion.

Suzanne spent her evenings with her fiancé. Selim, on his way to his first courtship visit, stopped to buy an expensive anthology of love poems. He had already sent the traditional *bonbonnière* filled with pastel-colored dragées, but to follow up with love poems would look well and pleased Mrs. Hakim.

He drove to Suzanne's house, bent on making his visit as short as possible, for Doudi, his pretty blonde mistress, was expecting him. He smiled, thinking of the scenes Doudi made when he kept her waiting. Well, he regretted that Suzanne wasn't pretty too; it would have made for a pleasant life. But after all, she did bring money, and at thirty-two a man should marry. On the whole, it wasn't a bad bargain.

When Selim arrived, Suzanne and her mother were in the grand salon. He gave the book to Suzanne saying, "Pour ma bien-aimée."

Mrs. Hakim remarked, "How thoughtful of you, Selim. Suzanne, thank Selim and tell him how moved you are by the poems."

Suzanne repeated after her mother, "Thank you. I'm very moved by the poems."

Mrs. Hakim said, "I know you two young people want to be alone . . ." She winked as she left the room.

The engaged couple sat in the garish grand salon while the rest of the household discreetly tiptoed by, joking in hushed voices about *les fiancés* alone in there. Meanwhile, Suzanne and Selim checked the dates of the dinner parties various members of their families were giving for them. When this subject was exhausted, there was nothing more to say.

Suzanne's eyes wandered around the room and stopped on the picture of the peasant girl filling her jug. She remembered the time she had made a hole in the pink brook by shooting darts at the jug. She had patched the hole with a pink bandage, hoping her mother would not notice. For fifteen years Mrs. Hakim had not seen the adhesive holding the brook together. She asked Selim, "Do you see anything wrong with that picture?"

He said, "No, it's a very nice picture. We have one like it in my parents' home, and we may find one like it for our house, ma chérie."

After another long silence, Suzanne said abruptly, "When are you leaving?"

Selim replied gallantly, "I'd stay all night, if I were allowed," and tried to kiss Suzanne.

She turned her face away and said, "Let's join the rest of the family in the petit salon."

Selim was puzzled when he left his fiancée. Her conduct was so peculiar. Did she expect him to be in love with her? He frowned and shrugged his shoulders. He wouldn't worry about Suzanne too much. He could still keep Doudi, and in the summer when husbands sent their wives and children to Europe or to the Alexandria beaches away from the Cairo heat, there would also be those good-looking *petites femmes* imported as showgirls by the Kit-Kat, the open-air cabaret. Selim gave a satisfied flick to the white carnation in his lapel. He was all smiles when he reached the little apartment he had set up for Doudi.

The Saturday following their engagement, Suzanne and Selim went to the Shepherd Hotel *thé dansant*. These teas were the weekly highlights of Cairo's social life, and no one aspiring to fashion ever skipped one of them. Although Suzanne disliked dancing, she had to go. As her mother said, "People would imagine things weren't going well between Selim and you if they didn't see you together at Shepherd's." So they went, watching the others dance, hardly speaking to each other. Selim, acting as a fiancé should, tenderly placed his arm on Suzanne's shoulders. He watched the pretty girls on the dance floor, and slowly his arm dropped away. He started, and remembering his duty, put his arm back where it belonged.

Suzanne had been engaged for only a few days when Mrs. Hakim told her husband, "You know, Joseph, I think we'll have to rush Suzanne's wedding. She's changing her mind, and you know her—she might actually refuse to go through with the business. She's already stopped wearing her engagement ring."

Mr. Hakim pondered and scratched his bald head. He had worked hard to rise from poverty to wealth, and he had not bothered much about the children. That was his wife's job. But he had a confused tenderness for Suzanne which he could never put into words, although it made him feel she was different from the rest of the brood. He pitied this girl, plain but clever, and vaguely perceived that her sensitive and intense nature only made things worse for her.

Clumsily, he tried to explain this to his wife. "Of course, you know best, Zaffira. I think Suzanne should get married. But maybe girls are different nowadays. If the girl is unhappy, do you think we should force her to marry the Basris' son?"

Mrs. Hakim had no such scruples. Her mother had forced her to the same duty when she was young and far prettier than Suzanne. "Tze, tze, Joseph, you're worse than she is," she said. "Suzanne will be married by the end of next month. I'll keep her so busy choosing furniture and trousseau that she'll be too tired to think and too busy to give me any more of her nonsense. I need you only to discuss the wedding arrangements."

Mr. Hakim sighed and his wife told him of her plans.

Suzanne's mother had decided that after the religious ceremony they would give a big reception, the most sumptuous Cairo had ever seen. Her husband had hundreds of important business relations, but he was too shy to invite them to his home, which he obscurely knew to be pretentious and in bad taste. Mrs. Hakim thought her daughter's wedding was an excellent opportunity to *faire la politesse* to all those people. Marcelle's father was lending them his large suburban garden for the occasion. Tents would be put up to hide the reception from the street. A dance floor would be built, and an American band hired, so that *la jeunesse* could dance. The buffet, she said, would be superb, everything provided by Groppi, the most expensive caterer in Cairo. Of course, it would amount to a lot of money, but wasn't it worthwhile, when they were getting Suzanne off their chests and at the same time impressing all Cairo? Mr. Hakim grunted that perhaps it would be worthwhile.

*

The day of Suzanne's wedding came. After the wedding ceremony the guests poured in under the bright oriental tents. Arabs clustered in the street, yelling congratulations, helping people out of cars, calling the women Madame la Duchesse—unless the tip received was too small—then they cursed. Under the tent decorated with potted palms, Sudanese Negroes passed trays of ice cream and dragées.

A discordant crowd, speaking ten languages incorrectly, swirled on the lawn. The divisions of Cairo society were maintained—between natives and foreigners, Moslems, Christians, and Jews, between the new rich and the old rich. Groups snubbed each other, although they were so much alike. Most of all, they snubbed the shabby people the Hakims had reluctantly invited, relatives and friends from the old days of poverty. These avidly stared at the Cairo upper crust lacquered in riotous splendor.

When Suzanne and her husband arrived, the band struck up Mendelssohn's *Marche Nuptiale*, the guests cheered and congratulated the newly wed couple and their parents, and the Sudanese servants passed champagne.

The older women, with too much make-up and an arrogant display of jewelry on their copies of Paris creations, sat around the dance floor watching the young people. The young ones, slightly intoxicated, danced, laughed, and flirted. Some girls danced "cheek to cheek" to the American tunes, and the mothers commented sourly, "Cette petite tournera mal," unless their own daughters danced that way. The girls, intent on snatching this hour of pleasure, did not care. They averted their eyes when they saw Suzanne, unlovely white ghost floating in all this revelry. Most of them had the radiance of a flame shining through an alabaster lamp. Now they were still free, beautiful, courted. Soon they would be married off as Suzanne had been. Their fragile beauty would vanish, leaving them like their mothers, dilapidated flesh, with only their luminous dark eyes to remind them of loveliness they had once had. So they refused to see the sad little shadow in the sumptuous bridal gown. Even Marcelle turned away from her friend dancing stiffly, aloof in Selim's arms.

The excitement reached its peak when the buffet was opened at nine o'clock. People rushed to it madly, pushing, stepping on each other's toes, fighting to be first at the long laden tables. They sniffed and piled their plates high with whatever they could snatch. The poorer guests had never seen such fanciful foods, elaborate French delicacies with names unknown to them. Their mouths full, they shouted to each other over the tables, "Did you get some of this? Fight for it, it's worth it!"

The rich people, used to this kind of food, stood a little apart, shocked and disgusted. "Such behavior," they said in French. "I wonder where these people come from!" They forgot that at their weddings they were plagued, like the Hakims, by their own inglorious relatives.

As servants constantly brought in new dishes, people whispered that this must have cost old Hakim a good thousand pounds.

At ten, Suzanne went into the house to change. She came out in her traveling suit, ready to leave on her honeymoon. Both families, flashing their new clothes, looked proud and happy as they kissed Suzanne and Selim good-by. As the couple entered the Hakims' big Buick, the guests shouted wishes of eternal happiness and threw rice at the departing car before returning to eat, drink, dance, flirt, and gossip.

Suzanne sat by her husband in the back of the car. The velvety Cairo night enfolded her in caressing arms and rocked her with its gentle touch. She yearned to be held thus in a pair of human arms and impulsively said to Selim, "Take me in your arms . . ."

He dropped an arm on her shoulder as he had done at Shepherd's Hotel.

"The idiot," Suzanne thought. "He can't even understand I mean both arms."

At home that night, Mrs. Hakim, elated but dead tired, gave her impressions to her husband while struggling to get her swollen flabbiness out of her girdle. "Ouf!" she said. "I'm glad it's over. Joseph, I don't like to boast, but, parole d'honneur, we have done things magnificently. No one in Cairo ever saw such a reception. God bless their appetites, did you see all they ate? And everybody came, the best of people, and all the snobs. Wallahi, I feel so relieved. You know, to the last minute I was afraid of what Suzanne might do. Imagine the scandal if she had tried to run away! Well, let her husband worry about her now. I only hope we don't have as much trouble marrying the other girls. Joseph, why don't you say something?"

Mr. Hakim, shoes and socks off, was thoughtfully rubbing his tired feet. He mumbled, "Suzanne didn't look happy, and she's alone with him now . . ."

"Don't worry about that," Mrs. Hakim replied, as she plumped herself in the shiny brass bed. "Suzanne will get used to it. All women do."

*Nine*

# Europe from Afar

*Like the previous story, this essay describes the unsatisfying options available to the young, bourgeois Levantine women who had completed their formal education and were awaiting marriage. Not permitted to attend university abroad or pursue a career, Kahanoff and some of her friends dabbled in legal studies and philanthropy, opening an ill-fated medical clinic in the impoverished Jewish quarter of Cairo. Published in 1959 as the second installment of the "Generation of Levantines" cycle, this article's depiction of the cultural and social ferment in late 1930s Egypt is viewed through the lens of the upheavals yet to come—the decimation of European Jewry by the Holocaust, and the displacements of Middle Eastern Jewry following the establishment of the state of Israel.*

I remember my philosophy class, the last one at the Lycée Français. Few girls, many boys, Jews, Greeks, Armenians, Copts. Not one Moslem was left among us, and in the Catholic schools it was almost the same, except for the predominance of Syrian Christians. There was a French girl, Françoise, whom we envied for the elegance of her writing style and rosy complexion. Moslem boys studied in English or Arab schools, but Western culture was, almost exclusively, a minority concern. Education widened the gulf that separated us. The daughters of Turkish pashas and Egyptian doctors with whom we had played in childhood had gradually withdrawn into the harem, then marriage.

We exchanged a few words with them at Groppi's, the Swiss caterer's tea room, dancehall, restaurant-bar, the center of social life in Cairo, or at the smart charity balls in the famous tourist hotels—Shepherd's, Semiramis, Mena House. Most of them had cast away virtue together with their veils. They appeared, generously made up, in clinging satin dresses, defiantly asserting the most precious of all freedoms, the easiest to conquer—conjugal infidelity. The virtuous wives led their secret lives and never appeared in public.

We learned then that a girl who sat at a bar was putting her reputation at stake, and that she should never accept a dance with a Moslem, however high his social standing. Some Jewish girls, our parents warned, became mistresses of Moslems, but never their wives. At the sumptuous balls given by the various communities to help their poor, each community occupied a separate section of the ballroom, and if, by chance, a young man crossed the room to invite a girl from another group (everyone knew everyone), people stared and gossip started. It was only in the upper reaches of society that people mixed naturally, as a matter of course.

We, the studious young girls of the minorities, began to attend these balls. Virtuous, ardent feminists, aggressive, we were proud to sit in the classroom with our male contemporaries, taking notes on Descartes, Kant, Spinoza, and had a distressing tendency to discuss philosophy even while dancing La Cucaracha (never cheek to cheek).

In the classroom, our professor introduced each philosopher, who made a brief appearance, stating his views. The one who followed invariably tore his predecessor to pieces. Philosophy was supposed to give the key to understanding life, but I thought it was as good as useless, since we would start living long before we knew how to use this key. We never read any of the books cited in our textbooks, and knew no one, with the possible exception of our professor, who ever had or would. Who then read the books which had made people so famous? This was one of the mysteries of Levantine culture. One had only to know their names to be considered "cultivated." Two or three years later, when I went to the Comédie Française in Paris, I was surprised to find in the audience both younger and older people who since leaving school had obviously read and reread their classics.

After class, in the schoolyard, we used to spout quotes from *L'Humanité* and other publications of that kind.* So excited were we, that we hardly realized that we were all saying the same thing. At these moments, Françoise's equanimity was quite infuriating. Here was a girl who attended mass, collected recipes and poems, and even embroidered, almost as if women were not fighting to be liberated from domesticity. She wasn't an empty-headed girl either. Her parents were known to be less reactionary and anti-Semitic than other high-level French officials and businessmen, the cream of Egypt's foreign colony. Her serenity made us feel as if we were pretending to understand something which in fact eluded us, and although we never admitted it, we hated her.

We heard a great deal about Darwin in class. Yes, Darwin worried me. I worked hard to find arguments to indict him. Whenever I smelled the scent of a flower or tasted the flavor of some fruit, I marveled at the miracle that made every living thing create something out of the juices of the earth—to become the perfume, the form, the color, the taste which made the world a wondrous, marvelous, colorful collection of unique objects. And, when killing for the sake of survival was necessary, the wolves, even among human beings, never killed all the sheep. Had they done so, there would not be thousands and thousands of beggars in the streets of Cairo, but only millionaires.

If Darwin were right, then the Nazis were right. There was a master race, and when it had destroyed all mankind it could only destroy itself. The last man would die, triumphantly asserting his dominion over the devastated earth. How could our professors, good Socialists most of them, waste our time on Darwin? What was there I didn't understand? Throughout our years of acquaintance with Western thought, we seemed to progress backwards from Jesus Christ's "Love

* In the period about which Kahanoff was writing, *L'Humanité* was the daily newspaper of the French Communist Party. In the early twenty-first century it is still in circulation as a Communist-leaning independent newspaper.

one another" to this barbaric nonsense. Perhaps that was what was wrong with Europeans. They had brains, philosophy, science, but a brute lust for blood was always there. Darwin, like Nietzsche, led to the swastika, and it wasn't the Jews alone who would be crucified on it, but Christian Europe itself—limbs broken and twisted in this burlesque caricature of the Cross. The twilight of the Gods.

Yet, it was important to know these things, and we Jews, Greeks, Syrians, Copts, the studious minorities, the truly civilized, we would take their place, if we could but learn the secret of their power without allowing ourselves to be poisoned by it. From us would come the shape and color of tomorrow, and it would not be stained with blood if only we remembered the commandment "Thou shalt not kill." We were the people who knew that every man is born to live in darkness and journeys painfully to the light of ultimate grace, and that no one has the right to shorten another's pilgrimage, be it even by a day.

What then of patriotism, heroism, honor, the courage of those who gave their lives? Of course, there was an essential difference between a martyr and a soldier, but still, weren't they justified in saying that we were the crafty, cowardly Levantines? Didn't we, the minorities, say contemptuously of the Egyptians that the rioting mob would never make a real revolution because at sundown everybody scampered off? I didn't know the answer, but a whole life was given to me to find out. It was perhaps our destiny to learn to think anew, the Greeks with their clarity, the Jews with their passion, the Phoenicians with their adroitness, to pass on what we learned and to grow.

We had a religious approach to the problems of our day, transposed to the secular world, for we despised the stale old beliefs. It seemed to us that Judaism was the whole family gorging itself to celebrate events the young found meaningless and derided with queer rancor, as if resenting that they could never quite escape from their past. With Catholics, it was no better. I had lost sight of my childhood friend, Marie, until Sylvie, then my closest friend, invited the two of us to tea together. Sylvie was passionately pro-Blum, pro-science and the Spanish Civil War. Over dainty sandwiches, pastries, and a superabundance of silver passed around by a magnificent Sudanese in gold and red regalia, we discussed our latest enthusiasms, Jules Romains, Roger Martin du

Gard, Ilya Ehrenburg.* Sylvie and I lived in books, but Marie demurely shook her pretty head: No, she hadn't read any of them. "What do you read then?" we inquired, dismayed. "The lives of saints and generals," she replied seriously. "You know, Saint Thérèse, and the Marshals Foch, Joffre, Pétain."** We split our sides laughing, and although we later met at parties, we no longer tried to be friends.

Friendship and intellectual exchange between girls was important in our lives, perhaps as a carryover from a society where men and women had little, except sexual, intimacy. Our relationships were freer than our parents' had been, but we did not know what attitude to adopt toward young men—partners, but also enemies. Adolescence passed, and the boy-girl relationship was confusion, conflict, and ambiguity. We relied on girlfriends for a sincere, satisfying relationship, and confiding in each other took a great deal of our time. We talked, almost with terror, about what we should do after school. Our parents took our studies seriously: education was the ideal of the leisure class. For girls it served absolutely no practical purpose and was, in that respect, pointless. We had known this, but had hoped for some kind of miracle, some great love, perhaps, or a new courage, which would fire us with the strength to rebel.

After graduation we enjoyed the lazy life at the beaches, and the stormy pangs of loves, innocent and perverse. Fall took away most of the boys we had known at school, severing the last bond of childhood. They would come back from European universities knowing much more than we did, and treated us like our older sisters. We'd go to parties, flirt and drink, outrageously bored, disappointed, waiting for husbands, tempted, but without daring to cut the silken cords which tied us to our well-to-do families. We'd read, play cards, be pessimistic, and continue in that vein through marriage, child bearing, adultery, and possibly divorce.

* Jules Romains (1885–1972) was a French poet. Roger Martin du Gard (1881–1958) was a French novelist and recipient of the 1937 Nobel Prize in literature. Ilya Ehrenburg (1891–1967) was a Soviet writer and journalist.

** Marshals Ferdinand Foch (1851–1929), Joseph Joffre (1852–1931), and Henri Philippe Pétain (1856–1951) were all French heroes of World War I. During World War II, Pétain served as prime minister of Vichy France, and in 1944, in the face of the advancing Allied forces, he retreated with the German Army. After the war he was found guilty of treason and spent the rest of his life in prison.

"There is so much for a girl to do," my mother would say to console me. "Parties, nice clothes, sports, concerts. Learning to sew and cook. Yes dear, I know you hate it, but when you marry, you must know how to run your house. You can also attend literature courses."

"Some Ashkenazi girls go to study in Europe, why can't I?"

"You aren't an Ashkenazi," Mother would reply, "and if you are too clever, our young men will be afraid to marry you."

"Then I'll marry an Ashkenazi. They are a thousand times more intelligent than we are. Freud, Trotsky, Bergson, all Ashkenazi Jews. We haven't one famous man to boast of since Maimonides.* Not one. Besides, take Sylvie. She isn't Ashkenazi, but her father allowed her to stay in Paris and go to the Sorbonne."

Mother laughed. "Whatever she does, she's rich enough to find plenty of young men willing to marry her. Besides, geniuses don't make good wives."

"Let me work then."

"You can't. People would think your father was ruined."

Similar arguments went on in every home. Our families consented to let us learn first aid in a clinic, on condition that there were no contagious diseases. We were also to attend French law school in the afternoon, wedging it neatly between tennis and parties.** We thought we had won a victory of sorts, but of course one doesn't learn two professions simultaneously, and we had neither the work discipline nor the need to earn a living, although we envied the girls who did. Why should one grind through the Code Napoléon when so many pleasures were available to us? and in any case, in a few years foreign courts would cease to exist in Egypt and European-trained lawyers would find themselves out of work. We attended the lectures without much enthusiasm until the students in Egyptian institutions of higher learning went on strike to protest, as usual, against some aspect of Britain's continued occupa-

* Moses Maimonides (1135 [Cordoba]–1204 [Egypt]) was a prominent Jewish philosopher and physician.

** From 1875 to 1949 there was a seperate legal system in place in Egypt to try civil and commercial cases involving foreigners. This system, known as the Mixed Courts, operated in French under French legal codes. Under the terms of the 1937 Montreux Convention, the Mixed Courts were disbanded in 1949.

tion. Their delegates rushed into the sedate precincts of the French law school—another minority stronghold—asking for a solidarity strike, and when a roomful of them had gathered, they locked the door. It was a growling, nasty meeting, and for most of us, it was the first time we saw Moslems at a mass meeting, eyes blazing, mouths distorted, prey to a fanatic collective emotion. The professor huffily explained in French that as a civil servant in His Majesty's government, he could not go on strike. He would lecture to empty halls, but we students were free to follow the dictates of our conscience. One of my Greek classmates, now an important man in the International Labor Organization, translated into Arabic, his face a masterpiece of irony, as his voice swelled emphatically: "Fellow students, you are free to make your choice! The door is locked!" The Moslem students were in an uproar. I rushed to the door and shouted to one of them over the din: "It is not right to lock girls up with so many men. You wouldn't like it to happen to your own sisters. Let us out quietly." (In personal relationships, they were always decent, though still Levantine enough to know that a person, however worthless, counts more than principles, however sacred.) They let us go.

I remember running through the dark, empty streets. Not a car in sight, and most of the lampposts smashed. Policemen patrolling. A volley of shots. I thought, "It's well after sundown, and it isn't over yet. Maybe there will be a revolution after all, and independence." There was ferment among them, as among us, but it was not quite the same. I wondered how those young Moslems intended to change conditions in Egypt if they did not even realize that learning what the Europeans knew was the most important thing of all, and if they continued wasting so much precious time on their political agitations.

We thought they imitated Europe in its most superficial aspects, without making the effort to grasp the superiority on which its dominion was founded. The wealthy ones among them paraded their foreign-made black Buicks and very blond mistresses, while those who had to earn a living dreamed of the diploma which would allow them to swish flies in government offices. Few applied themselves to becoming the elite needed to bring Egypt into the modern world. It was no accident that what there was of modern industry in Egypt was created by foreigners and members of the minorities, seldom by Moslems, however rich. To them, European civilization was too often merely something whose external trappings bestowed on them a coveted class privilege.

Thus, even though we sympathized with the Moslem nationalists' aspirations we did not believe them capable of solving the real problems of this society, and for this they could not forgive us. As Levantines, we instinctively searched for fruitful compromises, feeling as we did that the end of colonial occupation solved nothing fundamental unless Western concepts were at work in this awakening world, transforming its very soul. We knew that Europe, although far away, was inseparably part of us, because it had so much to offer. These radically different attitudes toward Europe and toward our conception of the future made the parting of our ways inevitable.

The strike lasted for weeks. We had completely lost our bearings. When we finally returned to law school, the professor had continued to lecture to almost empty benches, but unlike the young men, we had not spent time on our textbooks. But now, when we read books about the period preceding the Russian Revolution, the similarities with our kind of society irritated us, although not so much as the feeling that we too were old-fashioned, slightly ridiculous, and out of step with our times.

Some of us worked in the clinic regularly as volunteers. In that crumbling Arab district, the misery of women—many of them prostitutes just out of childhood and already victims of syphilis—and of their babies was so abysmal that whatever we did seemed useless. Most of the volunteers were Jewish or Coptic girls. The Moslem girls who had registered turned up only to curtsy to Queen Farida when she visited the dispensary,* after the least depressing-looking patients had been washed, dressed up, and lined up in rows, smiling.

The doctor in charge, one of Marie's cousins, who was exhausted from overwork, barked at patients in a voice raw with angry, desperate tenderness. Years later, in America, when I saw pictures of the faintly living corpses in Auschwitz, they reminded me of the tiny, still faintly breathing skeletons on the dispensary's tables, and of the doctor bawl-

* Queen Farida (née Safinaz Zulfiqar; 1920–1988) was married to the Egyptian monarch, King Farouk I, from 1939 to 1949. Farouk (1920–1965) ascended to the throne in 1936 and was deposed by the Free Officers revolt in 1952.

ing us out hoarsely: "Go to Palestine, where the Zionists are building a society that makes sense." Indeed it seemed to us that in Palestine a new social order was being built from the ground up, while in Egypt, one started from the top floor, hoping the foundations would take care of themselves.

Although we were not Zionists, since we were searching for universality, we discussed Zionism almost as ardently as Marxism. Our point was that a "European education" separated from religion was necessary before people could choose "objectively" for or against Zionism, and one could not jump from the *harat al-yahud* (Cairo's poor Jewish neighborhood) to the kibbutz without any preparation. This intermediary stage is what we tried to create, or at least, what we stood for. We resented the moralizing of the local Ashkenazi Zionists who, we said, talked a lot about Palestine, the Jewish People, and Nazi persecution, but were not concerned about the conditions in which Jewish people lived and died under their very noses. They were middle class in a solid, hard-working, virtuous way, which was foreign to us, and we found it rather selfish that they denied us the satisfaction of newfound freedoms that their parents had known in Eastern Europe, when breaking out of the ghetto. They built solid, middle-class fortunes in this Egypt, once so generous to those who were not of her soil, and for twenty, thirty, or forty years lived there, temporarily, always on their way to Palestine. "Next year in Jerusalem as free men . . ." Their idealism was to us just sufficiently tainted not to give them the right they freely abused, to criticize our Sephardic softness and *laisser-aller*. Later, more mature, less sensitive, we came to better appreciate the work they did, familiarizing us with these ideas, and we learned of the extremely useful work they did, propagating the faith right in the *hara*, helping an advance group of young pioneers to reach Palestine unofficially. Many people who had seemingly professed anti-Zionism had discreetly and effectively helped, with money or with the proper contacts, to hush up investigations.

Eventually we Jewish girls started our own clinic in a school in the Jewish quarter, where conditions were almost as bad as in the Arab quarters. We discussed earnestly if this was betraying "the masses," but decided that since there were fewer Jews, we would at least see some results, and that the pashas' daughters could do their own social work.

Then, if our people went to Palestine some day, they would at least be in better health, and could be more useful.

People laughed at our clinic, but helped us, surprised by the results we obtained without much experience. We caused a minor revolution by paying rates unheard of in the *hara* to the girls who worked with us. That was our undoing. We knew nothing of the organization of the Jewish community, and were astounded when the Sheikh al-Hara (head of the community) made veiled threats. It was rumored that we advocated birth control and Zionism, to which we retorted that the second allegation was a lie. We learned that parents whose children came to us were barred from the Sheikh al-Hara's list and were no longer helped by the community's funds. Nasty little articles appeared in some papers and upset our parents, who did not want us to be known as well-meaning but dangerous revolutionaries. One by one, we quit. We should have fought, but that was exactly what we had not learned to do. We were too self-indulgent and lacked the perseverance needed to create from our dreams and potentialities the solid facts that would have a bearing on reality.

Without the clinic, our lives seemed more futile than ever. Parties and flirtation were not quite so exciting once the newness wore off. We attended courses according to our inclinations—painting, stone cutting, philosophy, dancing, yoga—dropping one thing to start another, never finishing anything. We despised ourselves and the smug young men who at least had the satisfaction of making money. Some of us, in our usual amateurish way, joined antifascist groups, leagues for democratic action, debated Stalinism and Trotskyism in meetings of various degrees of secrecy with unmarriageable, fascinatingly disquieting young men—Henri and Raoul Curiel, Albert Mosseri, writer Georges Henein, and Lotfallah Soliman—almost all from the minorities.*

* Henri Curiel (1914–1978), from a wealthy Jewish family, founded an Egyptian Communist organization, in which his older brother Raoul also dabbled. Albert Mosseri (1868–1933) was a journalist and founding editor of the trilingual Egyptian Jewish newspaper *Israël*. Georges Henein (1914–1973) was a Francophone Egyptian surrealist poet of Coptic and Italian parentage. Lotfallah Soliman (1919–1995), a writer and journalist, was also a member of Henein's literary salon, Art et Liberté.

I published my first sketches, oddly unreal because all reference to any social context was carefully omitted. I also visited Palestine, where I was tempted by the kibbutz. One did not need money there, so I could do without my parents' consent, having just turned twenty-one, and thus would be saved from the soft, stifling, corrupting life of Egypt. Something held me back, which was not only attachment to an easy life. First I had to know Europe from the inside before I could make my choice. Only then could I go to Palestine as a whole person. I loved Egypt, but could no longer bear to be part of it, however conscious I was of its queer charm, its enchantment, its contrasts, its ignoble poverty and refined splendor. I had to break the spell.

One summer afternoon, we sat on the floor in the handsome library of a friend's house, around a mountain of petals from her father's rose garden, from which her grandmother would soon be making rose water. The roses had a pungent scent, and someone remarked, "Our grandmothers knew how to make rose water, and we, not even that." The girl who spoke was Turkish, the daughter of a princess and a pasha who had been ambassador to many Western capitals. Having lived in Europe all her life, she had trouble adjusting to the life of the Turkish aristocrats. It was rumored that she had refused to become Farouk's queen, making him angry and her family distressed. She perhaps alluded to this, telling us that while undoubtedly there was *noblesse oblige*, it was asking too much of a woman to live locked up for the rest of her days in a harem with bitchy court ladies.

We were silent, drowsy with heat and the scent of dying roses, when one of the girls stretched her big, well-built body and exclaimed, "I wish I had the guts to be a cabaret dancer, naked between two fans. We all behave like whores anyway once we're married—except for the poor queen." Soon after, she announced she was off to Turkey, to find herself a husband. "A true Turk," she said, "and not one of those degenerate Turks from Egypt. I'd prefer someone with a real profession. Engineers, for instance, are not much fun but, come the revolution, we would at least never lack a loaf of bread." Perhaps she meant it as a joke, but her words were prophetic.

There was another girl there, about whom a few days later an enormous scandal broke out. A married assistant professor of philosophy, not yet divorced, had dared ask for her hand. Her outraged parents kept guard over our friend and fought the professor for months, a burlesquely dramatic battle which kept all tongues wagging. She became a heroine because she did not give up her man, and her name was the rallying cry of a generation of young women who wished to be masters of their own bodies as they saw fit. If any young men dared to criticize her conduct, they were left cold on the dance floor by young women who told them, "The system is all to your advantage, but we won't stand for it any more." In the harem section, on streetcars, humble black-veiled women discussed the girl they did not know, enthusiastically comparing her to the Duchess of Windsor. "Ya Allah! Amour! Amour! Those are men! Ready to lose a kingdom for the woman they love." I wondered how they knew that the professor had lost his job. Older people could not understand what evil wind was blowing, and parents feared they would have dishonored, unmarriageable daughters forever on their hands. "Elle est casée" (she's been married off), they would say with a sigh of relief when a reluctant damsel flashed an enormous diamond engagement ring.

The time had come to make our choices. One of us married a professor and went off to teach in a French school in Indochina. My Turkish friend married a Turkish engineer of noble birth. Yet another of our group ended up doing social work in a village near her father's sumptuous villa, teaching women to use a sewing machine, and to knit, all the while talking of Lenin, Trotsky, Stalin, and of the Red Star which would bring salvation from the East. The one who was really envied by all came to Egypt for short visits during holidays, spoke knowingly of Hegel, patronized our misguided efforts and corrected our so-called "faulty interpretations," for she supposedly had the key to all understanding. She talked about the French *normaliens* students,* and used their jargon with ease while we had to be content to know about them only through Jallez and Jerphanion, in Jules Romains's *Les hommes de bonne volonté*.

I married a young Jewish doctor of Russian origin who was going to

* Graduates of the École normale supérieure, a prestigious French institution of higher education.

settle in the United States. The gate to freedom . . . Perhaps, one day, I would be able to write about this Egypt I both loved and hated, the frail little world, seemingly so perfect, but in reality so rotten that it had to fall apart—to give birth to one of which I might feel a part. But, first I would have to assess my generation in search of itself, and this I could do only from afar.

The Second World War broke out, and from the distance of another continent I could see how much the Egypt I had known was changing. My younger sister went to university without the slightest objection from my parents. I proudly thought that I had paved the way for her. She, like many other young girls, worked. It was considered smart, even patriotic, to work for the British and the Americans. With all those uniformed young men about, the girls thumbed their noses at the local boys and at their parents' counsels of moderation, secretly wishing the war would never end.

When I returned to Egypt to visit my family in 1946, I came in the thoroughly enviable position of a young divorcée who had won a literary prize in the United States. "It can only happen in America," my left-wing and violently anti-American friends would say contemptuously.

Many of the girls I had known had left Egypt to marry Allied officers, preferably from smart British regiments. Such husbands were hard to find, and many settled for less. A few of the other young women wheedled their influential fathers into getting their Communist friends out of jail. The words of these elegant Marxists, spoken in beautifully converted Arab houses above the Red Stairs, were whispered softly in the young officers' clubs. The seeds sown there sprouted and bore fruit, in fields that had long lain fallow. It was later rumored that one of the group, a Stalinist of the highest Turkish aristocracy, had a hand in grooming young Nasser himself.

I was fascinated by the Egypt I now saw as if from the outside, which afforded freedoms I had never known as a girl. I sniffed at the desert wind, spiced with orange blossoms, dung, dust, fruit, and flowers, filled myself with it, feeling alive again. The very air in America by comparison seemed odorless, sterilized, polluted. Everything here seemed real, dreadful, magnificent, as nowhere else. We all felt that the end of the world we had known was close at hand. Sumptuous cars on their way to some expensive pleasure were merely detoured, to avoid the streets where rioting had broken out. At a poker table, King Farouk was heard to remark, "Soon, there will be only five kings left in the world, the four kings in a pack of cards and the King of England." He was a bad king but a good prophet.

# *Ten*

# A Culture Stillborn

*As described in this essay, Kahanoff hesitantly started her writing career as a young woman by composing comic sketches of her social set; however, she was never encouraged to pursue her craft while in Egypt. Indeed, as she articulates, members of the foreign minority communities produced little literature of note while living in Egypt. After their dispersal, some, like her friend the noted Francophone poet Edmond Jabès (1912–1991), whom she mentions in this piece, were able to memorialize the culture that no longer existed. This essay was published in two parts in the Israeli newspaper* Davar *in April and May of 1973.*

Many European languages were spoken in Egypt's main cities, both by the Turkish Egyptian aristocracy and among the minorities. English was the language of the occupying power, while French tended to be the language of culture. But Italian and Greek maintained strong positions. Within the Jewish community, as the switch from Arabic and Ladino took place, some inclined toward English, others toward French, while the Italian Jewish community continued to send its children to Italian schools, at least until fascism profoundly divided the Italians settled in Egypt. Many of these Italian Jews were the descendants of those Khedive Isma'il had invited as doctors, engineers, architects, technicians when he started Egypt on its dizzy course of Europeanization and indebtedness to European powers. The Italian Jewish community was the most genuinely European, and it was particularly prominent in Alexandria, where it gave the Jewish community its tone. Its members were intermarried with the prominent local Jewish families. Many people in this milieu were well-read in all three languages, Italian, English, and French. This complexity gave this minority culture a subtlety, diversity, and refinement rarely matched elsewhere, but no ethnic element or language was actually strong enough to weld these disparate groups into some kind of unity.

Even so, now and again, a brave attempt was made to start a literary magazine in French—which usually died after a few issues were published. What struck me about these magazines (I wish I could remember their names) was their poetic romanticism about the Orient, its perfumes and mystery; otherwise, they were curiously vague about people, their status and station in life. This was particularly evident in the love stories. It did happen in real life that a Jewish girl had an affair with a Moslem man; there was always an aura of scandal about her, but that kind of story was never written about. In Alexandria's high society, it was quite the fashion for Jewish men to have Greek mistresses, and Greek men to have Jewish mistresses, but no one wrote about it. Educated Jewish girls had a mania about falling in love with French professors who taught at the lycée or the university, and it was never quite clear whether they were in love with the man or the culture he represented. One of my friends, who read *Thus Spake Zarathustra* with passion, called this "living dangerously," for indeed, having a lover before one's parents had got one safely married and off their hands was a rather risky business, and just about the only way a girl could live dangerously. A book could be written about the ludicrous, funny, tragic, or perverse stories which occupied a society with enough money and leisure to devote much time to sex and love.

Some people in Egypt were wonderful mimics and storytellers; why they didn't write remains a mystery. I suspect there was a strong taboo about not upsetting the delicate balance which allowed people belonging to various communities and religions to live together in fairly good harmony as long as various accommodations with the facts of life were never openly acknowledged. So these vague stories about next to nothing were written in a stilted "cultured" style, quite unlike the language one spoke. One could have written funny pieces about our various linguistic mixtures, and in real life, every group made fun of all the others. But this too was never written about. It seems to me that this same sociological indefiniteness characterizes films and television shows produced in the Arabic-speaking countries, as if, in spite of their revolutions, they still considered it indelicate to mention class, ethnic, or religious factors, which in fact play a determining role in shaping people's lives.

In Cairo, Kish-Kish Bey's popular theater provided the one setting where people of various backgrounds met and laughed together at themselves and one another.* These unpretentious, lively, funny, partly improvised playlets were produced by a young Jew called Mizrahi. Vivid, recognizable types were portrayed on the stage: the Greek grocer, with his funny lisp in Arabic, having a passionate argument with his customers, the Jews from *harat al-yahud*, with a rose or twig of jasmine behind his ear, which he passed under his nose whenever he felt embarrassed or told a fib; and the middle-aged, veiled Moslem lady, venturing in a department store, entranced by Western goods, asking the cheeky little Italian salesgirls whether one put a girdle over or under a petticoat, and at what moment one puts on or takes off a bed jacket in bed. Kish-Kish Bey reflected our simple origins, stripped of pretense, and bound us together by its affectionate mockery. On my last visit to Egypt, just before General Muhammad Naguib took power,** Kish-Kish Bey's theater no longer existed. It was the sign we could no longer laugh together.

Of course, I too had attempted to publish some of my writing in a local magazine. Feverishly, we discussed the need to honestly portray life in Egypt. The young man, who was called Albert, as was practically everyone I knew, asked me whether I would contribute, and I agreed to do so, but he must promise nobody would know about it beforehand. With a beating heart, I'd meet Albert in secret, in the back room of a little pastry shop called Loques, between two and three o'clock in the afternoon, when nobody was around, except lovers meeting on the sly. "I can't understand why you must visit your girlfriend in this blazing

* Naguib al-Rihani (1889–1949) made his name playing the role of Kish-Kish Bey, the mayor of a fictional rural village whose encounters with modernity and city life formed the basis of comic sketches on stage and screen.

** Naguib (1901–1984) was a member of the Free Officers group that implemented the coup overthrowing King Farouk in 1952. He served as president of Egypt from 1953 to 1954.

heat, do you girls never rest?" Mother would protest before turning in for her siesta. Finally the magazine appeared, with my sketches about girls in Egypt: sixteen with its silly giggle, eighteen with its torment as we left school and felt the future closing before us, twenty with our despair and revolt against a society that permitted us to get an education but forbade us to use it. Defiantly, I brought it home, telling my parents, "Look, my signature. In print."

Consternation spread over their faces. Why hadn't I said a word about this? "What was the point of asking permission for something I knew you wouldn't allow?" I retorted.

My sketches were not bad at all. My mother brought me those yellowed pages torn out from the magazine when she and my father joined us in Israel after the Sinai Campaign.* She did not know I had left them behind because they reminded me of a cruel humiliation. For weeks, the young men I danced with at parties would remark ironically, "I didn't know you were a Proust in petticoats." And women of my mother's generation were incensed because an ad for contraceptives figured on the same page as my sketches. That sly Lebanese had done this intentionally, to suggest that Jewish girls needed contraceptives before they were married.

A few years later, in the United States, when my first short story, "Cairo Wedding," was published, I received letters from publishing firms to the effect that if I was planning to write a book, they were interested and had fellowships to help beginner writers. I remembered the reaction in Cairo, so denigrating toward my first efforts. After all, I reflected, the United States did not need me to have a literature, but Cairo should have needed me. Yet, it was in America that I received encouragement. How many budding artists were nipped in the bud in Cairo and Alexandria, perhaps also in Tanta and Damanhur? I tried for a fellowship and won it. My novel, *Jacob's Ladder*, was finally written

* Also known as the Suez Crisis. In 1956 Egyptian President Gamal Abdel Nasser nationalized the Suez Canal. Egypt prevented Israeli ships from passing and implemented a blockade on Israel's southern port, Eilat. Israel, in collusion with France and Great Britain, retaliated by launching a military attack on the Sinai Peninsula.

and published. As it was "sociologically honest," it upset my family immensely. I never finished another book.

Why did we have an attitude at once so touchy and denigrating toward ourselves? I think we considered ourselves too inferior—or, as we say in Israel, too "Levantine"—to dare express ourselves in writing. Gide and Malraux were our standard, but it didn't occur to us that the point was not to emulate them, but to tell our own story, in our own words. That could be only our beginning. Once we had left Egypt, it broke our hearts to think that practically nobody had done this; that a whole community, one of the most complex and interesting, disappeared without leaving a trace. The one significant work about Egypt's Levantine world, the *Alexandria Quartet*, was written not by one of us, but by Lawrence Durrell, an Irishman. But then, he had a language at his command, perhaps also a vitality, a naïve self-confidence we lacked. He could describe our failure of nerve just because he didn't suffer from it. It was as if something in us had broken, long before we reached adulthood.

Even so, I've known a number of women writers and painters who were born in Egypt—rather talented ones too: Andrée Chedid, who writes novels; Joyce Mansour, who has written some quite beautiful poetry; Nadine Gorse, the wife of France's ambassador to Algeria. Their work is interesting, but never quite lives up to its promise. All of them published only after they had left Egypt. Among the painters, I'm particularly fond of Donatienne Sapriel, who lived in Kyoto many years and whose art is very much influenced by Zen Buddhism. She once told me, "We're incomplete, unfinished. The most charmingly disappointed people I know of." These women live in Paris, as do the Egyptian-born journalists who write about the Middle East, Georges Henein, Albert Fakri, Eric Roulean. Some of them, who have known each other since childhood, form a loose, nostalgic little community. They do not have the support of a large, fairly cohesive community to back them, as the North African Jewish writers who have settled in France.

Not surprisingly, the best Egyptian-born writer, the poet Edmond Jabès, found his essential theme once he had left Egypt, and settling in France, felt dreadfully, irremediably, the full weight of exile. His theme is death, a slow death through attrition. The three volumes of *Le livre* *des questions* is an extraordinarily evocative achievement, mixing surrealism, *Kabbalah*, and the dialogue and sayings of his imaginary rabbis. These are interspersed with poems and prose pieces which explore the plight of the Jewish people. It is an arid world of utter desolation, but with nothing of that vitality which allowed the Jews to survive, no matter what. It is also a book about writing, but here, the act by which man's creation reflects the divine creation is a desperate interrogation about a world where man is alienated, lost. The love story of Yudkl and Sarah, who lose their sanity before losing their lives, haunts the mind of the writer, who once traced letters on the shifting sand drifts of Egypt's deserts, letters the wind erased as if everything inevitably dissolved into nothingness, and the human cry of anguish, echoing in the void, remained forever without an answer. *Le livre des questions* starts thus: "Marque d'un signet rouge la première page du livre, car la blessure est invisible à son commencement," Reb Alcé.*

Some of these imaginary rabbis bear the names of Jewish families from all around the Mediterranean basin (Acobas, Panigel, Segré, Chemtob) as if the poet were engaged in a secret dialogue with ghostlike witnesses of this Jewish past who are still alive, although it is dead.

I remember Eddie as the handsome, dreamy, charming young man he was, his blue eyes lost in the distance. His first published book of verse was titled *Je bâtis ma demeure*. There had been a time when he believed a house could be built. Nothing remains of it but those broken figments in the poet's memory.

"Eddie," I asked when I saw him and his wife Arlette in Paris, "how did you come to invent those imaginary rabbis?"

"I think they were always with me, but they spoke only when I learned what exile is," he replied.

In most Jewish homes I know there are a few dearly loved relics rescued from a former life: pictures, candelabras, a rug. In Eddie and Arlette's small living room in Paris, I recognized the tapestry representing a child squatting among wild ducks half hidden among the rushes of

* English translation: "Mark the first page of the book with a red marker. For, in the beginning, the wound is invisible." Edmond Jabès, *The Book of Questions*, trans. Rosemarie Waldrop (Middletown, CT: Wesleyan University Press, 1972), 15.

the Nile. These tapestries, depicting Egypt's village life, had been made by the children of fellahin in a school founded by the Wissa-Wassefs, one of Egypt's prominent land-owning Coptic families. The children made up their own designs, chose their own color schemes. Nothing I've ever seen is more evocative of Egypt's melancholy mud villages, barely emerging from the Nile silt, than these naïve, intensely poetic tapestries.

So we talked about the present where our bodies live and the past where something of our souls remained. Arlette was working as a bilingual secretary, and Eddie was a representative for a film company, writing his poetry on night trains. And as we spoke, I could see, superimposed on that image of village life which had been the ignored yet haunting background of so many of our extravagances, Eddie and Arlette running down the rose marble staircase of the villa where her great-grandparents had given the famous ball for Napoleon II and Josephine, who had come to Egypt for the inauguration of the Suez Canal, that very canal whose closure had coincided with our final liquidation as a community.

"You know," I said, "other communities have suffered beyond anything we thought conceivable. But at least they had writers to record their lives. We have left nothing, and you, Eddie, tell of our death, not of our lives. It is like dying twice, in the spirit as well as in the flesh. I have tried, written so many beginnings. But something stops me long before I reach the end."

A couple of years later, when Eddie and Arlette came to Israel for a holiday and brought Arlette's mother along, I persuaded her to tell me her recollections, which I registered on a tape and sent to the Institute of Contemporary Jewish Studies. Edit Cohen, the granddaughter of Cattawi Pasha, who had been Khedive Isma'il's banker, was by then a frail old lady, nearly eighty years old. Her voice was hardly audible as she spoke of people so long dead. She told me wonderful stories about her maternal grandfather, Dr. Rossi, whom the khedive had invited over from Ferrara. The khedive had sent Dr. Rossi to survey Arabia, and in the Hadramout the doctor and his party were attacked by tall, savage-looking marauders.* Dr. Rossi, thinking his last hour had come, threw

* The Hadramout is a region of Yemen along the Gulf of Aden.

himself on the ground and recited his *Shema Yisrael*. It turned out the savage tribesmen were Jews, and upon hearing the *Shema Yisrael*, left Dr. Rossi and gave him and his party shelter. The doctor returned to Egypt convinced he had discovered one of Israel's lost tribes.

Then she told me a lovely story about Joseph Cattawi Pasha, her grandfather. He had refused to raise a large sum of money the khedive urgently needed by Sunday because he asked for it on a Thursday, and Cattawi Pasha never transacted business on a Sabbath. When the khedive sent his carriage, drawn by the horse he had imported from Vienna, to invite Cattawi Pasha to drink coffee with him, the latter took leave of his family, thinking his last hour had come. Poison was sometimes slipped into coffee cups in those days. The anguished family waited for his return. But before sunset, in time for the Sabbath, the khedive's carriage brought Cattawi Pasha back home. The khedive had only wanted to chat with his friend; not a word was said about the loan.

The shrunken little old lady evoked a hundred years of what had been the life of Egypt she knew, until she reached the end. She did not cry, although tears came to her eyes when she spoke of her husband. "Il était superbe," she said, and something of the passion she had known as a very young woman vibrated in her voice. By then she was faint from exhaustion and I was worried to see her so prostrated. "I'm glad," she whispered. "In this way, at least, something of us may be remembered. The record will be preserved in Jerusalem."

One evening, we roamed in Jaffa, which reminds one of Alexandria. The same types of churches were built at about the same time by Italian masons. We heard Greek music and had arak and mezze of olives, goat cheese, and anchovies at Ariana, which was so much like Greek casinos which had once been strung along Alexandria's seafront. Then we watched the starry night and listened to the sea. Eddie said, "Here in Israel, there was once a place called Yabetz, which we are supposed to have come from. The name Yabes [Jabès] is a distortion of Yabetz." Perhaps, I thought, one of Eddie's ancestors had studied the *Kabbalah* in these parts and spoke through the voice of imaginary rabbis in *Le livre des questions*.

Our ancestors trod through the desert and cities of the East, crossing and recrossing them. Our Sarahs and Jacobs, our Elivars and Moshikos, our Victorias and Alberts rest in these sands. It covers the letters of their names in abandoned Jewish cemeteries by the desert's edge. The sand hides and preserves our names, for our stories from time immemorial were written on this sand. Insatiably, it eats us up, for our stories belong to this sand, the desert which encompasses the green oasis of hope. The sand remembers us.

⁂

It is possible to see the promise of a beginning of Levantine literature—rooted in the realities of the Middle East and influenced by European culture—in *Le livre de Goha le Simple* [*Goha the Fool*] by Albert Adès and Albert Josipovici. This sad and cynical love story, which employs the prototype of Goha, the hero of many Middle Eastern tales, describes the lives of the common folk of Cairo before the spread of Western cultural influence. The innovation in this novel was its description of local realities in the context of a European novel; it was written in French. Adès was born in Cairo in 1833, and Josipovici, the son of a doctor, was born in Constantinople. They both studied in France and lived in Egypt. They wrote the book together in 1913, and it was published by Calman-Lévy Press in 1919. The book was a great success and almost won the Goncourt Prize, which was granted with all honor to no less a writer than Marcel Proust that very year. *Goha* has been translated into seven languages and made into a play produced by Odéon in 1937.

Albert Adès died in 1921 and Albert Josipovici died in 1931; no one followed in their footsteps. Their deaths caused deep sorrow within the Egyptian Jewish community. I recall my family grieving when Josipovici died. That was how I heard about *Goha the Fool* for the first time. If Adès and Josipovici had remained alive, they would probably have gathered a following of a school of writers from Egypt who would have used local realities as the subject of description in a modern style.

That is in fact what happened in Arabic literature launched by the memoirs of Taha Husayn about the village of his childhood, written in the Egyptian dialect and not in classical literary Arabic rhetoric.* But

* Taha Husayn's memoir, *al-Ayyam* (*The Days*), like all of his other works, was written in literary Arabic.

the direction of the educated elite of the minorities was different. Their European cultural orientation was obvious. They read what was published in France and gathered at literary salons and lectures, but never created any literature of value. The Greek poet Constantine Cavafy was an exception in this regard, but it is worth mentioning that the rich, multilingual Greek community lived in Alexandria from ancient times and held on to the Greek language and maintained close ties with Greece. Cavafy belonged to a very specific literary and cultural tradition. The Greeks who lived in Egypt learned French and English but spoke Greek and sent their children to Greek schools.

The situation of the Jewish community was different. Members of the community who were born there were in the minority. The community grew as a result of Jews coming to Egypt from other Mediterranean countries, some for economic reasons—the prosperity that the Suez Canal brought to Egypt—and some for political reasons, because life under the rule of the British protectorate was more secure than under the regimes that had sprung up after the fall of the Ottoman Empire. The Jews who lived in Egypt before and after World War I came from Syria, Iraq, Lebanon, Turkey, Greece, North Africa. Later, Jews came from Romania, Russia, and finally from Austria and Germany. The Sephardi Jews already spoke Ladino among themselves. The Jews from Middle Eastern countries spoke different Arabic dialects. The Jews in Egypt did not have a single shared language like the Yiddish of the Eastern European communities. The connection between them was French culture, which was spread with the help of the network of the Alliance Israélite Universelle extending throughout the Middle East and North Africa.*

The Jews were so intoxicated by French culture that they did not pay attention to the advice of the Alliance for the Jews to learn the language of the land in which they lived. In the eyes of the middle-class Egyptian Jews of my generation, speaking in Arabic was considered out-dated and old-fashioned. Only the lower classes, that is to say the

* Alliance Israélite Universelle [French], an organization established to protect the human rights of Jews, was known principally for establishing a network of Jewish schools in the Middle East.

Jews of the ghetto, spoke Arabic. With time, they, too, mastered French in the schools offered by the community. The language of instruction was French, and Arabic was taught as a "foreign" language, as was English. A dual French-Arabic educational program was implemented in the schools just before the Arab-Israeli war.

Even the Jews who came to Egypt from Central and Eastern Europe learned French and English and didn't bother learning Arabic. There were several positive aspects to acquiring French culture, but after all was said and done, French and English were not local languages in which people could easily or spontaneously express themselves. To a great extent we were a people without a language. There is no doubt that this lack was a barrier to written expression. Furthermore, we were appreciably carried farther and farther from reality. We had a vague sense of uneasiness because of the difficulties of our position, or perhaps because of the fundamental deceit within it. But we could not nor did we want to confront these things. At the same time Egyptian nationalism adopted a more explicit antiforeign, pan-Arab, and religious-Islamic character. The Moslem majority and the minorities drifted farther apart in their language, their cultures, their aspirations, and their outlooks until nothing shared remained. The resentment and suspicion of the Moslem majority toward the minorities (some of whom were natives, like the Copts) intensified. The minorities scorned the failures of the Egyptians, their degeneracy, and the rest of their faults.

The potential writers from the minority groups could not, therefore, anticipate a local readership. They could not create a meaningful connection with the Egyptian majority, not through their language, and not through the content of their writing. The Egyptians who wrote in Arabic, of course, had no influence on their writing. We didn't even know of their existence, except for Taha Husayn, who was married to a French woman and did not live in a closed Moslem environment. If the name of one of these writers came to our attention, we would dismiss him contemptuously. Their presumed inferiority compared to what we read in French made them not even worth reading. We forgot that we could not read their works even if we wanted to. We did not ask ourselves if perhaps they had something to say that we should know, not only because we lived in the same country. It seemed as if we were afraid to admit to ourselves that we lived in the same cultural, political, spiritual realm. It was as if the explorations of Adès and Josipovici toward symbiosis were a stillborn experiment.

Why and how this symbiosis died is a long and complex story. I would say that in a symbolic way, the era of crisis began with the death of the Egyptian leader Sa'd Zaghlul in 1927.* The British, who had earlier deported Zaghlul, returned his body to Egypt and saw to it that a national funeral of vast proportions was held for him. I was a big enough girl and received permission to watch the procession. Members of my family crowded onto the balcony of my grandparents' apartment overlooking Qasr al-Nil street along which the procession passed. The length of the street, all of the balconies were full of people. The silence was impressive, sincere emotion and sorrow.

Members of all religious sects participated in the funeral, not just the Moslem sheikhs, but Coptic priests, Greek-Orthodox, Armenians, Syrians, Maronites, and representatives of the important Catholic orders—Dominicans, Franciscans, Jesuits (in those days I knew how to identify the members of different churches and orders by their clothes, or head coverings, or even how they grew their beards)—and among them our chief rabbi, Nahum Effendi. There were also representatives from the different schools and I recognized the students from the Jewish orphanage school and the Greek school by their uniforms. I didn't know then how to express it in words, but I felt that all of us—people who differed from one another by religion, national origin, and language—all of us were part of an Egypt that aspired to freedom and mourned the death of Sa'd Zaghlul.

About forty years later I saw Nasser's funeral on a television screen in a restaurant on the outskirts of Haifa. The waiters, young Israeli-Arabs, cried bitterly. I noticed the greater community that surrounded Nasser's casket was only Arab. Perhaps representatives of the minorities that stayed in Egypt were also present, but the television crews did

* Zaghlul (1857–1927) was an Egyptian national leader who agitated for Egyptian independence from Great Britain. Exiled in 1918, he returned after the Egyptian Revolution of 1919. He served as prime minister in 1924. Contrary to Kahanoff's contention, Zaghlul died in Egypt, not in exile.

not choose to film them this time. They were no longer in fashion as they had been in Zaghlul's time, a time in which the unity of all of Egypt's inhabitants seemed very important. The idea of a liberal, pluralistic Egyptian nationalism which included the non-Moslems and was accepted by them had died in the intervening years.

This all seems very far away from literature; but there is a deep connection between culture and politics, especially in societies which underwent such radical transformation, always attached to a new self-definition. After Zaghlul's death, Egyptian nationalism became harsher and less tolerant of any "foreigner." It chose to forget that Sa'd Zaghlul, the Egyptian, had opposed the idea of a treaty between Arab nations, flirted with by King Fuad like the other Middle Eastern monarchs. "Zero plus zero equals zero," is how Zaghlul explained his opposition. These same years granted the minorities the opportunity to ignore reality. The more they feared the hatred of the Moslem Brotherhood,* the more they relied upon the British presence in Egypt, and became more isolated. Only the Syrian-Lebanese Christians supported Arab nationalism without pangs of conscience, and they gained advantages from this support. To a certain extent, it was their device, their means of winning the hearts of the Moslem rulers and persuading them to drop the other minorities. They owned widely influential newspapers in Egypt and expressed in them Arab-nationalist themes, anti-Semitism, and anti-Zionism with a venom not present in the other newspapers of the day that were owned by Moslems.

Thus, they shared the linguistic, political, and cultural bases of the Egyptian majority, and the minorities disappeared in stages. The potential writers from the minorities did not know how to say anything meaningful or interesting to upper-middle-class Arabs. Potential writers—and there were many among the minorities in Egypt—had to write to people, even if to a very few. To whom could they write in Egypt? Jews to Jews, Greeks to Greeks, Armenians to Armenians? And in which language? The opportunity to create a shared, complex culture

* An Islamic political group founded in Egypt in 1928. In the early 1940s an armed branch of the organization carried out violent acts, contributing to fear among the religious minorities in Egypt.

that would permit connections and fertile, enlivening exchange, which seemed so close when *Goha the Fool* was written and when Taha Husayn began to write, was missed.

Egyptian men of letters from the middle class were angry with the proud, detached culture of the minorities and rejected it, even though it was a window to the world. The more sophisticated culture of the minorities was not drawn from local sources and existed in a strange empty space, full of self-doubt and self-loathing, at the same time as it was full of the anxiety of not belonging and lacking connection. Its potential writers who lived between the two world wars even distanced themselves from the topics of alienation and estrangement. These were fearful topics, and the youth did not dare to deal with them. A strange escapism characterized the few attempts at literary expression which appeared, white-washed, here and there in short-lived amateur journals, which are the natural habitat of most beginning writers. Edmond Jabès, the man who wrote—finally—about Judaism and alienation in *Le livre des questions*, did this after he emigrated from Egypt and settled in Paris, when he was already middle aged.

*Translated from Hebrew by Deborah Starr*

*Eleven*

# To Live and Die a Copt

*In 1964 an Anglophone, Egyptian-Coptic writer, Waguih Ghali, published his first and only novel,* Beer in the Snooker Club. *Kahanoff first became aware of this book nearly a decade after its publication and several years after its author had committed suicide. Featuring a Coptic protagonist and a Jewish love interest, the novel, set in the 1940s and 1950s, moves between England and Egypt and traces the struggle of Egyptians to hold on to their disappearing cosmopolitan, Levantine world. Kahanoff's essay, published in April 1973, serves as both a belated review of the novel and a reflection on Jewish-Coptic relations in Egypt. Kahanoff was apparently not aware that Ghali had spent time in Israel from July to September 1967 as a freelance journalist for the British press.*

A friend of mine lent me the book *Beer in the Snooker Club* (Penguin) by the Coptic-Egyptian writer Waguih Ghali and asked for my opinion of it. The author's name sounded familiar and brought back memories. The Ghalis were a very wealthy and influential Coptic family, owning large estates in Upper Egypt. A young girl called Mona Ghali attended the same French high school as I did and lived not far from us, in an apartment block on the other side of a small square, in the Garden City by the Nile—the neighborhood was called Qasr al-Dubarrah. One summer I discovered she had a brother. A tall, dark, very handsome young man would stand on the balcony of their house, dressed in an all-white linen outfit, a red tarbush set rakishly on his head. He would smoke as he waited for his friends who came to pick him up every day at five in the afternoon in their fancy sports cars. I heard that the young man had just returned from England, where he had obtained an education, that he was not prepared to do any work whatsoever, and that he led a rather extravagant life.

When I read *Beer in the Snooker Club*, I wondered whether Waguih Ghali was the same young man I remember. There are many similarities between him and Ram, the hero of the book. Like that young man, whom I recall quite clearly though I never spoke with him, Ram had lost his father and belonged to the poorer branch of the family; otherwise, he would have lived in a palatial villa, rather than an apartment block, and would have had his own sports car. If indeed the young man of my recollections is the author of the book—how strange, how symbolic of our particular situation, that both of us, wielding our pens in the night hours, lived so close to each other, both of us trying to put on paper our impressions of Levantine Cairo and our problems as residents, while neither knew this of the other. Would Egypt's cultural scene have been different if the members of our generation had been able to associate with one another? Communal-religious boundaries were not easily crossed in those days, and what one knew about a member of another community was mostly gossip, and usually negative. It would have been interesting to talk with that clandestine writer, who seemed as desperate as he was reckless and charming. The heroes in Ghali's book, surviving from the pre-Nasser period, are so familiar.

Ghali's testimony seemed all the more valid when I was told he had taken his own life, unable to adjust to Egypt under Nasser, nor to England, where he saw himself as a foreigner. "I am an Egyptian," Ram declares in *Beer in the Snooker Club*, but Nasser's Egypt did not claim him as its own. The Copts are descendants of the early Egyptians, most of whom were Christian in the Byzantine era. Those who refused to convert to Islam after the Moslem conquest did not fully integrate with the Arab newcomers nor with converts from other communities. The Copts remained apart, but they were certainly Egyptian, members of the lower middle class, at least, and as highly skilled artisans they were hard-working and thrifty. Those with a higher social standing had considerable influence in the pre-Nasser period. As nationalists, they hoped that Egypt would develop into a liberal democracy and that religion would not be the factor determining national identity. But the time was past for that early form of Egyptian nationalism, which was personified in Sa'ad Zaghlul. Egyptian nationalism became a pan-Arab Moslem movement with which the minorities could not entirely identify, and which in turn shunned all the minorities, even if they were—like the Copts—indigenous. The phenomenon recently returned, when a zealous, frustrated Moslem mob set fire to Coptic churches.

## Suicide as a Way Out of Ethnic Conflict

Copts from the upper classes were often given the names of gods from early Egyptian mythology: Isis, Osiris, Horus. Some of the most talented among them committed suicide, like Ghali, because they could not find their place in Nasser's Egypt, and were not capable of living in another country. Perhaps they lacked the flexibility that Jews have acquired through necessity. The Copts are like the reeds on the banks of the Nile: they bend as the storm passes over them but are well-rooted in the mud and cannot easily be transplanted.

Despite the sadness, *Beer in the Snooker Club* is an entertaining book, overflowing with indefinable Egyptian humor. Its sharp-eyed author mocks everything, himself included, with a fascinating mix of acerbity and good-humored wit. A melancholy envelops Ghali's book, the way Egyptian dust covers the landscape. Like the silent desert, the great stone monuments, and the dead gods that weigh upon human lives, the heaviness cannot be shaken off. There are those, like Nasser, who try to escape it by feverish activity and dreams of greatness—but the burden of eternity wears them down and makes every human endeavor pointless. Egypt is a country whose inhabitants find it hard to believe in themselves or their future; everything in it seems to turn to dust. Sometimes I wonder whether the most egregious errors committed by its political leaders might not derive, to a certain extent, from that same fatalism, a fatalism that overwhelms them when they act stupidly, believing as they do that nothing can really change.

But let us return to Ram and *Beer in the Snooker Club*. Ram is a well-read young man, a nationalist, easily offended, Socialist in his sympathies. His heart is in the right place, but when he has to act he is paralyzed, as if pulled in opposite directions by too many conflicting forces, feeling a constant despair and seeing all action as basically futile. Young Ram and his mother live comfortably, thanks to the wealthy branch of the family, which does not want the shameful burden of poor relatives but is not especially pleased at having to cover Ram's debts. The elderly uncle, who lives on his rural estate, likes to enjoy himself in the company of young women when he comes to town. His mean and snobbish daughter Mary, who speaks only French, insists that her cousin Ram should find work or marry a young heiress. Both matters can be arranged through the family's connections. But Ram prefers to go to parties, play cards, read, drink, and smoke. How to occupy himself during the minutes or hours ahead: that is the question liable to distress him most. Much of his time is spent at the Sporting Club, in the company of those who "belong," such as American diplomats and representatives of American firms—or in the company of their wives. They all exemplify the kind of lifestyle in which Nasser's democracy took shape. The author has a fine ear for the absurd, bombastic things people say to hide their intellectual inadequacy. Sometimes Ram gambles in the basement of the Snooker Club. There he meets those who do not "belong"—including cocky, downtrodden Armenian storekeepers, and his best friend, Font. Font withdrew from the university and from society and was selling vegetables from a cart before he agreed, with lofty contempt, to serve at the bar of the Snooker Club.

Ram is in love with a wealthy young Jewish woman of Communist sympathies who was tortured on account of the activities of her former husband after he fled to Israel. He is also friendly with the daughter of a rich pasha, who received her education at the Sorbonne and lives alone, with flowers and book-binding as hobbies. Ram and Font need a change of air, and Edna, the young Jewish woman, pays for their trip to England, then disappears. But once there, the two young men cannot get their visas renewed. Luckily for them, they meet some liberal British intellectuals, the sort who are always ready to help foreigners in trouble. Together, the young people, English and Egyptian, drink, argue, and make love. Their unexpected encounters are entertainingly described, with a fine feeling for dialogue and a sense of the absurdity inherent in certain situations.

Ram's conversation with a tough and passionate elderly woman who collects tickets on the tram, and his exchange of views with an English soldier who fought at Port Said* — these are gems of irony. The soldier's version of events is very different from that of the young Egyptian patriot, and both men try to remain polite despite being very drunk and acutely irritated. Each of them, of course, sees the Suez situation in an entirely different light.

## A Sophisticated Minority Culture with No Purpose

Ram and Font return to Egypt. It is their home and they cannot adopt any other. But they are not the types who become involved in political struggles and risk arrest and torture. They were educated in the wealthy sector of society, where the privileged had no duties beyond the obligation to be charming. With the declining status of the class to which they belong, they are left with no grip on reality. Something in them breaks and will never be mended. They are without faith or vitality. A cultural aimlessness and exhaustion pervade the milieu of those who belong to the upper strata of the minority groups and who flee the phantoms of a shared heritage to meet on a more personal level. Hopelessness dogs their clever discussions on politics, as well as their gossip and half-hearted love affairs. Their exchanges have no anger and no enthusiasm. Although they are still well-off, these people find themselves marginalized, gradually pushed aside by Egypt's Moslem society, with its newly privileged class of officers and bureaucrats.

Looking back, it seems a great shame that educated, talented people like Waguih Ghali were wasted and lost. For it is as if the whole country was silenced. Was it a failure on the part of society, which indulged its

* The Anglo-Egyptian treaty of 1936 permitted the British to maintain troops in the Suez Canal Zone. In 1951 Egypt revoked the treaty, and clashes along the borders of the Canal Zone in and around Port Said broke out between Egyptian anticolonialist demonstrators and British troops. In the novel, Font is injured during one such skirmish.

children to the point where they believed in their ability to stand up and fight, even though they had never attempted to do so? Is the flaw to be found in the sophisticated minority culture, which led nowhere for those who did not belong? Or was it the fault of history, moving at too fast a pace? Egypt's problems had been neglected for so long that perhaps it was impossible to believe in a gradual move toward modern social structures, toward a culture that was both deep-rooted and at the same time open to the world. In addition, the minorities were Egypt's intellectual mainstay, but their formal, exclusively European culture put up a barrier between them and the Egyptian populace. They were unable to create a rooted, open culture, and the rift between the Moslem population and the European-educated minorities only deepened. Those minorities, while sharing certain elements of European culture, were constrained by their communal or religious loyalties, and hence there were mutual suspicions, prejudices, and quarrels that prevented them from coming into contact with each other, not to speak of creating ties with society at large.

## Anti-Semitic Christian Minorities

The Christian minorities—Coptic, Syrian, Lebanese, Armenian, and Greek—were sometimes anti-Semitic. The Lebanese and Syrian Christians owned newspapers and on occasion waged aggressive, pan-Arab campaigns with an openly anti-Semitic, anti-Zionist tone, thinking this would give them an advantage over other minorities, especially the Jews. Egypt was different from most other colonial countries in that it had many European cultures intermixed or living in mutual hostility. In Iraq and Palestine, for example, English was the dominant foreign language. In Egypt, cultured people from all the different groups spoke both English and French, and there were also large Italian and Greek communities with their own schools and other institutions, linked to the mother country and reflecting the different political positions there. Fascism, for example, split the large Italian colony and even the Italian Jewish community. In other words, there was really no dominant group among the European-oriented minorities, which were separated from each other by religion, political inclination, and language. This phenomenon made Egypt a complex, fascinating place, but at the same time prevented the consolidation of a minority "Levantine" culture as an alternative to the Moslem-Arab culture.

The Moslem "revolutionaries" in Nasser's ruling group repressed all the minorities en masse. The question remains: was anything at all gained by such repression? Egypt does not seem to have improved as a result of Waguih Ghali's suicide, or as a consequence of many others giving to other countries all they had to give.

Those who did not have "other countries" were silenced or lost. The case of Waguih Ghali is especially symbolic and sad, since his talent was indisputable, and he could not stay alive to develop it.

He no longer believed in anything—and that was fatal, because a writer has to believe at least in his work. For the Egyptian Copt, not even that belief was possible.

Part of Ghali's tragedy was that he wrote in English and felt himself to be Egyptian. But there is another way of looking at the issue. After all, Tawfiq al-Hakim and Naguib Mahfouz write in Arabic,* and still Sadat has virtually silenced them, along with two hundred other authors and intellectuals. They not only expressed support for the student riots, but also dared argue that Egypt had to relinquish pursuit of the pan-Arab dream and perhaps, in addition, reach some agreement with Israel on the issue of opening the Suez Canal. Waguih Ghali, too, though not exactly a supporter of Israel, claimed in *Beer in the Snooker Club* that Egypt had more pressing problems than the war with Israel. It seems, then, that the earlier version of Egyptian nationalism, which had found expression in Sa'ad Zaghlul, and which was more liberal and humane, open to Western culture, and not hostile to the minorities, is not yet altogether dead in Egypt. It has just been forcibly silenced. The war of attrition on the Suez Canal was not the only war Sadat lost: there is also a war within Egypt, and its losses are perhaps even greater. The canal may one day reopen, but the writers and intellectuals who

* Tawfiq al-Hakim (1898–1987) was a prominent Egyptian dramatist. Naguib Mahfouz (1911–2006) was a leading Egyptian novelist who won the Nobel Prize in literature in 1988.

have died—whether in body or spirit—will not be easily replaced. Even with all the doubts that beset him, and with all his perplexities, perhaps Waguih Ghali could have given the Egyptians more than is offered by those who have silenced people like him.

*Translated from Hebrew by Jennie Feldman*

*Twelve*

# Wake of the Waves

*In 1937, three years before her departure from Egypt, Jacqueline was invited to accompany a friend's family on a trip to Palestine. This essay records her first reactions to the land that was later to become her home. Ideological debates between Jacqueline and her friend Sylvie offer uncommon perspectives on the Zionist enterprise during the interwar years. Published in* Amot *in 1962, this essay frames Kahanoff's reminiscences of the youthful journey with the perspective she later gained while living in Israel as an adult.*

This is my first trip abroad after living in Israel for seven years. The Mediterranean Sea, which is much bluer than I remember, whips up foam—a dense white foam that thins out, disperses, and disappears. I have often been on voyages like this, watching the ship's greenish wake as it dissolves, amazed again and again by the way these expeditions of ours leave nothing behind them, even the memory of them erased, unless something happens, a tremor that sends bubbles rising to the surface of our minds. How strange it is that we wander over this vast expanse until one day we reach some shore, some place, which disappears behind us when we set out on our way. The wind stirs and carries back to me, like the spray of sand or water, scenes of our life together, and now we know that everything we have assembled will scatter like a wave, and soon our fragments will be cast up at random. I try to find some shape in those scatterings, like the fortune-teller on the beach in Alexandria many years ago, who with her henna-stained hands would toss shells onto the sand to read our future and would say, as we children listened in rapt attention: "Long journey . . . sorrow . . . good luck . . . love . . ." And indeed, who among us did not know all of these?

And now that I am going to meet again, after such a long time, some of the people who were closest and dearest to me, there comes to mind with particular sharpness a memory of my first visit to the country, then Palestine under the British Mandate, which was much closer to our native Egypt than it is now.

On this Israeli ship, with its cargo of middle-aged Jews, most passengers speak a variety of languages, though a few are more proficient in one of them, and an even smaller number still live in the land of their birth. Once we were also fluent in many languages, none of them really our own tongue, and although we too would be dispersed in all directions, we were quite unaware of it at the time. Our wanderings were still bounded by the margins of the Levant, and the routes crossing it were like the corridors that connect rooms in a familiar house.

In those days my best friend was Sylvie and we loved each other with the complete devotion of girls too protected to dare show much interest in boys. Now we are going to meet again in Paris, we will no doubt have to rack our brains to come up with polite questions even as scenes whirl across our mind's eye—scenes of the street we lived in next to the majestic Nile; the classrooms where we shared a bench; the study in her father's spacious house where we were supposed to do our homework, but where in fact we would sit and talk and talk and talk. Now things were going to be different, as neither of us would want to hurt the other or be hurt. My moving to Israel—a considerable factor in what divides us—was a crucial decision, its significance more profound than had been anticipated.

Sylvie, as is the custom with emigrés, had maintained most of her old friendships, while I had severed them. When in Israel I do not miss them, but in Paris—I knew—it would be a source of pain, which I would try to alleviate as best I could. Not many people manage to keep into their mature years the friends of their childhood; friendships that develop afterwards are never as meaningful.

Our ways have parted, and so we shall now salute each other like two ships meeting out at sea, whose horn-blasts sound cordial enough, but whose chief concern is to avoid collision.

But we barely managed to avoid colliding when we parted in Paris seven years ago. "Whatever happens, we'll always be as we were," I said to Sylvie.

"No," she replied, "not you. You will have to change if you want to live with the people there. Don't you remember how strange they seemed to us when we visited Palestine in 1937?"

"Something has changed since then," I pointed out, and our leave-taking was decidedly chilly.

I think back now to that trip to Palestine, because even then, as we returned from Jerusalem to the Canal Zone, our viewpoints differed, though we did not know, of course, how distant we would grow from each other over time.

*

It was in our final year at the French lycée in Cairo. During the Easter vacation, Sylvie's parents invited me to join them and spend the Passover holiday in Erets Yisrael. When my parents gave their consent, my joy knew no bounds. The trains in those days were slow steam trains and the journey took an entire night. At dawn, I remember, I was wakened by the wonderful, intoxicating scent of orange blossom and by the swaying of the train as it came to a halt somewhere. We were right in the midst of the orange groves—as we saw when we opened the curtained windows and the fragrance struck our nostrils even more acutely. The air was crystal clear and dew sparkled on shining leaves and blooms that glowed like precious stones. Never had morning seemed brighter or more joyful. Every fifteen minutes the train would stop to take on crates of citrus fruit, and the trees were so close it seemed I could just reach out and touch them. The people working in the groves waved and called "Shalom!" and my heart lifted at the thought that this was the fruit of Jewish labor, that this was the fragrance of Palestine. I do not recall the names of the kibbutzim the train stopped at; they are no doubt still there today, somewhere near Lod or Rehovot. But now when I smell citrus blossoms, the scent is not as sharp in its freshness, and no plot of land looks the way it did then. Impressions grow dim with time. And apartment blocks and industrial areas have all but crushed the rural innocence that marked the Jewish settlements, while the hands that gathered citrus fruit may now be busy signing official documents.

The Judean hills, that spring, were the hills of the Song of Songs: the blossoms have appeared in the land, the time of the nightingale has come; the song of the turtledove is heard. Arabs, their white keffiyehs fluttering in the breeze, sheltered in the shade of a fig tree with its ripening fruit, and grapevines scented the air. Such biblical charm has almost entirely vanished, and with it the delightful simplicity of the Jewish settlers. Gone too are the decorated Arab cafés, painted blue and roofed with vines, where now and then an Arab would dismount from his donkey to sip cool water from the large earthenware pitcher standing in the shade.

Already then, in those days of naïve faith, the Jewish farmers were creating—in contrast to the dirt and neglect of the Arab village—settlements that were clean and well-organized; instead of the Arab cactus—the Jewish eucalyptus; instead of apathy—energy and resourcefulness. While this was a source of pride, we were at the same time saddened to hear comments that recalled the colonial attitude of the British toward "the natives." We were full of admiration for their desire to work for their own salvation, and maybe ours, too—though privately we still had doubts on the matter; we admired the spirit of Socialism and equality that inspired them, and which—sad to say—was still unknown in our society. At the same time, we had reservations about anything we regarded as the prejudices common to all white settlers. The colonial reality we lived in had a greater influence than we realized, and in the simplistic mode of thinking that we adopted, we could not decide which category Zionism belonged to—the whites, the natives, or the Jews. We were surprised that the nationalist Jews of Palestine felt no kinship with the Arabs, their Semitic brothers. Even though—as I said to my friend Sylvie—Arabs were the sons of Ishmael, these Zionists were not in the least religious; moreover, right from the beginning, from the story of Cain and Abel, the Bible is scattered with episodes of hatred between brothers, whether over the issue of birthright, or because the father loved one above the others. The same was also true for most Jewish and Moslem families, and although such feuds have always gone on, the families do not split up. It is strange, then, that the Jews acknowledge this shared origin and yet do not settle such conflicts, old or new. Perhaps they have not thought about it, being away from here for so long.

The two of us never ceased to marvel at the true Socialism of those Zionist pioneers in all matters relating to social status, though at the same time they appeared to us "reactionary" in their attitude to people. It seemed that everything outside their camp was to them "goyish" and "Ishmaelite" and that we Sephardic Jews were also flawed on account of our links with the step-brother. During those ten days in Palestine, Sylvie and I often debated as to whether the Jews there were "reactionaries" or "Socialists."

⁎

Accompanied by a guide—from the Jewish Agency, I assumed*—we saw everything in the country that Jewish tourists were supposed to see. The arrogance of the tour guides and of most of the people who showed us around their kibbutzim; their inability to let their achievements speak for themselves; the sense of superiority they always showed in the comparisons they drew with other peoples—all these made one want to smile, but at the same time were irritating. "They have no tact," Sylvie would say when we were in our room getting ready for the evening meal. "There's something about them that is distorted and narrow-minded. Their English is awful and they don't know any French at all. And they keep on preaching about the importance of learning Hebrew. They all say *exactly* the same things. It's so boring."

I now understand what we could not have known then, that beneath those lofty assertions lay hidden wounds, and that as long as their pride could be expressed aloud, the wounds were quite forgotten. And they were sure we would understand as much without being told. So when I meet again with Sylvie, I will not say: "You know, they are still saying more or less the same things and sometimes it gets rather tedious." At that time, though I conceded that many of the things Sylvie disliked also disgusted me, I would also argue that there was no reason Jews from Eastern Europe should speak French, and since they had dedi-

* The Jewish Agency was established in 1929 by the Sixteenth Zionist Congress to oversee the settlement of Jewish immigrants in Palestine.

cated themselves to reviving the homeland, it was their right to demand that everyone learn Hebrew.

"But what does it matter to them? They know we have only come for a few days," she would reply.

"With them it's like the Gospel: the mission to spread the good news. They believe no chance should be missed."

I did not dare tell her how much I envied the young people who, whether or not they wanted to, learned at least some Hebrew for their Bar Mitzvah. The good thing about Zionism was the fact that it made no distinction between boys and girls. Sylvie, however, was more taken with the idea that religion is the opiate of the masses than with equality for women. And so I said half-heartedly, "If people speak Hebrew, the language could be revived."

"Maybe . . . but if they speak only Hebrew, they will be totally cut off from the world." The very thought made Sylvie shudder.

"But they speak many other languages, even if not the ones we know. They speak Russian, German, Yiddish, Polish."

"Yes, but they are also against that. And anyway, all those languages, apart from Russian, sound awful. The worst is Yiddish. Could you ever marry someone who spoke to you in Yiddish?"

Afterwards we would debate late into the night on the little we knew about Marxist doctrine, those scraps we used to gobble up, together with reports on the civil war in Spain, from our favorite reading matter—French leftist weeklies. Sylvie, who spent part of the year in France and had Communist classmates whom I secretly envied, used to read Marx, Trotsky, and Victor Serge. Those books were on display even in the room of our Jerusalem hotel, much to the annoyance of her father, who said it was simply ridiculous for a well-off girl to be Communist, to which Sylvie retorted that that was his fault, not hers—and besides, a person's objective ideas had nothing to do with whether or not his father had money. That, she said, was a typically bourgeois comment. Her father would roll his eyes skyward or start arguing with her, and I would try hard to make my presence as unobtrusive as possible.

When we visited the kibbutzim, with their green rectangular fields and straight lines of huts and houses, someone would always tell us: "First we put up houses for the children—the most precious asset we have; next we build sheds for the cows, the source of our livelihood, and only then do the parents move from the huts into houses."

We were ill at ease in the company of Sylvie's father—a banker who wore a silk shirt and felt hat, and leaned on an embossed walking stick. We felt uncomfortable listening to the enthusiastic account of respective statistics on the yield of Hebrew cows and Arab cows, on the size of Hebrew and Arab eggs. The kibbutzim reminded us of the colorful cardboard scenery that children position around their toy train sets. Everything seemed too rigid to be real. We never spoke with the young people of the kibbutzim, who would stare scornfully at us until we felt embarrassed at our silk stockings and our hands that had never known hard work. Time and again we were told about the openness of those youngsters laboring to revive the soil of Israel and to liberate the Jewish people from their parasitic occupations in banking and commerce—and such things put us to shame.

Sylvie, although shy and polite, never hesitated to call a spade a spade. "Isn't it slightly anti-Semitic," she asked, "to regard banking as a Jewish monopoly? And what about the Morgans?"

I had never heard of the name, but I assumed they were richer than the Rothschilds—and not Jewish.

When we were on our own, Sylvie's father rebuked her. With supreme forbearing, along with a kind of humility, he said that although they could be extremely annoying, we had to relate to them with respect and even be grateful for the extraordinary things that those Polacks were doing in Palestine. Sylvie retorted that capitalism was the enemy in any case, and it would take more than the small kibbutzim in Palestine to destroy it. Especially since these were being supported by money from various Jewish donors such as the Rothschilds.

Only rarely did Sylvie's mother join us on these trips, and when she did, she would retire to her room at mealtimes on account of her mysterious indisposition, putting an end to such arguments by reminding us all of the terrible headache that was torturing her.

*

Sylvie and her father were similar in appearance—tall, pale, and fair-skinned, with pensive eyes. But they seemed farther apart from each other than were my father and I, though I would never have argued with him over what I called my "ideas," for I knew they were beyond the range of the education he had received at the Kol Yisrael Haverim school in Baghdad. We had a feel for our Jewishness, and so did Sylvie's father; as for Sylvie herself, she was uncertain. She had very much wanted to come to Palestine, but at the same time I had never seen her so rebellious.

Our reactions were also different when we visited the Western Wall* in Jerusalem, which we reached by way of the Old City's vaulted, noisy alleys. Young Jews dressed in khaki passed by us, and our guide did not lose the opportunity to compare their proud, upright bearing with the stooped posture of the idle peddlers, religious Jews who took no notice of the marvels wrought by hard work; we were sorry to see that most of them were Sephardic, and we tried to appear unruffled when he asked us rhetorically: "How long have they been praying for the Messiah to come, and what have they gained till now?"

When we reached the Western Wall, the guide was taken aback.

It was an appalling sight: the Arabs grinning and jeering from above, leaning over the wall of the Mosque of Omar; the British soldiers, polished and composed, guarding the entrance; and all those hundreds of people trapped there, in rags and tatters, their eyes diseased, their bodies deformed, their wailing beating upon the wall in wave upon wave, their hands pressing the black stones. Ugly weeds like wild beards sprang from cracks in the wall, and the sour stench of that impasse was like the stench of *harat al-yahud*, the Jewish quarter in Cairo. The irony of lamenting the destruction of the Temple was all the more grievous when we remembered it was Passover, when we celebrate going forth from Egypt. Suddenly I felt I wanted to burst into tears and flee the place. Sylvie's father, with his ornate walking stick and other finery,

* The Western Wall is a remnant of the Second Jewish Temple in Jerusalem that was the center of ancient Jewish worship and sacrifice. After the destruction of the Temple by the Romans in 70 CE, the Western Wall became a site of Jewish pilgrimage. The Roman-era wall was augmented by later construction and now forms part of the wall surrounding the Muslim holy sites the Dome of the Rock and the al-Aqsa Mosque.

leaned on the wall and sobbed, and Sylvie retreated to stand next to the guide. My fingers touched the dirty stone, but I could not put my lips to it. I thought: How terrible it is that this, here, *this* is the Jewish people, and I was sorry I didn't know even one prayer in Hebrew to help me feel closer to it all. The only Hebrew words I knew were *Shema yisrael, adonai eloheinu, adonai ehad* [Hear O Israel, the Lord our God, the Lord is One], but it seemed that here, before the Western Wall, it would be more fitting to pray with the words, "Hear, O Lord, hear, enough is enough!" The four questions from the Haggadah came to mind and I silently prayed that I would not be like the "wicked son" who says "them" and not "us," and sets himself apart from the others. I tore my handkerchief in two and stuffed one half as far as I could into a crack in the wall, and with the other half I wiped my right hand, the one that should lose its cunning if I forgot Jerusalem. All the time my head was buzzing with lines from the Haggadah that I remembered in the English version, but which came unbidden and accusing; all the same, I was relieved I was not standing apart, cut off . . .

*

On the ship we still speak a medley of languages, and the passengers' attempts to strike up conversation with each other often end in confusion. Nevertheless, I have the impression that many of them are returning from a pilgrimage more heartened than we were on our return from that trip of ours to Jerusalem. Marc, a young man of twenty-two studying medicine at Lausanne, tells me in hesitant French, only recently acquired, that he photographed the Israeli flag proudly flying from the masthead, and as he spoke his pleasant young face lit up. He came to spend his vacation in Israel, took photographs of everything he saw, and is preparing an album to send to his parents. He has decided to settle in Israel and hopes his family will move there. Yes, his parents did well in Bolivia. They had fled from Poland to France and had managed to leave there in time. In Lausanne he lives with three other Jewish students from Bolivia who were born in Poland. "Now that Israel exists, you don't have to be a stranger any more, standing on the outside," he says. His face grows sad when he tells of the immigrants he saw on the ship bound for Israel. "They were shouting and arguing in

Arabic, with dozens of children and all sorts of bundles and packages. They were much more like Arabs than the Algerian Moslem students at Lausanne University. If only I could have felt something in common with them, but I couldn't."

Naturally I began to deliver a lecture, Israeli-style, but when I remembered how Sylvie and I had reacted twenty-five years earlier, I realized the absurdity of it, and told Marc a little about that unforgettable trip to Palestine.

"Do you mean to say that for you and your friend the Jews who spoke Yiddish seemed *strange*, that you did not love all Jews?" At first Marc was somewhat shocked, then he burst out laughing and finally came to the conclusion that actually it was all rather sad, not to say stupid.

"What else did you see besides the Western Wall?" asked Marc

Hebron, Rachel's Tomb, the University on Mount Scopus . . . I told him about the places, but not about the things we experienced there. That, too, seemed sad, not to say stupid.

⁎

In Hebron we had seen the ruins of the Jewish quarter: torn pages of scripture blew about in gaping, wind-strewn alleys and drifted across the dirty floors of the small, gloomy dwellings. We stared, petrified with fear, at the brown stains on the pages, knowing it was the blood of people killed while praying.* Even our guide fell silent before the imposing stillness of that place. Did the Moslems really do such a thing? I wondered. Shaken, I could not believe it. Pogroms, Hitler—those were things that happened in Christian countries. The Moslems, though, had never thought we killed their prophet, who died a peaceful, natural death. Hence they could not be as cruel as the Christians, who were taught to believe we crucified their messiah.

Our forefather Abraham was buried there; at least, that is what the tradition says, and his tomb is holy to Moslems, who claim that they

* Intercommunal violence erupted in Palestine in the summer of 1929. In August, the violence spread to Hebron, where sixty-seven Jews were killed and the remaining members of the Jewish community fled.

too are his descendants. Only a few Jews were given permission to visit Hebron after the massacre, but Sylvie's father obtained the necessary permit and so we arrived accompanied—or protected—by armed Arab guards. The air of tension and hostility around us was so intense that I said to myself, "We are here alone, and they could easily shoot us." Indeed, the guards threatened to open fire on anyone who tried to go higher than the seventh step of the stairway leading up to the Cave of Machpela. Sylvie's father and the guide stood below and kept an eye on the guards while we two girls climbed the stairs. When we reached the seventh step, there came a warning shout. Sylvie turned to go back down. I could not—it was disgraceful that we were the ones forbidden to visit the grave of our forefather Abraham. On an impulse, I went up one more step. The guards yelled, a shot was fired, and I stumbled back down the stairway shaking with fear. The guards looked shame-faced, Sylvie's father shouted something about all of us risking death, and the guide tried to calm us down. It was with relief that we retraced our steps through the streets of Hebron, under the wrathful, hostile gaze of the local people.

"I am not religious," I kept repeating to myself. "I don't believe in holy relics. The bones in that tomb are surely not the bones of Abraham. So why does all that matter to me?" What angered me was being there on sufferance, like a delinquent child whose rights are in question. Maybe that is why Sylvie's father and the guide did not want to go up the steps, but I did not dare pursue the matter.

On our way to Jerusalem we stopped by a small, white-domed building, where tradition says the matriarch Rachel is buried. As a child I loved her dearly; she was my favorite Hebrew, there beside the well—fine-looking and blithe as one of the young Bedouin girls. Jacob loved her so ardently, and Joseph was her son. She was the mother of the Jewish people, not a stern, forbidding figure, but a woman with the charm of eternal youth.

Many years later, when I went to Ramat Rachel, I looked across to Hebron and Bethlehem, and remembering that day when we saw the tombs of Abraham and Rachel, I thought of the Jewish cemetery in Cairo where our dear ones lie, mine and Sylvie's, and no one goes to visit them any more. That place had been called Fustat, and the Arab conquerors had given the burial ground to the Jews in perpetuity, for their help in defeating the Byzantines, when they opened up to them one of the city gates. Not that we had any idea, at the time of that trip to Palestine, that as an indirect effect of the storm gathering force in Europe, we too would be uprooted from where we belonged. There is no denying, of course, the part played by chance and convenience in the paths finally chosen by each of us, but it seems that even then there were early indications of a parting of the ways when we were young girls of seventeen.*

⁂

It was our last year at school, and filled with trepidation and hope we made plans for when our studies ended. Naturally we had this in mind when we visited the Hebrew University on Mount Scopus, the day we were due to return to Cairo. The view was harsh and impressive; you could even see the Dead Sea in the distance—a vivid strip of water in the oppressive wilderness. The idea that here in Jerusalem a university had been founded, where scholars would pave the way for a Jewish revival, was very exciting. Hence I barely listened to the answers given by our erudite guide in response to Sylvie's questions regarding the subjects taught, which she compared to those at the Sorbonne where she was going to study the following year. In the library we were taken around by the librarian's assistant, who had a strong German accent, and as he showed us the bookshelves he boasted that this was the finest and biggest library in all the Middle East.

We scanned the rows: Hebrew books, German books, some books in English and in Arabic, but very few in French. Sylvie expressed disappointment. "This Hebrew University is too Germanic. Nearly all the books are in German, and all the professors and students were born or educated in Germany."

The librarian did not say that few professors or students who were not from Germany were willing to come to Jerusalem, but he declared

* In the essay "That Day in May in Chicago" (*Ma'riv*, 3 May 1968), Kahanoff notes that she visited Palestine in 1937, making her nineteen or twenty at the time of her visit, not seventeen, as indicated here.

that the world's best scientists and researchers were German, and the best scholars in Jewish and Semitic studies were also German.

"There can be no doubt that Germany has great scholars, philosophers, and scientists, but do you really think that France and England lag so far behind?" asked Sylvie, in a tone of meek deference toward the librarian, who could not have known that Sylvie was never more sarcastic than when she couched her words in this manner, and so promptly fell into the trap.

"Ach," he said gravely, "the French are far too superficial, and the English have no imagination and none of the thoroughness and seriousness of German scholars."

"I see. Well, do you think you can suggest anything for students whose training is not German?"

The librarian responded shortly that every educated person had to know German.

I was surprised by the fact that she had appeared to take a serious interest in the Hebrew University, as if here, at least, she had hoped to find something closer to her thinking. This was, for her, the critical moment.

"No," she said, as we were packing that evening, "this mixture of German arrogance and Yiddish chauvinism, together with the Hebrew language—no, it's just too much. It's not for us. It's so suffocating! I want to be part of the wider world, not shut away here. It would be a backward move! And now of all times, when nationalism is giving way to internationalism. This . . . culture here!"

Our discussion continued on the train as we sipped lemonade in the buffet car. I'm not sure, I said, that nationalism is a thing of the past. After all, countries like Egypt and India are also striving for independence.

Sylvie claimed that first there had to be a nationalist bourgeois revolution, and only afterwards would the masses realize that they had to liberate themselves from their feudal landlords and from their capitalistic middle-class status.

Her father, who was conversing with a rich pasha at the next table, signaled to us that we were talking too loudly.

"So what will happen to people like us?" I whispered mildly. There was a considerable difference between us as regards wealth, even though we both belonged to the "bourgeoisie," and being afraid that this disparity made me "petit bourgeois," I was less enthusiastic than Sylvie on the question of the revolution.

"As a class," she whispered to me, "we will of course be eliminated; in a time of revolution, that's essential. But people with useful occupations, such as engineers, chemists, manufacturers, will come to no harm since they are needed."

"And I thought you wanted to study philosophy, not manufacturing," I remarked.

Sylvie was furious: "Why do you have to bring it down to such a personal level? Sometimes I think you are absolutely incapable of understanding wider issues."

Again our voices rose, and in despair Sylvie's father motioned to us to come over and meet the pasha. After the usual pleasantries we went back to our fierce exchange of whispers at our table.

I asked why the Jews had to be the only people without a land. Would it not be better to settle their country and to bring about the revolution afterwards, if indeed that was what all the other countries were going to do?

Sylvie replied that since we are not a colonial people, we have no need to go through that phase. Moreover, had I given any thought, she asked, to the dangerous situation Jews in Arab countries would face if Palestine became a Jewish state?

It was my turn to whisper back, when I caught sight of the pasha's enormous ears, sticking out on both sides of his red tarbush. If it is such an urgent matter for other Jews, I said, then our own security is of secondary importance. We too will be able to go to Palestine if it becomes necessary.

We deployed all the arguments of the French left-wing press and added some of our own as well. It all sounded unreal and even rather alarming: here we were, two serious, idealistic young women, sitting and eliminating ourselves, Sylvie because we belonged to the middle class, and me because our worth as Jews might perhaps be less than that of Jews from Eastern Europe. I could find no way out of the imbroglio.

"We will never feel at ease among those people in Palestine, and don't pretend you like those Polish and German Jews any more than

I do," said Sylvie. Thinking back, it seems to me we gave the Jews of Russia a sort of back-handed compliment in forgetting to include them with the others.

"Actually," I argued, "how can one blame the Jews of Eastern Europe for living by different standards from ours; the great suffering they endured, far worse than our own, made them more fervent and narrow-minded, and besides—they are passionate about German culture exactly as we are about French culture. The Russian literature we so loved began to appear only in the nineteenth century, long after the decline of Islam. Although Russia has taken great strides forward since then, it was for a long time considered an Asiatic, barbarian country, and is still seen as such by reactionaries in Europe. So it was inevitable that Jews in those countries would be somewhat backward and uncultured, that they would look to German culture as the only one in the world, since it alone had left its mark in Russia, Poland, and all those countries. It isn't fair to regard it as a shortcoming on their part if German Jews seem to us arrogant and 'antipathetic,' and we should not forget that we were taught in French schools to loathe everything German, as a matter of course, and that was because the ruling powers in both countries decided their peoples had to hate each other, so that arms dealers could increase their wealth. We should not be taken in by such things.

"At the same time, if we believe that the Latin-French influence is needed to counterbalance the rigid, heavy German-Yiddish atmosphere we found in Palestine—how can that happen unless French or French-educated professors and students come to the Hebrew University and leave their mark on it? Perhaps it is our task as French-educated Sephardic Jews to help Zionism acclimatize to a new, modern, progressive Middle East."

When I had had my say, very pleased with myself, Sylvie, who had been listening patiently, asked with her usual tone of mocking enquiry: "If you could continue your studies, which university would you choose—the one in Jerusalem?"

I was obliged to answer frankly, though it was not easy: "No, I would also choose the Sorbonne. But after finishing my studies I would have to—so it seems to me—live and work in Palestine."

"Don't you see how inconsistent your attitude is?"

I could not deny it, but I was also unable to explain something I felt obscurely but profoundly beneath the illogicality of my words. I knew that Sylvie was closer than me, by one or two generations, to the European world, and so could take greater risks. If I were to obtain a university education some day, I would perhaps be able to probe more deeply into the French culture that I knew—to some extent at least—and loved, but I would be utterly lost, I would sink, in an atmosphere so completely foreign to me, in the Hebrew-Yiddish-German mixture of Palestine.

*

When I reached Paris a few days later, I rang Sylvie.

"At last you've arrived! You wrote that you were coming, but you didn't say when. Where are you? When can we see each other?" The genuine affection in her voice was heartwarming.

We met in a small bar where we used to talk in years past—up to 1954, in fact—about such events as the fall of King Farouk and the rise to power of General Naguib, our anxiety mingled with gaiety.

Of course, we both had changed, and so we declared to each other, "You've hardly changed at all."

She said the situation was good overall, especially for that turbulent period, and I agreed with her wholeheartedly.

And then we fell silent. Sylvie had grown very thin, and blue veins stood out on her hands. Their tense, quick movements, with fingers and joints bending at strange, sharp angles, were more characteristic than her pale, expressionless face; this I had quite forgotten, apparently.

She met my gaze; all of a sudden her hands trembled and she said, "Do you also find it hard to believe that youth is so much shorter and life so much longer than you thought?"

Again I agreed with her. Between long, awkward silences, we asked each other about everyone we could think of.

Suddenly Sylvie said—her voice sharper, like in the old days when we used to argue so passionately: "I've just finished a book that I am sure you would like. It is written with a lot of wisdom. A really brilliant book. It's about a woman who at a certain moment in her life realizes she can no longer change anything. Everything is fixed and static, *frozen* at a particular point. So she retraces her path, and with every backward step she takes she remembers the different possibilities that had lain before her, possibilities that multiply the farther back she goes. And so she discovers how, in choosing one of the several paths open to her, she had closed off, one by one, all the others, without ever experiencing them, until she reached that narrow passage, that point, where she now stands and from which she cannot move." Sylvie's hand moved through the air describing all the possible paths narrowing down to that one point. "Would you like to read the book?"

I said: "Yes," pointing out that even if we had chosen roads completely different from the ones we did take, in the end we would still have reached that one fixed place, and that every choice a person makes necessarily blocks off all the other possibilities.

"Have you ever had the urge to live every possible life, have you ever felt that the choice you made deprived you of the possibility of going down other roads?"

"Yes," I replied, "sometimes I have felt that way." Again I was agreeing with her. I thought to myself: how good it was when we used to discuss things and disagree on them.

We looked at our watches at almost the same time and decided it was time to go our separate ways.

While I was in Paris I met with Sylvie a number of times. We both knew, of course, that for each other we were no longer living people but dark mirrors in which we caught glimpses of our childhood and everything that had vanished with it. I did not ask for the name of the book or its author, and she did not mention it again, though I am certain we both thought of it from time to time.

*Translated from Hebrew by Jennie Feldman*

# *Thirteen*
# Reunion in Beersheba

*Although Kahanoff left the United States in the early 1950s, throughout her career she continued to publish in American Jewish journals. This article, published in 1957 in the* American Israel Review, *a publication of the American Jewish League for Israel, describes the arrival in Israel of a family from Egypt and offers a picture of the lives of recent immigrants in the early years of Israel's existence. A telling sidebar published with the article asks the journal's readers, "What are Egyptian Jews like? Are they backward Orientals or modern Westerners? Or a mixture of both? Few of our readers are aware of the fact that the Egyptian Jewish community is—or was—a melting pot in itself."*

*Because of the enmity between Egypt and Israel following the 1948 and 1956 conflicts, the Jews who remained in Egypt were careful to distance themselves from the state of Israel. In the period between 1954 when Kahanoff immigrated to Israel and 1958 when her parents left Egypt, she published under assumed names to protect her parents from any possible repercussions. As much as relating the story of a happily reunited family, this article, published under the pseudonym Louise Sassoon, expresses Kahanoff's own anxieties about the well-being of her parents in Egypt.*

When I saw a pile of suitcases on the veranda of the Lombrosos' ground floor flat in Beersheba, I immediately knew that their relatives had arrived from Egypt. I hesitated to butt in on the family reunion, but while I lived in Beersheba, Regina and I had talked so often, with such longing, about those we loved who were still in Egypt, that now, when for her at least these anxious years of separation came to an end,

I wanted to share this joy with her. It seemed to bring closer the day when mine would come too.

When Regina answered my knock, she, her husband, and the children greeted me with excited shouts, "They are here! At long last, they are here."

Regina, round and motherly, immediately asked, "Have you heard from your parents? Are they coming? Oh, don't despair! It will be like with us. After we'd almost given up, they were suddenly here on our doorstep. See, my husband's brother Maurice and his family have just arrived, and they tell us my brother and his family will soon be here too."

Maurice Lombroso, a quiet, gentle-mannered man, looked very much like his Beersheba brother Albert. But while the newcomer was dressed in a good flannel suit, a cashmere sweater, shirt, and tie, the Israeli brother wore khaki pants, a mended woolen shirt, and a faded sweater. Yet, it was Albert who would have to support his brother's family until Maurice found a job and a home. It was striking to see how the refugees looked more prosperous, more "middle-class" than the Israeli relatives who offered them shelter in their home.

The children were different too. Regina's had lived for many years among new immigrants from Yemen, Persia, North Africa, Romania, and Poland, and they had not had the chance to acquire that polished, almost Parisian demeanor which was very much in evidence when their newly arrived cousins from Egypt greeted me so politely. These youngsters had obviously been to French secondary schools, while the Lombroso children, who had grown up in Beersheba, had had to start working to help their parents as soon as they had finished primary school.

Regina resented her family's lowered social status. She suffered and often regretted the pleasant, easy life she had known in Cairo, where her husband had been an accountant for a Jewish-owned department store. It was only now that she suddenly realized all that had been achieved during those difficult years of adaptation. Loans obtained from the firm employing her husband and her oldest son helped the family add a large room to the standard Beersheba new immigrant flat of one and a half rooms. Later, they had added a large kitchen, a proper bathroom, a veranda, and had had the concrete floors entirely tiled. Since Adda, their sixteen-year-old daughter, had started working as a salesgirl, the walls had been painted, curtains hung over the windows, bedspreads and gay pillow covers decorated the many couch beds. It had taken them seven years to make this home they could now put at the disposal of their relatives.

"We couldn't have done all this if Dan and Adda hadn't helped us," Regina proudly explained. "Next year, we'll be sending Yossi to high school, and later, we hope, Carmela will go too. Their older brother and sister fought right along with us to make it possible for them."

Without having quite realized it while it happened, Albert and his family had been pioneers. Not only were they among Beersheba's first settlers, but, like so many others before them, they had paved the way for those who came later, making the followers' start in Israel easier than their own had been. Now they had a feeling that their past struggle had not been in vain. This new perspective, in which they saw themselves, mixed with their happiness at the family reunion in Israel, gave their faces new expression of smiling self-assurance.

*

"Where's Danny?" I asked, following Regina into the kitchen. After the proper exchange of greetings I noticed the absence of Regina's eldest son.

Her face beamed while anguish flickered in her soft brown eyes. "Danny? He is with the army. But he is stationed in a camp nearby and sometimes gets leave to come home in the evening. I hope he comes tonight." She sighed as her plump, skillful hands worked away, peeling vegetables. "There's so much to tell! You know, of course, that he was working for the army as a radio operator. He was to be called up last October. But his induction was postponed. They thought he would be more useful as a civilian technician. He's been all over Sinai and the Gaza Strip. We were almost mad with worry . . ."

In the next room, the record player ground out a French song. Regina rushed out. "Children," she announced firmly, "sorry, but those are Danny's records and nobody touches them without his permission."

After she took the records away and hid them, she returned, explaining, "Those records are, with Danny's guitar, his priceless possessions. You remember, don't you, how Danny gave us most of what he earned to build that extra room? Well, the little he saved for himself he used to buy those records. The last thing he did before joining the unit he was assigned to was to arrange to get his pay, and run home to bring it to us. We felt so bad that we needed it, and so moved that he had thought of us in this way. It's foolish superstition, I suppose, but I feel that as long as his records are whole, Danny is safe."

Her busy hands stopped, and her eyes lit up with the thoughts crowding her mind. "You remember," she asked me, "how I found fault with everything about Israel? Since the Sinai Campaign, all that has changed. Danny came home once, black as a scarecrow, thin, exhausted. He threw himself on a bed and slept for hours. We all walked on tiptoes. I looked at his face. He was only eighteen, but it was the face of a man, not a boy. I understood at last that this was my children's country and from then on loved it with all my soul. I thought of those living in Egypt, whom we loved, who would have to pay for the Sinai Campaign. But I was glad that we were all here, however hard it is, and not there."

She bustled around the kitchen, called in her daughter and her sister-in-law, and soon everyone was seated around the table. One empty place was set, just in case Danny might come after all.

*

Through the stories, told in a great rush of words around the family dinner table by people eager to bridge the gap of the intervening years, the newcomers heard about the difficulties of settlement in Israel, the demands it makes, the mistakes to avoid. The conversation of these "Egyptian" Jews was carried out in French, Italian, and Spanish. The Lombrosos were Sephardim whose parents, like many other Jews from Mediterranean and Near Eastern countries, had settled in Egypt during the prosperous era which followed upon the opening of the Suez Canal. The older people still spoke Ladino, the old Castilian dialect used to this day by Jews whose ancestors were expelled from Spain in the sixteenth century. As youngsters they had attended the Italian schools established by Catholic orders. (Regina's parents had come from Italy.) Their children had attended the fine schools established in Egypt by the French government. These schools, plus the excellent

French-language schools supported by the Jewish community itself, accounted for the predominantly French culture of the Egyptian Jews.

"I hope you were able to bring some silverware," Regina remarked, while looking over the table she had arranged for this festive gathering. The number of plates, forks, and knives was obviously inadequate. "We left Egypt in a rush," Regina explained. "Albert was getting in trouble as a Zionist; we left as tourists and I had to leave behind all our household goods so as not to arouse suspicion. I never thought these things would be so difficult to replace. Everything one brings is a help."

Her refugee sister-in-law told Regina that they had been able to take out a little silver and were allowed fifty pounds' worth of jewelry per person. "With clothing, blankets, sheets, and a very little money, that's all we have now," she said.

"It's a matter of luck," her husband explained. "We bribed everybody; they all expect it as their due. But the officers and customs' officials don't always perform the favors they're supposed to; they know we are helpless. Corruption has always existed in Egypt, but never like now. People used to be ashamed about it. Now, whatever one asks for, the officials openly and brazenly demand, 'how much?'"

The wife said that all day and all night long, people had banged at their door, asking what they had to sell, and they had been terrified, fearing a police raid. Maurice said he had tried to take some of their rugs, but these were held back at customs, as well as his wife's sewing machine. "They kept whatever caught their fancy. But, even so, some of the inspectors were decent. The one we had at least let the kids take their bikes."

Maurice, who had been department head of an export firm, began inquiring about the possibilities of finding a job.

"You must first learn Hebrew," his brother told him. "But we'll find you something to keep you going in the meantime. In Israel, one sort of graduates from the shovel to the fountain pen."

Blank, rather frightened looks spread across the faces of the newcomers. Regina, ladling out plates full of spaghetti, remarked, "That's the way it was with Albert. He broke stones on the roads and washed dishes in restaurants while he learned Hebrew at night. Then he got his accountant's job."

Just at that moment, the front door opened, and in came a uniformed young man, lanky, deeply tanned. I was barely able to recognize the baby-faced Danny I had seen a year before. But as he scanned the group around the table, recognition flashed in his eyes and he rushed toward the newcomers with boyish exuberance. "Uncle Albert! Aunt Sorine! Raymond! Laura!" They embraced, fired a thousand questions back and forth, and Danny's smile was sweet and innocent, exactly like his mother's.

When calm was restored, Regina proudly pointed out the ribbon on her son's chest. "Sinai Campaign. Danny was there. Even though he wasn't a soldier, he was in the most dangerous spots with them, so he was awarded a ribbon too." She beamed and looked around the table. "Well? You see what our Israeli boys are like?" she demanded triumphantly of her nephew and niece. "They gave the Egyptians a good trouncing! Our hospitals were full of their soldiers and officers sprawled on their tummies because they got shot in their behinds while they were running away."

Everyone laughed, but Regina was rebuked by her husband and son. "Mother, where did you pick up such nonsense? Our government was careful not to make them look ridiculous. You shouldn't invent such stories."

Regina held her ground. "They fled, didn't they? They couldn't have been shot anywhere else! I could tell our government a few things about the Arabs. None of their rulers have done a thing to provide them with enough food and education. They smoke hashish to forget their misery, then start dreaming of empires and Holy Wars. If the U.N. started by curing them of drug addiction, we'd have peace." She ladled out the spaghetti, which, with cheese and olives, and oranges for dessert, constituted dinner.

*

It was a revolution in the family's way of life. In Egypt the food had always been lavish, particularly on such festive occasions as a family reunion. Until a few months ago, Regina's budget was always out of balance because she could not bring herself to adopt the simpler Israeli fare. Now she jokingly told her relatives, "Don't you repeat the mistakes we first made in Israel. Those were the years of austerity—there was nothing to eat. But I wanted the children to be fed as well here as they had been in Egypt. So we spent all our money on the black market, and had none left when it came to fix up the house. Now I see that the children fare as well on a plainer diet."

She passed a dish of margarine, which the newcomers tasted for the first time. "We haven't had butter for months—it came from the United States. We don't get it with our rations any more, and it's too expensive to buy." Her eyes rested on her son. "I would have forsaken butter gladly to the end of my days, if it could have rid us of the fedayeen."

Regina mused inwardly at the change that had come over her.

"At first I hated this country. Now I love it as if it were my child who gives me a lot of trouble. I used to ridicule the schools, the teachers, the Hebrew language. I wept, I found fault with everything. I'm partly to blame that Adda didn't do so well at school. But with the baby it's different. Now that Carmela goes to kindergarten, she teaches me Hebrew—and I'm learning it with pleasure. This country grips you—through your children."

Albert reminisced, "When Carmela was born, we couldn't even afford to buy her a crib. We had to fix up an empty orange crate for her. We felt awful because we could not give her what the other children had had."

All eyes turned to Carmela. She had slipped away from the table and curled up around her only doll, and now was fast asleep on a couch.

"She's a fine looking child," the aunt from Egypt said, moved. "We knew about her birth, because Regina wrote to her sister in Australia, and she sent the news to us. We even had a party to celebrate Carmela's first birthday. But we had no idea you were having such a hard time."

"At first, in Beersheba," Regina related, "Albert worked at building roads. He also washed dishes in a restaurant. He studied Hebrew at night. As soon as he knew the language well enough, he found a job as an accountant, but he kept right on studying. Now, he's chief accountant, and since he knows Arabic well, his firm put him in charge of business transactions with the Bedouin tribes in the Negev. His courage pulled us through."

Maurice looked puzzled. "But you had money when you left Egypt.

You couldn't have spent it all on food. Whatever happened to bring you to such a pass?" he asked.

"We made many mistakes," the Israeli brother explained. "In France, we spent too much money having a good time. Then, with a group of Egyptians, prospective settlers in Israel, we bought some machines, intending to go into the clothes manufacturing business. We paid tremendous duty on those machines, but we did not get the authorization to set up shop. The government was worried about all the newcomers wanting to settle in the big towns. The policy was to push people into agriculture or development areas. So we had to sell those machines for next to nothing, and start from scratch."

Regina had a different interpretation. "In Israel people think that Jews from oriental countries are all uneducated, and are only good for picking peanuts. If immigrants from Europe had come with those machines, they would have been helped. We Sephardim are considered a lower breed of Jews."

*

This had been a point argued at our very first meeting when, as fellow-Egyptians starting a new life in Beersheba, Regina and her husband had flung open to us their home and their hearts.

"She doesn't have her mother here to spoil her," Regina would tell my husband, although she and I are only a few years apart in age. Each time she came to see us, she would arrive laden down with samples of her remarkable cooking and baking. "Besides, you should be thankful I'm not one of those stingy Ashkenazim who lives on herring and sour cream and keeps everything under lock and key," she would say, mischievously. While Albert would glance nervously at my husband, who was born in Russia, she would quite disarm all of us by saying, "It's different with him. He grew up in Egypt and became one of us," and off she was on her favorite subject.

"Now, now, mother," her husband soothed her. "Don't start on that again! Don't give our nephew any such ideas!'"

Regina persisted. "Now they send the Egyptians to the tough new places, but not the Hungarians. Wasn't Maurice sent to Ofakim although he asked for Beersheba? We had to go to Ofakim ourselves to bring them all here. When the buses arrive from Haifa, I go to see the people. There are three or four families from Egypt for every ten or fifteen Hungarians. Albert, you can't say it's not true."

Albert gently put his point across. "I find it wiser not to count. I just rejoice that other Jews have come."

Young Dan interposed, "Those who fought in Sinai, and those who died, fought as Israelis, as Jews; they did not think of themselves as Poles or Moroccans, Egyptians or Hungarians. We must remember that."

The newly arrived relatives were impressed. "Were you in Sinai?" his cousin asked Dan.

"Yes. Until we evacuated, I was there most of the time. I'm a radio operator in the army. I should have been called up just then for my two years' service, but it was decided that I'd be more useful as a civilian technician in my job. Still, I'll get the medal of all those who participated in the Sinai Campaign."

Awed, his cousin asked Dan some pointed questions, but was told, "Sorry, I never speak of my work."

Albert explained how, with the help of the town's mayor, he had obtained a subsidy for Dan to get this training, during which the youngsters were paid while they learned. As he spoke, he glanced at his wife significantly, as if to say she should not forget the positive help her family had received.

Dan turned to his cousins, "Tomorrow, I'll take you to the trade school. You'll learn Hebrew, acquire some technical skill, and get a small grant to keep you going."

"But I wanted to become a physicist," the lad protested. "I needed only a few more months to graduate and qualify for university."

Dan reasoned, "It doesn't work out that way. You can't afford to devote a whole year to the study of Hebrew, and then pay university fees, board, and lodging in Jerusalem. But if you take a year of technical training, then you can continue it in the army. It has courses of all kinds available. You may even prepare for a Hebrew High School degree in the army. After your discharge, you have a skill you can depend upon to earn your living, and then, while you work, you can study at the university. Believe me, that's the best way."

Because this was explained to him by someone his own age, the boy agreed, without feeling unduly disappointed. The family conference decided his young sister would go to high school, and that Maurice would start Hebrew courses. Albert would busy himself with helping his brother find a job and a home. "After all, there are a few strings I can pull. I'm one of the first settlers here, and have some influence," he said, smiling.

Albert was a poorer man than he had been in Egypt, but here he counted more in this community, and he knew it. Maurice knew it too, and said, "Look, Albert, if the only work I can get now is to pick peanuts or build roads, I'll do it. We'll start from the beginning."

*

As I took my leave, wishing them all the best of luck, Regina escorted me to the bus station. "There'll be ten of us sleeping under our roof tonight," she said. "But, suppose, just suppose we had only come now. We couldn't have done a thing for them, and who could have done anything for us? Ah, this Israel of ours, it makes sense after all, and hang all that we left behind us in Egypt. It would have been lost anyway."

We waited in the dark, and I could feel her fretting to say something. It came out at last.

"I know you are worried about your parents," Regina said softly. "But they won't do anything to old people. Only try to understand what it means to them to leave their homes, their habits. Yes, yes, their habits are important to old people, the shell that protects their frailty. And then think what it means to parents to receive rather than to give. Remember the Arab proverb 'Love goes down, never up'—that is, the parents' love of the children is stronger than the children's love for them, and that is as it should be. Then, too, they are fearful of imposing upon your husband, however kind and ready to love them he may be. Quarrels between people who love each other do occur, but when the old are dependent, the slightest quarrel means that they are not wanted, and sometimes they aren't. Young couples want to lead their own lives."

She was holding my hand, and its agitation told her I was going to protest. Her gentle pressure silenced me. "We are all like that sometimes. It's human, and doesn't mean we don't also love. But in spite of all these things they are thinking about, your parents will come, because their love is stronger than their pride."

From around the corner, my bus came into sight. She hugged me and said gaily, "Let me know when they'll be arriving! I'll drop everything and come a day ahead to prepare a dream of a dinner while you go to Haifa to them. It will be the sort of dinner they would have had in Egypt—a dinner none of you will ever forget to celebrate their homecoming, and your reunion." Her voice vibrated with happy anticipation. As the bus rolled away I wondered at my friend Regina whose heart was so rich she could give to everyone and never be poorer.

*Fourteen*

# A Letter from Mama Camouna

*Letters that crisscross the Mediterranean trace the routes of dispersal of Kahanoff's family. As this essay relates, the family of Kahanoff's mother, Yvonne Chemla, hailed from Tunisia. "Mama Camouna" was the second wife of Yvonne's grandfather, Jacqueline's great-grandfather. Kahanoff's maternal grandfather, Joseph Chemla, and his two brothers left Tunis for Cairo where they established a department store named Chemla Frères. While Joseph and David, the elder brother, oversaw operations in Cairo, Clément, the youngest, was responsible for purchasing and shipping merchandise from Paris, where he settled. As Kahanoff writes, Mama Camouna's letters from Tunisia kept the family connected to their collective past and to one another.*

To those of us who were born in the communities of the Orient, the names of places which were once familiar—Baghdad, Damascus, Cairo, Tunis, Algiers—are now the faraway places in that mythical geography of hearts and minds, where distances do not correspond to those on maps. And I wonder sometimes how the cousins, *shlishi be'shlishi*, ever got to places like New York, Montreal, and São Paolo when for countless generations their families had been rooted in the ancient communities of the Orient. Even before the establishment of Israel precipitated a mass exodus, our grandparents or great-grandparents suddenly packed up and left their ancestral homes. Cairo, Paris, London, then Jerusalem, and now New York, became crossing points of these caravans pursuing their peregrinations through space and time.



Gathered around our festival tables here in Israel we rejoice to see the increasing number of grandparents and even great-grandparents living with their children and grandchildren. Perhaps to them the ring of our faces constitutes that fortress which in childhood appears impregnable. But together with the rejoicing, a sadness, a kind of anguish, creeps in as we remember those who are no longer, who rest in abandoned graves in lands we cannot visit. And somehow we would like these children descended from them, wherever they now are, to remember those who sat at the head of the table when we ourselves were children, in other lands, in other times.

The parents whom we, of the middle generation, knew in their full vigor, and against whose authority we often rebelled, are now these frail old couples who look so much like the pictures of their own parents which decorate their rooms. We feel an immense, aching tenderness for them, our parents, no longer strong and powerful, more often vulnerable and dependent. We become aware that they, and we, and the pictures of the old people on their walls belong together to a world which those who are now children can only know about by hearsay, if they are prepared to listen.

These old couples are all the more defenseless since they came to Israel at an advanced age. It isn't only a question of finding their way in unknown surroundings, but that we, their adult children, have become their only link with their past, and feeling disoriented, they project us backwards into their own world. That can be unnerving, particularly when, as immigrants struggling to build new lives in Israel, we feel we ought to concentrate our energies on a present open on the future. Nostalgia for the past appears a luxury we cannot afford. We know there is no going back, nor really do we want to. From that point of view, Tel Aviv can be just as much an exile for the aged as Ottawa or Montevideo.

When my parents came to Israel from Egypt after the Sinai Campaign, and we lived in a two-room apartment which was not even paid for yet, I'd become annoyed as I cooked our meals over a kerosene burner when my mother, unpacking her suitcases, would call to show me dresses she had worn at various family weddings, back in the 1920s, or photographs of her parents, or of my sister and myself as children, or would insist on reading to me one of those famous letters Mama

Camouna used to write, and which were always read aloud as we all gathered every *motsa'e shabbat* in Uncle David's house. I didn't want to remember the time when we were this huge, exuberant family, quarrelsome and gay, that assembled in my great-uncle's house, because it hurt more than I could admit.

All her life, Mother had kept all the letters she had ever received tied up in little parcels, which went into boxes, bearing the names of people who had written them, sometimes over a period of fifty years. And the cupboard which held this huge correspondence, more than anything else, was what delayed her and my father's departure from Egypt. It had been difficult to carry on my own correspondence with them through third parties and I had been torn between two conflicting needs: on the one hand to transmit correct information about life in Israel, and on the other to make sure that this information should never point to Israel so clearly that Egyptian censorship might give them trouble with the political police.

Mother would write, "I'm going through all the letters in the big cupboard in the hall. With every letter I read, I remember the best years of our lives. Every letter I tear up is like tearing my heart away. I'm going through the correspondence so that I can later select the strict minimum I want to take to our new home. I also found a box of letters from your friends. Would you like me to keep it for you?"

I'd write back via Paris or Rome, with someone changing the envelopes so that the postmark "Israel" would not figure on the letter. "Our apartment is a small one with absolutely no storage space. Nowadays people live with the bare essentials. Don't keep any of my letters. Burn them. Nowadays it's best to travel light."

I had kept this correspondence with friends who had studied or married abroad, or rather, had left it at home, and being very much my mother's daughter, it hurt to give it up. But I thought that only by sacrificing my treasure—the record of our generation, really—could Mother be encouraged to prune hers more severely. She wrote a letter so tear-stained I could hardly read it of the auction sale at which all that had been our home had gone for nothing like its value, and I could see Mother and Father wandering in this big empty apartment with the bare minimum left, and Mother still sorting out the letters and pictures she could not bear to be separated from. As time passed, our correspondence became more frantic, and prudence was thrown to the winds. A German-born friend of mine in Tel Aviv urged me: "You must push them harder. It was just the same with my people. They couldn't bear to leave their home. It seems that the more the outside world threatens, the harder older people cling to the illusory safety of memories. It is a form of paralysis. My family got out on the very last ship that left Hamburg for England."

What worried me most was the thought of an illness or accident which might make it impossible for them to travel; then they'd be completely cut off from us. Finally, after months of waiting, they were with us. Safe. For me, that was the main thing. But Mother didn't see it that way. She'd say, "Who else do I have here except for your father and you with whom I can share my memories? I only brought one suitcase of letters and photographs, and I brought them for you and your sister, thinking that you, too, would like to have souvenirs of home. But you won't understand. You've become so hard in Israel, your father and I don't recognize you at all." She'd begin to weep.

Sometimes I'd indulge her. But there was no end to the flow of memories connected with each letter, picture, or object. And during that time, of course, I wasn't getting on with the household chores, or with the articles I was writing for the Jewish Agency on integration and absorption of immigrants and the happy, happy family reunions in Israel. It hurt too much to write about happy family reunions in Israel if I allowed myself to think of what had been home being sold at an auction, or about the fun we used to have in Uncle David's house, a band of cousins skating down the immense corridor, or playing savages with great war whoops, or running to be fondled by our grandparents sitting in the big room. And as I typed stories of people I interviewed in Dimona, Ashdod, or Kiryat Shmona, who often had been crying their hearts out—although the photographer managed to get them to smile for the cause—I'd think angrily, "as if the people who left their villages in Poland or the Ukraine to settle in the Lower East Side of New York, or the South Side of Chicago did not have their hearts break, just as my mother's does now, at the tearing apart of this organic tissue called a family." It was on such occasions that I would recall the big, jerky, clumsy alphabetic characters filling the letters Mama Camouna used to write.

Mama Camouna was a great power of a women, and totally illiterate. How was it then that she could write letters? Well, that's the story.

My grandmother had lost her mother in infancy, and her father, my mother's grandfather, had remarried. This second wife was Mama Camouna. She was a *Tunshi*, a member of the local Jewry that spoke a Maghrebi dialect and which the upper-class Tunisian Jews, who claimed to have hailed from Livorno and who spoke Italian, looked down upon as distinctly lower class. Mama Camouna had many children and it was said she had been rather rough on my grandmother. Nevertheless, families are families. When my grandfather and his brother and their families left Tunis to settle in Egypt where they opened a department store, Mama Camouna suffered to be separated from her stepdaughter, whose family had become hers. She found it intolerable to have to rely on the goodwill of others to write what she had in her uncommonly strong head to say. So Mama Camouna, watching her grandchildren in Tunis doing their homework, got it into her head that if those little brats could write, so could she. It was simple: they'd teach her. They teased, "How can you learn to write, Mama Camouna? You don't know how to read and you hardly know any French." But Mama Camouna said she didn't need all that. All she wanted was that they teach her the "signs that show the sounds." My grandmother's half-sisters, with whom their widowed mother lived in turn, would write to us in Cairo describing those epic lessons. The grandchildren would get impatient as they guided the old woman's hand on the paper as she learned to write her name, and they'd run away. She'd chase them, catch one of them by the scruff of his neck, plunk him down by the table, and warn, "You aren't going to play until you've taught me to write the sound *SSSS*." And so it came about that Mama Camouna learned to write her Judeo-Arabic dialect with French letters. Her letters were incomprehensible to those who did not know the Maghrebi dialect, and the writing was so completely phonetic that it made no sense until read aloud. She wrote exactly as she spoke.

So, one Saturday afternoon, in Uncle David's house, there'd be this tremendous excitement when my grandmother would say, "Guess what I have in my handbag?" and we'd all exclaim, "A letter from Mama Camouna!" Even the small children would drop their games, as rolling with laughter, or with tears in our eyes, we all listened as Mama Camouna expressed her feelings in her rough-simple way, in that impossible jargon of hers. For the best part of thirty years we were truly thrilled to receive those few lines that took Mama Camouna hours to write.

She died in her nineties, during the Nazi occupation of Tunisia. Of grief perhaps. What made her slip out of the house in a cold winter night we cannot know. She was found dead in the morning on a park bench. Jeannot, her favorite grandson, had died in the meantime somewhere in the Libyan desert after having joined the Free French Forces. Jeannot had been the grandchild she had battled with most, until he understood what it meant to this old woman to write and taught her, not because he was forced to, but willingly, moved perhaps by that sense of justice which made him join not only the Free French but also the Communist Party. And because he had taught her as a little boy, she had been able to write to him, and to other members of her brood who left Tunis, one by one.

A short time before his death, Jeannot had turned up on leave in Cairo, and of course, was fêted by those enormous couscous meals we used to have, and he brought with him one of his Moslem comrades in arms who, like him, had joined the Free French full of hope about the world that would emerge after the war, bringing independence, freedom, and justice for all. I was in New York at the time, and Mother had written to me, telling about Jeannot's visit. Grandmother was dead, so was Uncle David, but the family still met every Saturday afternoon in the house of Uncle David's widow, and there Jeannot read to the assembled families and his comrades what must have been one of Mama Camouna's last letters.

I remember Jeannot from the days when we went from Egypt to Tunis for the marriage of one of my aunts. We must both have been five or six at the time and we immediately fell in love. Some branches of the family were well off, others poor, but it made no difference. There was such warmth and gaiety as every family in turn fêted my aunt and her fiancé. Jeannot and I considered ourselves engaged as we exchanged cigar rings as wedding rings, and in a family where so much of private emotion was in the public domain, everyone called us "les petits fiancés." This embarrassed me greatly in later years when, after much writing back and forth, our dispersed tribes would meet for a glorious orgy of familial affection in some alpine resort, and I'd be asked, "Don't you remember Jeannot, your little fiancé?" But Jeannot's family was too poor to come, so I never saw him again after that memorable visit to Tunis, where together we had discovered something about the relationship of light and love. During the hot afternoon hours, we'd play in a darkened room, where just one ray of light with millions of tiny specks of dust dancing in it passed through the nearly closed shutters. We played at capturing the sunray in the palm of our hands, and offered it to one another. We began to dance, spontaneously as children do, drinking in the light, and when it fell on my face, Jeannot would steal a kiss, and sometimes I'd dodge, and sometimes I didn't. Of course, we were caught at it and scolded. We didn't feel we had done anything wrong: after all, we only kissed the light.

So, many years later, Mother wanting to read me letters from Mama Camouna seemed determined to pull me back into that region of the mind which is still, where time is abolished, where separation, sorrow, death do not exist. But time abolished by its very immobility foreshadows death, and we must live, all of us, in the world as it is, where no love, be it as strong as Mama Camouna's, is as innocent as that which Jeannot and I felt for one another dancing in the pure dancing light.

On occasion I'd tell my mother, by way of consolation, "In Israel, so many people lost so much more than we did, we must consider ourselves lucky in comparison. So you left your sisters, brothers, nephews, nieces, and innumerable cousins. But you'll see at least some of them again, someday. Think of those families who perished, whole families with so few survivors left." I didn't really believe it but that was what most people said.

Mother, stubborn in her sorrow and sensible in her way, didn't take to that line of argument at all. "I suffered to be separated from you and now I suffer to be separated from them. And please, don't tell me we are lucky in comparison to people whose families perished in concentration camps. Do you think those survivors would not prefer to suffer being separated from those they love than to forbid themselves even to think of them? How can you accept what happened in concentration camps as if it were a normal condition of life? I refuse to. I never shall.

The normal thing is for families to be happy when they are united, sad when they are parted. But we, we are always torn."

Our neighbors, who had just arrived from Poland, treated my parents when they met in the staircase as something infinitely precious and fragile, as if made of spun glass. My father was rather uncertain on his legs, and when the children raced up and down the stairs, our neighbors would hold them back and help him. One of the women said, "Our children will never know what it's like to have grandparents. In Poland, life was too harsh for our old people. Almost none survived. You are blessed to have them, blessed to have been able to save them. There's nothing more beautiful than old age. They say Israel is the only place where a Jew can live fully. May it be the place where Jews live to become old, surrounded by their families."

With the passing of years, a few members of the family settled in Israel; others, including my sister, came to visit. There were times when the feeling of exile was unbearable, and times when Israel was a link between us in our dispersal, increasingly part of the fabric of our lives. Among the most memorable of these visits was that of my father's favorite sister, whom he had not seen for twenty-five years, when she had last visited us in Egypt. She had married in Manchester a good half-century back. Aunt Rose had a dream, imperatively ordering her to visit her brother Joseph. So she came, accompanied by her daughter, Amy, whom I hadn't seen since we were both toddlers, on one of our visits to Manchester. Amy looked incredibly British and behaved with old-style Victorian decorum, when very formally shaking hands she said, "How do you do?"

Aunt Rose said, "Really Amy dear! Don't you remember your cousin? When they stayed with us in Manchester you pushed Jacqueline down the stairs!"

"I'm so sorry. That was very naughty of me," Amy said. There was that twinkle in her eyes, so much like that of her grandfather—and mine—when he teased, and we both laughed. It was fascinating, this extraordinary family resemblance we came to discover, not so much in looks but rather as something very deep in our natures, which made us react almost exactly in the same way and share the same likes and dislikes. Amy and I went on a few excursions, but Aunt Rose saw nothing of Israel. That was not what she had come here for. Every morning, from her hotel, she'd take a taxi to see my parents, and they'd talk, remembering.

It was in this way Amy and I had heard how our grandmother had gone to Egypt with the smaller children after our grandfather had set up a proper house for them in Cairo. He had crossed the Syrian desert in a caravan, but Grandmother, after visiting one of her sisters in Basra, went all the way round the Arabian Peninsula up to Port Said, on one of those famous British Peninsular and Orient liners. It was a long trip. She was ultra-orthodox, and it was out of the question that her family should eat in the ship's dining room. Grandmother had come on board with a Primus stove, a sack of rice, and one of lentils, among other provisions, and every day she cooked *mujaddara* on the deck, the only cooked food they ate on board. Father, who was almost seventeen at the time, rebelled and went to eat in the dining room. He found the non-kosher food delicious, but it made him very sick. After so many years, those two old people with their dark brown faces, white hair, and thick white eyebrows whooped with laughter as they revived that old Primus stove on which their mother had cooked that long-ago *mujaddara* on the ship on which they had made their crossing to the Western world.

Then Sammy came to visit from New York. His father, my father's nephew, had wisely put him on the immigration quota to the United States some time before "the events." Sammy, whom I picked up at his hotel, had a Ph.D. in economics, worked for a big investment firm, and talked expansively about finances, American style. He was mad about the United States, contributed to the U.J.A., attended bond dinners.* He had "integrated" fully. He was trying so hard to be ultra-American. Yet, when he saw my father, not only was he moved, but the old patriarchal tradition in which he had been brought up spontaneously expressed itself. He kissed my father's hand and received his blessing, exactly as it had been the custom in the house of his great-grandfather

* The United Jewish Appeal (UJA) was a Jewish philanthropic organization founded to help Jewish refugees and communities in need. In 1999 it merged with other organizations to form the United Jewish Communites. "Bond dinners" refers to fund-raising events to promote the sale of Israel bonds to wealthy American Jews.

who had left Baghdad to settle in Cairo. So we began to talk about the numerous branches of the family now settled in the United States. Most of those in their thirties had managed to get university degrees while they worked, and had eventually brought over their parents, and cared for them. "There's a time they decided things for us, now we decide for them," Sammy told me in an aside. And the younger girls, those in their twenties, were all going to college, doing well, even brilliantly. They were five generations removed from the ultra-orthodox and illiterate old lady who had cooked *mujaddara* for her children on the way around Arabia. We told Sammy the story, and he said he'd tell it to his sister's children, so that they remembered. Of course, he spoke of Aunt Rose's visit and exchanged the latest news about the branch of the family in England. Then Father told Sammy he wanted him to write something down. It was this: our family had moved from a town called Anna to Baghdad 735 years before they left Baghdad to settle in Egypt, which was in 1911. He wanted those in America to know. Skeptical, I asked my father, "How can you know without any records? Seven centuries is a long time." And he said that nothing written could be more exact give or take a few years than oral tradition. People might cheat with written documents. But when the head of a family knew he was approaching the end of his days, and passed on what he wanted his sons to remember and in turn pass on to their sons, he was careful to calculate exactly, and one must not cast doubt on what was thus solemnly transmitted from mouth to mouth, throughout the generations.

I asked Sammy if he saw much of his cousins in New York, and he gave an answer that was typical, "When our parents wanted to force us to, because it was the family, and hold us by the old rules, we wouldn't have any of it. But actually, some of us see a great deal of each other, guided by a natural affinity and common interests, something which draws us together. On the whole we've made quite a society of cousins. It's strange. There's something deeper than the culture we acquire from the countries we live in. We adapt to them, of course. But there's a kind of kinship that's hard to describe but that seems to persist, no matter what." "Kol yisrael haverim,"* my father answered, recalling the motto

* [Hebrew] All the people of Israel are friends.

of the Alliance Universelle Israélite, which had been instrumental in bringing about the emergence of the old communities of the Orient into the Western world.

Not long after Sammy's visit, my father died after a long illness. My mother's sorrow and mine were compounded by the fact that there were not ten men who had known him in his life to stand by his grave and recite kaddish for him. Seeing we were so few, some strangers at the Holon cemetery visiting their own dead did the mitzvah of coming to recite kaddish for this Jew they had never known. This was the time when we felt that Israel can be exile most bitterly and cruelly. But telegrams and letters poured in from so many places in the world where Father's brothers, nephews, and grand-nephews lived. In New York and in Manchester there were enough of them to gather in his memory and do things the proper way, as he had done all his life for others. And when some of them now come to Israel, and ask to visit his grave, there is a more gentle sorrow, a kind of peace over the fact that he is remembered by them. Sometimes, I go alone, and this loneliness seems incredible when once we were so many.

Then I remember my grandmother telling me when I was a child how Mama Camouna and the other women would take the children to the Jewish cemetery in Tunis, so that the dear dead ones would not feel lonely. "At first we lamented and tore at our cheeks, and then we'd settle down for a collation, and the children would play hide-and-seek among the graves. And we'd remember what our dear ones had said and done and told stories about them. Oh, we'd laugh so much remembering your great-uncle Fragi, because he was so gay, always playing pranks and at weddings he'd compose songs, honoring the bride and groom and their families, with funny refrains about everybody." Then Grandmother and her daughters would remember those weddings in Tunis and what everybody wore, some of the women still in their traditional dresses, wrapped up in big white silk shawls, and those who already dressed in the style that was "modern" before the First World War. Their infectious laughter sometimes seems to echo among the cold rectilinear alignment of the graves in Holon, and they all seem to be there, and I the surviving witness of something marvelously warm, vital, and alive, which I knew but which no longer is.

Nowadays, even the dead seem regimented in these straight-lined cemeteries, so different from the old ones, where families kept together, in death as in life. And yet, somehow, life continues, reasserts itself, and some of the old ways still survive. After my father's death, my mother stayed some time with my sister in Paris, where she saw many of her cousins, some who had left Egypt after the Sinai Campaign, and some who, in the meantime, had left Tunis and other North African cities. Then she stayed with my father's relatives in England, and each of his nephews and nieces brought their children and grandchildren to see her, exactly as it was done in the old days. She wrote: "They still cook the same dishes, some of them, at least for the holidays."

She returned to Israel having seen them all, appeased. In Paris, her cousins, the daughters of Uncle David, who are now old ladies, still meet every *motsa'e shabbat* and read the letters they have received. Anyone who passes through Paris joins the circle. The younger people sometimes come and sometimes don't. Perhaps this will be the last generation to keep up the custom, but in the meantime it holds.

And so it was that Gerard, a great-grandson of Uncle David, called me up one day from his kibbutz. A little mockingly, he said, "Grandmother said that if I don't see your mother while I'm in Israel, she'll never forgive me. So when can I come?"

We make arrangements for his visit. He arrives, a handsome boy of eighteen, a student, who, trying to look serious, tells me that he, too, paraded with the black flag of anarchy during the student riots. We laugh. With his long blond hair he looks very much like a beatnik and his pink outfit is very dirty.

"Would you like to wash?" Mother suggests.

Gerard looks scandalized. Then his eyes begin to rove over the pictures hanging on her walls and he recognizes some of the old people he knows when they were still young, and of some he asks, "Who is he? Who is she?" For a brief moment they live again as part of our lives, mixed up with what we say about the Six-Day War, and what Gerard tells us of his kibbutz, and the family in Paris, and the student riots. And Gerard tells my mother, "Aunt Yvonne, you should have seen the crowd that came to hear your letters being read. Aunt Louise called us all up, and said 'A letter from Yvonne!' and we all went. We heard all about your visit to Jerusalem. It was very moving. But your letter about the visit to the Golan Heights drew crowds three Saturdays in a row! It was a masterpiece. You can't imagine what it means now, to have family in Israel."

Mother was very pleased. "I'm only an old woman. I just wrote about what I saw and what I felt about it, and wanted to share it with those I love."

Gerard knits his eyebrows and asks, "But how did it happen that for the last three or four generations we've been constantly on the move? And it's not finished yet. How did it all begin?"

So mother tells Gerard how in her family it might have begun. "You see, your great-great-grandfather had an oil press in Monastir, a small village in Tunisia. The oil was stored in big jars, like those in the tale about Ali Baba and the forty thieves. One jar was kept for ablutions. There was of course no running water in those days. Well, one day, after he had worked hard and sweated and felt very hot, he had the jar filled with cold water and stayed in it too long. He died of pneumonia as a consequence. Times were already changing, and your great-grandfather, my Uncle David, the eldest son, decided to try his luck in Tunis, the big city, and gradually he brought the whole family over to Tunis. That's how it all began."

"Well," Gerard said, "it's not given to everybody to have had an ancestor who died taking a cold bath in an oil jar. I'll have to tell the cousins in Paris about it. I wonder why Grandmother never did."

"Perhaps," Mother said, at once gentle and reproaching, "because you never asked. How do you want us to tell, when you young people nowadays are really not interested in those old tales, when you can't really be bothered with the past, because the world you live in is so different? So it's wiser to wait until you ask." She glances at me, a little slyly. "Isn't it so, my daughter?"

I say yes and I think it's always the same caravans crossing and recrossing. Perhaps memories are like water in a well, that well Rachel uncovered for Jacob when he came to his Uncle Laban. Perhaps that is when it all started, and since then it is only the means of transportation that have really changed.

*Fifteen*

# Rebel, My Brother

*In the years following Kahanoff's arrival in Israel in 1954, communication with her parents, living in Egypt, was limited. After her parents moved there in 1958, they were able to share information they could not get past the Egyptian censors. This essay, the third of the "Generation of Levantines" cycle, reveals the surprising story of how Kahanoff's parents came to provide refuge in their Cairo apartment for Tunisian and Algerian revolutionaries during those countries' respective struggles for independence. The Shohets' interactions with their boarders reveal the complexity and multiple affiliations of their mutual Levantine loyalties. It is clear from this essay, published a few short years after the events described, that the polarized rhetoric of the Arab-Israeli conflict and the Algerian struggle for independence from France already gravely threatened the possibility of Levantine coexistence.*

When my parents joined us in Israel, after the Sinai Campaign, we spoke as a matter of course about people and events that had been important in our lives in order to make up for the intervening years when it had been difficult to exchange letters between enemy countries. It became apparent from Mother's account that another drama had unfolded alongside our own, which had been different from and yet implicated in the events we had endured. Mother's grandfather had been in his day a cobbler in Monastir, the small town in which Habib Bourguiba had been born,*



* Bourguiba (1903–2000) was leader of the Tunisian struggle for independence (1952–1956) and served as the first president of Tunisia after its independence from France.

and there was a time when we would receive from Tunisia oil, wine, and dates transparent as amber.

Vague feelings of jealousy welled up within me when Mother told me, after coming to Israel, about the patriots from North Africa who had lived in our home and had formed close ties with her and my father. She would mention in her letters "the enjoyable company of those young men—students from friendly countries—who managed to fill the vacuum left behind by the children who abandoned us." The implied rebuke annoyed me, and so too the thought of a stranger treating "my room" as his own. Oddly enough, I had the feeling there was some stranger reflected in the mirror on my dresser, a face encircled by the shining glints of the polished frame of the mirror. Friend? Foe? I couldn't say for sure. But I felt that there existed between us some sort of ambiguous connection.

My cousin Julian, who knew that my parents' days of prosperity had long passed, had asked my mother whether she would be willing to take in the Tunisian friends that Bourguiba had personally recommended to him. They had just returned, official representatives of their government in Egypt and the Arab League.* Being Tunisian, they were considered part of the family.

When I returned to visit my family in 1946 Julian told me excitedly: "These Tunisians are remarkable types. Like us they are steeped in French culture, we can exchange ideas, for we've read the same books. Moreover, they are secure enough not to feel ashamed at being grateful to France for giving them so much. They are utterly different from the Arabs here, who were all somewhat corrupted by Hitler, and are today anti-Semitic, because of this business about Palestine. Undoubtedly there are decent fellows among them, but not of the same type. The Tunisians hoped, and they are still hoping, that a free France, purified of its own reactionary forces, an uncontaminated France at whose side they fought, a France of the Revolution of 1789, will grant them their independence out of a generous fraternal spirit. France, you see, in spite of its colonial taint, is not England, which did not leave or create anything in this part of the world. France transformed these fellows

* Organization of Arab states founded in 1945 to strengthen ties and mediate disputes among its members.

into ardent freedom seekers, high-spirited, thinking fellows that she can be proud of. Would you like to meet my friends? This summer, if you pass through Paris before returning to that America of yours, I might be able to introduce them to you, especially one of them, you'll see, a remarkable fellow, bright, sharp-witted, deep and personable. I prefer not to mention names, after all you understand, they're involved in all sorts of things . . . most of them were also imprisoned for the cause."

I did meet with Julian in Paris, but not with his friends. One evening, when we were dining together in a small restaurant facing Porte de Champerret, the "remarkable fellow" was supposed to arrive, but hours went by, and Julian grew increasingly annoyed as his friend did not show up. In the end a young man entered and told him: "He's not coming. But he made it in one piece. He sends you his gratitude, mon chère. Without you . . . no, it's best I go . . ."

These go-betweens seemed to me somewhat frivolous and I put the incident out of my mind, but several years later, when I was living in Paris, other relatives from North Africa arrived and told me that Julian, in whose home Bourguiba had lived while in Egypt, had been enormously useful to him and other Tunisian nationalists and had helped them establish "ties" in Egypt, and that Habib Bourguiba, now president of the Republic of Tunisia, remained loyal to his friends. Might Bourguiba have been the man I was supposed to meet years earlier? When I read Bourguiba's declarations in the French papers, in marvelously limpid French prose, I imagined hearing Julian's voice saying: "We read the same books. . . . France can be proud. . . ." But it seemed that France was now suspicious of the very same strange fledglings over which it had brooded.

Some time later, in Israel, one of the Egyptian Zionist activists, who had managed to flee at the very last minute, remarked: "In that case you must know Julian? An affable young man who tended to talk a bit too much." A smile rife with insinuations. "He helped us once or twice, but didn't know it." I doubted Julian really "didn't know," given my knowledge of his complicated allegiances—Tunisian, Levantine, and Jewish, who in his youth dreamed of living on a kibbutz. He knew I was in Israel, but within the framework of his values this had no effect on his affection toward his Tunisian friends and my parents, for this was a personal friendship, and everyone should make sure not to let one set of loyalties get in the way of another, nor to speak of things that were best left unsaid.

*

My parents' recollections of their lodgers revealed unexpected discoveries about Arab loyalty. They spoke, for example, of Fawzi, the Iraqi medical student, who during the Sinai Campaign would rain down fire and brimstone on Nasser, and who insisted on "knowing the truth." Whenever the maid left the room he would crouch over the radio under the blanket and listen to the news broadcast from Israel, and upon emerging declare in a hoarse victory-whisper in the dimly lit room that the Israelis had invaded the Sinai Peninsula and reduced the Egyptians to scorn and derision and deserved to be applauded—and who do they think they are to rail against Great Britain? The Tunisians had only contempt for the Iraqi "wet hen," since at the sounding of every siren he'd whine that it was really complete folly to die for the Suez Canal. He returned to Baghdad in disgust to continue his studies undisturbed. Poor boy, what could have happened to him? My father claimed that he came from an upstanding family.

After the Sinai conflict the Tunisians treated Nasser, the ruling military hooligans, Egypt, and the Arab League with even greater scorn; the first was in their eyes "a novice," the second "foolish and arrogant," the third "hopelessly rotten," while the last seemed to them "corrupt, reactionary, and a complete failure." They laughed at the solidarity that stirred the brother Arab nations into hastening, so to speak, to Egypt's aid; they compared this to the positions taken by Bourguiba and Muhammad V, king of Morocco, who without severing their ties with France were patriotic supporters of the Algerians, and in contrast to Nasser were not dreaming of founding empires, being far too preoccupied with solving concrete and immediate problems to support the intoxication of words. The Israelis, they said, were fighting by right for their independence. They were "wonderful" and it was a great pity that the national struggle in Maghreb compelled the Tunisians to cooperate with Egypt and the Arab League. But once they achieved their objectives and the entire Maghreb was independent, it would not be enough to stand by France as equal partners, they should become friends of Israel as well. Unfortunately political power does not always coincide with feelings of sympathy. My parents were careful not to express their opinions, for after all there were Arab nationalists among their friends.

My mother proudly told us that the Tunisians had proved brave and loyal friends to the Jews of Egypt: "The Tunisian embassy would issue a passport to every Jew who could prove even a distant connection to Tunisia, and the Egyptian authorities were forced to cancel expulsion notices, for they didn't feel especially comfortable expelling citizens of an Arab sister-republic. The Egyptian newspapers accused the Tunisian embassy of turning into a Jewish consulate of sorts, an appendage to the Jewish Agency, and claimed its behavior did not befit an Arab sister-state. But the Tunisians paid no attention and went on helping Jews as much as they could, and in doing so proved that they were mature, cultured people with human feelings who deserved their own independence."

Significantly, these Tunisian nationalists deliberately chose to live not with a Moslem family but with Jews, with whom they would speak French, and though none of this was made explicit, they upheld the Levantine banner that shunned uniformity and safeguarded the dissimilar and the abrasive even within the framework of their national aspirations.

For these very reasons Bourguiba decided that pupils in all the elementary schools of independent Tunisia should apply themselves to the study of French. He explained that Arabic in its present form did not adequately convey thoughts and ideas essential to the times, and if children did not acquire such avenues of thought neither they nor their country could ever hope to bear up to the twentieth century. National independence does not achieve a great deal if it does not give to the entire nation the means to tap into the traditions of humanity as a whole. As a true Levantine he appealed to French teachers, while granting units of the FLN rebels refuge and the opportunity to train within his borders, and even after the bombing of Sakiet Sidi Youssef he did not sever his ties with France, but rather toiled assiduously toward mending the divide.*

* Front de Liberation Nationale (FLN), or National Liberation Front, led the Algerian armed struggle for independence from France (1954–1962). Sakiet Sidi Youssef is a Tunisian town on the border with Algeria. On February 8, 1958, the French Air Force, seeking Algerian operatives ostensibly using the site as a base, bombed the town, killing and wounding Tunisian civilians.

France, a Latin nation, which by means of the church had inherited the essence of cultured Levantinism as it was embodied in Byzantium, sent these teachers to Bourguiba, while at the very same time Nasser uprooted from his country hundreds of teachers, expelled the Europeans, and dispatched Egyptians to other Arab countries to chant a hymn of unity and to praise an old culture, as though they might be reinstated in the world by the power of incantation and invocation alone.

North Africa too is not lacking in weak-spirited zealots, white- and dark-skinned, devoured by the untamed winds of negativity, but even now there are also people who extend a hand to fix and to patch this inestimably precious tapestry of our lives, who are all an amalgamation, toiling over this amazing effort to develop new relations between nations, relations in which politics play only a small part.

My parents' Tunisian friend would tell them proudly that Bourguiba prefers to speak French over Arabic, for he recognized the importance of diversity and the manifold and thereby gave expression to the old tradition of Levantine humanism. The grafting of a new branch onto an old trunk is not easy, and the cut where the grafting took place is still swollen and sore. There also exists the rebel, who continues to be divided within himself, who plunges into action in order to flee from the rupture within him. I came to know him as well, as would gradually become clear from my parents, who spoke in their letters with warmth and deep admiration of the young rebel boarding in their home. They spoke of him so often that the selfsame reflection in the mirror still there, throwing me into confusion, finally grew clearer, turned into a face, a likeness, a familiar person.

*

I often got annoyed at my parents for speaking with such a complete lack of criticism in praise of one Khalil, who boarded intermittently in their home for two years. "Khalil is the most amazing person I ever met," Mother would say effusively. "So good-hearted and bright. We simply worshiped him. When he came home in the evening and noticed a light in the living room, he would ask if he could join us. I never met such an interesting man. He knew everything, read everything, Dostoevsky, Tolstoy, and had committed thousands of poems to memory, including, I think, all of Paul Valéry. He would speak about many other writers whose names I had never heard of, on Sorel and on one Russian called Bukharin or something of the sort. He was also so thoughtful. In the morning, before going out, he would always leave me a note, just to say something pleasant in a line or two of poetry, always on the mark, brilliant . . . oh, he was so sweet."

"Khalil was a genius and an angel," my father confirmed with gravity.

"Khalil also told me everything regarding Trotsky," Mother continued. "He read his books and told us that when Stalin murdered Trotsky he destroyed the purity of the Russian Revolution, its very soul. Khalil gave himself over completely to Algeria's War of Independence. His room was filled with newspaper clippings, journals, and books. He wrote a great deal and spoke so nicely. He devoted his entire life to the freedom of his native land."

"In the past you were fanatically pro-French, Mother, and our heroes were Joffre, Foch, Lyautey, and Franchet d'Espèrey,"* I jeered, upset at this young Algerian who worked after all in the Maghreb department of the Arab League and whose literary activities were known to me only as hearsay.

My mother blushed under her gray hair. "Khalil convinced me of the justice of his struggle. Not unlike our Tunisians, he loved France. When I reproved him once to his face: 'Khalil, how can a man as learned and sensitive as you advocate the rights of terrorists who kill innocent people,' he told me that the French were the ones who had turned him into a terrorist, a rebel, because in his youth his greatest desire was that he and all his countrymen become French. He joined the army at the onset of the Second World War, and later joined the rank of the Free French Forces. He fought in Italy, was wounded, and de Gaulle himself decorated him with the Croix de Guerre for his courage. He rose to the rank of officer and continued to serve in the army, and was charged with a battalion of North African soldiers. He told me how it all happened. Once, during Christmas, the soldiers from France received their

* Marshals Ferdinand Foch (1851–1929), Joseph Joffre (1852–1931), and Hubert Lyautey (1854–1934), along with General Louis Franchet d'Espèrey (1856–1942), were all French heroes of World War I.

gifts while the Moslem soldiers received packages half their worth. The North African soldiers were hurt to the quick and refused to open their packages, and Khalil, their commanding officer, went to the commandant to protest. The commandant said Christmas was a Christian and not a Moslem holiday, and Khalil answered, if so, the Moslem soldiers should have received a package of equal worth during Ramadan, which was not the case. They hadn't fought with their French comrades in order to be only half as important as a Frenchman. The commandant said he was sorry but those were the orders he received. Khalil then flung down his Croix de Guerre and said that France would have a reason to remember him. And he left the military. He then understood that assimilation-through-equality was not a feasible dream—Algeria would have to fight for its future independence within the limits of the possible, though he hoped with all his might that France would understand that Algeria must be free, 'before it missed the opportunity, before things got out of hand.'" I recalled reading about a similar case in *Le Monde*, even though I could not remember the name of the officer involved in the matter. There were undoubtedly hundreds and thousands of such cases, petty humiliations, feelings of wounded pride that had awakened and alerted the people who wanted "to be French," and to whom the French displayed a strange degree of indifference. Perhaps doing so was a way of declaring that our secular French culture taught us to accept the "Principles of '89" * in terms of absolute values of behavior but it did not teach us that—like St. Augustine of North Africa put it ages ago—"It is incumbent upon us to seek out like one who is obliged to find, and to find like one who is obliged to go on seeking." **

*

"How did you agree to lodge this terrorist under your roof?" I asked. "It could have put you in great danger."

"Well, at first we didn't know a thing. The Tunisians asked us if we were ready to accept their friend. He certainly had a strange business

* A reference to 1789, the year of the French Revolution.

** Although St. Augustine's writings explore the notions of seeking and finding, the passage that Kahanoff cites is either misquoted or improperly attributed.

that required of him to travel regularly; he traded in animal offal. To tell the truth, I had my doubts, but the Tunisians had recommended him with such warmth. I liked Khalil the minute he showed up, and the longer we knew him, the more I liked him. But we were surprised that a young man as pleasant and refined as Khalil dealt in the entrails of cattle, and even though he would talk about everything under the sun he never once spoke on that subject. Your father was so filled with curiosity that he finally asked him, Mr. Khalil, I can't believe that you, with all due respect, are a merchant of offal, and a wholesale merchant at that. Perhaps you are a journalist?

"Khalil admitted he was a journalist and begged to be forgiven for not telling us this from the start, but he had worried that if we knew his opinions we wouldn't accept him, and from what he had heard from the Tunisians he was very keen on boarding with us, as he wished to return to a place where he'd feel at home, and might live in peace, among friends.

"At first his explanation seemed reasonable enough, but later on I began wondering how it was possible that even though he wrote constantly no one ever saw an article under his name either in French or Arabic. I remember his lending me Menachem Begin's book *The Revolt*. He expressed deep admiration for Israel and said the Jews were perfectly right in their desire for their own state, and that achieving independence was a wonder. Begin, he said, was his 'Bible'; he had learned everything from the man. He also told us a great deal about kibbutzim and the Histadrut and the workers' government and social institutions there. He said Israel was a 'civilization of the avant-garde,' and when Algeria achieved its independence it would be possible for his country to follow Israel's example in many things in order to solve its own economic and social problems—except that at the moment Algeria had to ally itself with Nasser, Egypt, and the Arab League. It had no choice. And so, he was immersed head over heels in all these matters until in the end I could not hold myself back any longer and told him, 'Khalil, I can't believe that a person as dedicated as you is merely a journalist. You must certainly have an active part in these events—but you don't have to tell me.'

"He then admitted that he was an active member of the FLN and worked in the Maghreb offices of the Arab League. This worried me.

We were true friends, and so I told him, 'I understand and admire your idealism and I am proud that you trusted in me, in us, because you know how fond we are of you. But we are old and tired and hope to live one of these days with our children. It is our duty toward them to take care of ourselves. When you moved in you didn't tell me a thing about all this. I know, you couldn't. But I want you to promise me that if at some time or other we are endangered because of your boarding here, you will leave the house.' He promised—and he stood by his word. He also told me how important it was for him that the key of our home was always in his pocket, that whatever might happen and whatever he might do he knew there was always a place he could return to. When he left us in 1956 there were tears in his eyes, real tears. Terrorist, yes, maybe, but the sweetest and most sensitive young man in the world.

"He told me of his superior Amar, whom I approached in the Maghreb branch of the Arab League after one of his absences from our home. Once Khalil went missing far longer than he'd promised, and I worried for him, since according to the law I was obliged to report the matter to the authorities. What's more, our landlord, a French citizen, started to cause problems: he'd heard that Khalil was a terrorist and he didn't want his property to be blown up, nor did he want to commit a crime against the French, for he supported their policies, and only a few days earlier a bomb had exploded on our street. I told him: 'Mr. Soncino, bombs today are like fireworks during the *Bairam* holidays; they go off at every street corner and are in no need of Khalil, who is a journalist, who may get overenthused at times, as is the way of the young.' But I was worried. Khalil's girlfriend, who was madly in love with him, wrote to me that she was worried sick, as she hadn't had a word from him for such a long time. He had told me about her, told me everything—almost everything. And so I turned to Amar at the Arab League and asked him what I should do: should I report Khalil missing to the Egyptian police or the French Consulate, or what? After all he was a French citizen. And what should I tell the young girl? Amar laughed and said there was no need to tell the French or any other authority, since at that very moment he had received from Khalil a letter saying he would return in a few days. I could write to the young girl and tell her as much.

"Upon returning Khalil said he'd been under conditions that made it impossible for him to write. He was angry when I told him Mr. Soncino, our landlord, wanted him to leave. 'He'll regret his words,' he said. I protested: 'Oh, no, Khalil, and again no! This is beneath your honor. This person is entitled to his opinions just as you are, and remember—you promised me we wouldn't have any problems because of you.' He said I was right, he had gotten carried away. We have nothing to fear; to the contrary, the fact that he lived with us was our best defense against the Egyptian authorities, and he would always stand at our service. I told him it was also unfair that he'd neglected his sweetheart; couldn't he have at least written to her? Yes, I will write, he said, but he was so immersed in his affairs that for some reason women, love, and all the rest are no more for him. There were times he dreamed of peace, yearned to marry, to have children. But whom could he marry? Not a European girl, for he was an Algerian patriot. This may have been possible in Bourguiba's time, not in his own. But neither a Moslem girl, with no experience in life, who'd just found her way out of the harem, with whom you couldn't even hold a conversation. Ironically, only a European woman would be able to understand him. That night he told me he had called his girlfriend from Zurich and had written her a long letter as well. Were my fears allayed?"

All of a sudden I understood the bond that had formed between my Tunisian mother and this young Moslem, a bond so common between an Eastern woman and her precious son, whom she spoils, dotes on, admires, gives advice to, believes in, while for him she is the only woman he respects and completely trusts. My mother may have been closer to him than his own mother because of their shared European manners. We, Mother's daughters, could not give her our trust that easily: she always seemed disappointed when we did not behave in the conventional, acceptable fashion, when now and then we let ourselves be impressed by free spirits of one sort or another. She was astonished by our "independence," as she called it, as much as she was cautious and softhearted, but this trait which we possessed also shocked and frightened her. A man's fate was different; it was his God-given nature to be free, and whatever he may do there was no danger of his being rejected by society. Like France, she too was appalled by the chicks over which she'd brooded. And so Khalil, by rousing the "native" woman in my mother, succeeded where I had failed. In my time I had also wanted her to love the little Arab within me, and when because of her I cut myself off once and for all from that part of me, Mother was agitated and hurt at the emergence of my new personality, which she could not completely accept, not unlike what had occurred between Khalil and France.

I joked, "Ah, we don't have to worry about Khalil's love affairs. He'll return from Algeria one of these days—maybe he's already back—and will meet the nice girl that flung off her veil along with a couple of grenades, and who read all the thickly bound books."

"What will become of this world teeming with violence?" Father groaned. "But the unfortunate Ben Bella surely won't marry.* Don't you know that he still hasn't been released from prison?"

I jumped from my chair. "Ben Bella? The famous Ben Bella? The mastermind of the FLN, the brain that finessed the Egyptians and the Arab League to support the Algerian revolt? That was Khalil? But why didn't you say so immediately?"

"I didn't realize that you didn't know," Mother said. "True, how could you have known? We always called him Khalil, out of habit, and Ben Bella is now a name that belongs to history while Khalil is the young man we loved, who lived with us at home."

*

And so that was the reflection in the mirror, which is no longer, sold along with all the other things that had once been a home for me. Was it not a wonder that such important and mighty events took place in the very room where I had stowed my diary, with its dreams of the victorious revolt of the dark-skinned, and how another man had come to spur them into action, like the genie that pops up through the haze of dreams.

"Of course," my mother went on, "only after some time, after he left, only then were we told who Khalil really was, even though we knew that he was an important person in the FLN; this was a terrible shock for me when I recognized his face on the front page of *Paris Match*, accompanied by his entire life history and his imprisonment. What the

* Ahmed Ben Bella (b. 1918) was the leader of the Algerian struggle for independence. He served as the first prime minister and then the first elected president of the Algerian Republic after independence.

French did to him does no honor to France. He and the rest of the leaders of the FLN were to have stopped in Tunis, where Bourguiba was awaiting their return along with a huge, elated crowd. But they never got to Tunis. The plane took them by surprise straight to France, not for negotiations but to prison. Poor boy! It reminded us what he had told us about Trotsky. Ben Bella, too, was a pure soul. He believed and trusted in France, and if he hadn't been betrayed a second time perhaps this entire sorry affair might have ended."*

"Hold on," my husband mocked softly, "the French didn't kill him, did they? They may even have done him a great service. He is still popular, he wasn't overly defiled by his actions, and a halo of martyrdom hovers over him. At the right time they will be able to bring him out into the light. But you know, as a terrorist, and of such prominence, he spoke much too much, and God alone knows from what dangers you were rescued. The French were looking everywhere for Ben Bella. If they'd have found him in your home, or if Ben Bella's people had known that we were in Israel during these tumultuous years before the Sinai Campaign—anything could have happened. People involved in such affairs have no conscience to speak of, the stakes are too high. To tell the truth, it is unbelievable that you weren't thoroughly interrogated. As it turns out the inconsistency of the Arabs, their complete lack of a method, was your best protection."

Mother objected. "Can't you understand? We were friends. Apart from that we had nothing to hide—for sure, almost nothing. There was no point in telling him we had a daughter in Israel; we simply had to separate the two and be loyal to both. This way we behaved naturally and honestly, that's all. A short time after Sinai, when we told our Tunisian friends of our plans to leave Egypt and live with our children, they guessed where we were heading. They never bothered us

* On October 22, 1956, the plane carrying Ben Bella and his compatriots from Rabat to Tunis was intercepted by the French. He was tried and served prison time in France from 1956 to 1962. France's involvement in the tripartite aggression against Egypt, along with Israel and Great Britain, launched on October 30 was at least in part motivated by the French administration's desire for revenge against the regime that had harbored the FLN leadership.

and claimed we had nothing to fear. They said we were under their protection and the protection of the Arab League, thanks to Ben Bella, and that even Nasser would make sure that we weren't harmed since he knew who we were and how loyal we had been to Ben Bella and how happy he had been living with us. Our Tunisian friends said that in such matters one could always rely on the Arabs' sense of honor, but even if the worst should happen, after all, they, the Tunisians, would issue me a Tunisian passport for myself and my husband. And so, you see, we were completely reassured."

This way of thinking didn't make as much sense to my husband as it did to my parents. Even though he had lived many years in Egypt, he was not one of us, and it was difficult for him to believe that in the midst of all these political passions a semblance of humanity remained intact and to preserve it human beings had to make sure not to know the entire truth. I was eager to hear how my parents' involvement with Ben Bella ended.

Mother told us: "Khalil again vanished for a lengthy period, and when he returned his head was bruised and he looked like a hunted man. I pretended not to notice, but I wanted him to leave on his own. That was in November 1955; after that we saw him less and less. He would often sleep out and return home on the sly. He said his work was so demanding that it was easier for him to sleep at Amar's, though he regretted not being able to chat with us as in the past. We told him however much we enjoyed his company he was under no obligation and shouldn't feel compelled to hold on to the room, but he said no, he hoped that in a little while everything would return to its former state. He felt secure as long as the room was his to use and the house key remained in his pocket. In all honesty I was worried. I couldn't talk to him naturally as I had at first, and I wondered how he would be warned, should the time come, of any danger, but I didn't dare ask. When I read of a serious confrontation between the French and the FLN in Tripoli I realized the incident had occurred during one of his prolonged absences. His behavior changed more and more. He would arrive late, after we'd gone to bed, and sometimes the doorman would tell us that he'd come home while we were out. I started feeling uncomfortable. Then one day he came to visit me. He told me the time had come to keep his word: he was leaving. The French had laid in wait for him in Tripoli, and he had barely managed to flee, his head gashed. The Frenchman who had fired at him was killed; he felt sorry for him because that person had been the father of a family. He went to pack his things and then approached me with his suitcase in his hand and asked me whether he could leave some of his belongings as a symbolic gesture and hold on to the key, because it was his lucky charm and he didn't want to feel that he was leaving never to return again. I couldn't refuse, even though I wasn't happy with the matter, but really, if I had known what was to happen in the future, I would have told him to keep the key forever. He thanked me and said, 'I hope, I'm certain we will see each other again.' I wished him well, and told him even though I had my doubts that we would ever meet again, I was certain we would hear of his accomplishments, because he was destined to become a leader of his country, like Habib Bourguiba, and he answered that a person never knows what awaits him in the future, everything comes from on high. We never saw him again.

"But at times, at night, I heard the sound of footsteps. We had no boarders then, and consequently I knew it could be none other than Khalil. I never left my room until I heard the front door closing. That was in March 1956. Later, one morning in June, I found the key in the entrance hall. Only the key. I then knew Khalil would never come back.

"Shortly thereafter the doorman told us the house was being watched and that someone had asked about us and our tenant. What sort of person was he? What did he do? Did he still live with us? Was he called Beni, or Benah, or Bella? The doorman answered that he had never heard such a name, although the man described seemed to be Khalil Khalid, except that he'd gone and neither he nor we knew where he had gone. Later on I found in our mailbox a postcard addressed to Ben Bella. It was strange, after what the doorman had recounted. So I turned to Amar, and he told me that Ben Bella was a close friend of Khalil and was expected to arrive in Egypt soon. But since Khalil had already left Egypt Amar would send Khalil the postcard, and he would in turn pass it on to Ben Bella.

"I was relieved to hear that Khalil had left. He always made sure to keep his word. The matter no longer weighed on me. Then came the Suez imbroglio, and we all felt so insecure. Then appeared those photos in *Paris Match* and the Sinai Campaign. . . . My poor son! Locked up in prison in the prime of his life." Mother was distraught. "Would you like to see his picture?"

She fetched a bag containing photographs of her dear ones, and from among the faces that surrounded my childhood days she extracted a sheet of paper from which, adorned in bold-colored green and red Arabic letters, there stared out a brownish and pleasant face, with a delicately lined, sensitive mouth and melancholic, deep eyes, conveying a cultivated, quiet splendor. The face in the mirror, wreathed in fire, was the face of my generation. . . . Mother said: "The Tunisians printed and distributed these pamphlets immediately after Ben Bella's incarceration was announced." She was so proud, as if she'd had a hand in this act of protest. She nodded her head: "Just imagine, in my eyes he was far too sensitive and dreamy to be a leader. I was certain that Amar was the leader."

"Did you hear from him after his incarceration?" I inquired.

"Only vaguely. I thought perhaps in prison they didn't give him books to read, and as a result it must have been infinitely more difficult for him to serve out his sentence. So I handed over a bundle of books to one of our Tunisians who was about to leave, and afterwards I received from Paris an unsigned postcard which said that our friend was so glad we had remembered him. We frequently spoke of him with our Tunisian friends. I suppose they were a bit upset at me when I said he was a true hero. They insisted that they too had engaged in dangerous activities and had sat in prison, but I answered that although they were undoubtedly good, even wonderful fellows, Ben Bella was more than just another patriot—for he had carved out a place for himself."

Mother asked: "Would you like me to give you his picture?" I said, yes. After all, this is the face of my generation that fought such a desperate struggle to be free, to be whole.

"Of one thing I'm sure," Mother said. "Ben Bella is not the sort of person who sits back complacently, not even in prison. He needs to read, to think, to examine things. When he is released, then it is possible that he will achieve his full stature. Maybe he needed this time, even this terrible fate. Who can really know? Aren't our lives amazing, any life, in which we meet and part and again meet, this life that never ends?"

We smiled at each other over the swarthy face between us.

*Translated from Hebrew by Gabriel Levin*

*Sixteen*

# Israel:

## *Ambivalent Levantine*

*The previous chapter, "Rebel, My Brother," describes the end of an era of Levantine coexistence in Egypt. This essay, the final installment of the "Generation of Levantines" cycle, shifts focus from the cultural interactions among Jews, Christians, and Moslems in the Levantine world of Kahanoff's youth, toward defining Levantinism as a social model to be applied within the Israeli context. In Israel by 1959, when this article was published, the terms* Levantine *and* Levantinization *had taken on negative implications—the threat of integration of Middle Eastern cultures into Israeli society. Here, and throughout her work, Kahanoff attempts to rehabilitate these concepts.*

*In this essay, which is more politically pointed than the previous selections in this volume, Kahanoff likens the treatment of Jewish immigrants from the Arab and Islamic worlds by the Israeli establishment to that of a colonized people. This essay predates, and presages, the political organization and mobilization of the Sephardi and Mizraḥi populace in Israel.*

In Beersheba, those who live by Western time do not usually travel by train, a cheap but time-consuming form of transportation; those for whom time counts less than money, do. Most of the passengers I observed from behind my newspaper belonged to the oriental communities. An old woman, probably from Kurdistan, came on at some new village along the route. Torn, dusty skirts, coarsened, bare feet, straggling hair caught in some headgear that looked like a soiled bandage, a blue stone against the evil eye pinned loosely to her bosom. Her entire luggage was an egg basket, tied up in rags. After hesitating to sit on the floor, she settled down on the seat facing me, and, feeling uncomfortable, brought her legs up and crossed them under her skirts, Arab fashion. To Israelis this is a familiar sight—most people would move away for fear of catching fleas, or worse.

A beggar-musician passed. Watery blue eyes behind thick glasses, a raincoat, good shoes—an immigrant from Poland, I surmised. The old woman's stiff rheumatic hands fished out a little hand-sewn purse and she called out, "Wait! Wait!" as she fumbled to open it. The beggar continued on his way as if he had neither seen nor heard. The old woman kept the coin in her hand and said: "I'll give it to him when he returns. Perhaps he was ashamed to take it."

A tense watchfulness spread among the passengers, most of them young Moroccans, whose eyes were fixed on the door through which the beggar would return. "Grandma," one of them exclaimed, "keep your money for those in need, for that beggar is richer than you. Look how he is dressed."

The old woman shook her head. "If he has to beg," she said, "his need is greater than mine."

I lowered my wall of print, remembering so many old ladies, my ancestors, who had this immeasurable richness which I had lost in my struggle to live in a world which was not theirs.

The beggar passed through the coach again, but deliberately turned in such a way that the old woman could not slip the coin into his pocket.

"You see?" the young Moroccans shouted with passion. "You see how they purposely offend us. It is below the dignity of even an Ashkenazi beggar to take alms from one of us blacks." One of the fellows, who wanted to bring the beggar back and force him to take the alms had to be restrained.

"Perhaps he thought I wanted to offend him," the old woman said. "Who are we to judge? Through us, God gives, and Him we cannot offend." She turned to the young boy sitting next to me and said, "You go. From a child he will not refuse."

"No. No. No," the boy protested. "I will not beg him to beg from me."

The old woman looked at me. "Please go. You are dressed like him, so from you he will accept."

"No," I said. "I am not one of them."

But the old woman slipped her coin into my hand, and I went searching for the blue-eyed beggar to give him what was not mine.

"L'habit fait le moine" (clothing makes the man), the French say.* I cannot escape from the culture represented by the clothes I wear, I thought. Back in my seat, I brought up the wall of print, my prison and refuge, and heard one of the Moroccan lads remark, "Among all of us, only this old woman has wisdom and compassion. What we had of it, we are losing in Israel, to become hard, acquisitive, and mean. Power, knowledge, money, we don't have, and charity we have lost. We have nothing much left, perhaps not even hope . . ."

I knew what they meant. This old woman did represent the last treasure of our Levantine inheritance. Few among us, unlike the illiterate old woman on the train, have this inner certitude, born of faith, that human suffering, whatever its cause, weighs with equal heaviness on all of us.

A typical Levantine in that I appreciate equally what I inherited from my oriental origins and what is now mine of Western culture, I find in this cross-fertilization, called disparagingly in Israel *Levantinization*, an enrichment and not an impoverishment. It is from this vantage point that I wish to try to define the complex interrelated malady of both Israel's Sephardic (Jews of oriental/Middle Eastern origin) and Ashkenazi (East European) communities.

To begin with, one must remember that the Jewish people kept its identity through generations of dispersal, although it acquired many characteristics of the peoples among whom it lived, and bore the scars of its struggle to survive as a Jewish minority. The Jewish people long ago divided into two main streams, one which flowed into the Christian Western world, and the other, a Levantine-Islamic world; and although they are intermixed in Israel, they still have distinct histories and characteristics, ways of living and feeling, as well as different problems and hopes.

* Kahanoff misquotes the saying. In French, it should read "l'habit *ne* fait *pas* le moine," idiomatically translated by the common English saying, "The clothes do *not* make the man."

The negative aspects of oriental Jewry have been widely, if not always fairly, investigated in Israel. They are the same negative aspects attributed to Moslem countries in general—a gap in industrial development, and a lack of professional, intellectual, and technological equipment necessary to compete in today's world. This is not a specific problem of oriental Jewry, but rather that of the whole non-Western world in a period of violent readjustment in the relations between people at various stages of technological development. The oriental Jew should have no shame in having to undergo this evolution—no more than do the Arab, African, or Asian nations. The Ashkenazi Jews—so quick to offer technical assistance around the world—should realize that this kind of assistance can better be deployed right here at home.

While unable to solve the problems of a more complex social structure, and to rid themselves of the poverty which plagued them, the old non-Western societies nevertheless enjoyed a high degree of communal cohesion, emotional support linked to ritual, a clear relationship between members of a family and their social group, all of which enveloped the individual. Even if it did limit personal development, it was acceptable because of a deeply ingrained philosophy of fatalism and dependence, but also because it answered deep instinctive needs of human nature. When this inner balance broke down under the impulse of imperialist conquest and colonization from the West, masses of people were torn from their communal way of life.

At first, the colonizer's culture appeared superior, because it seemed to have the tools, the material resources, and the intellect to rule efficiently, even though quite ruthlessly. The native society was usually not so much primitive as it was decayed or ineffectual in comparison to a more aggressive society, which for all its professed "liberalism," organized life in relation to material rather than moral needs. The distinction is important, because in our time most people undergoing this kind of social upheaval have a sense of having fallen from a higher degree of civilization rather than being elevated to a more advanced one, or, these two attitudes become confused in an effort to create an efficient society on a Western model, while trying to preserve values better suited to the precolonial era.

In the initial stage of contact between two nations at different levels of technological development the native elite undergoes an imitative and acquisitive phase in absorbing the ideas and techniques of the dominating culture, and in so doing, first rejects with a feeling of shame the values of its own society. But, with the new possibilities offered by cooperating with the colonizer, this group increases in numbers, in influence, and in its understanding of what constitutes the colonizer's power, and hence its superiority. Gradually this new elite, native in its origin, but Western, at least partially, in its formal education, becomes surer of itself, better able to reconcile its various components in a fairly harmonious and coherent whole. It then becomes more independent in its judgments of the West, more critical toward the ideals it proclaims but does not live up to. Also it becomes more appreciative of the values of the old society, which can then be reappraised with greater sympathy and firmness. The new elite becomes increasingly impatient to share power with the colonizers, and wishes to apply Western techniques for its own benefit, and no longer exclusively for the colonizer. Before long, the colonizers begin to ridicule what they regard as a superficial imitation of foreign ways, and to idealize and sentimentalize the old native cultures they have in fact destroyed.

When the new elite's hopes for the help and cooperation of the Western colonizer in bringing about the desired new social order are dashed, and its demands for reform are either postponed or the reforms are seen to be dishonestly applied, it becomes far more aggressive in competing for power and in acquiring direct leadership and responsibility in the name of a new national identity which the Western colonizer created. Not only does the mass of the colonized people follow the lead of the elite, but the victory over the foreign culture whets its appetite to achieve a rapid social transformation for its own advantage. Because it has compared its standard of living to that of the Western world, the newly independent elite no longer accepts those religious tenets which sanction poverty as irremediable and "God-ordained." Unfortunately not always do they realize that it is not yet ready for the mass diffusion of Western concepts, and that it does not as yet have a large, technically trained force, or the capital, the machinery, and the necessary social organization which would allow it to achieve a higher standard of living. In this rush for Westernization it is also often forgotten that the

Western world's glorious expansion resulted from an evolution lasting many centuries. Hence, the social upheaval and the attraction to totalitarian ideologies, spear-headed by the self-same Western-trained elite, but which in itself is often overwhelmed by the magnitude of the new problems to be solved.

*

In the Middle East context, it was the Levantinian who acquired the new culture, at first as something desirable but external to him, then as an integral part of his own being. He has been derided by the Westerner mostly because he represented both a danger and a challenge. For all his weaknesses and self-doubts, the Levantinian is a potentially successful crossbreed of two or more cultures in our times, capable of applying what he acquired to the transformation and reconstruction of his own society, and able to compete with the Westerner on his own terms. He then effects a swing back to his native origins, now highly idealized. The increasingly Levantinized Arab nationalist is such a crossbreed, who idealizes Islamic or Pharaonic greatness. Similarly the Jew, regarded as a foreigner, both in Europe and in the Middle East, proclaims his ancient origins. In fact, both Moslem and Jew are far from these ancient origins, and have no intention of resuscitating dead civilizations, but are able to fuse elements of various civilizations into new dynamic patterns, characteristic of the Middle Eastern people—among them the Jewish people—from antiquity to our present day.

All this has directly affected the oriental Jewish communities, which were an integral part of the Islamic world. They learned to use the advantages offered by the colonizing power and, in many cases, achieved a high degree of economic well-being and a higher social status, outside the old minority-community framework. They Westernized and created their own Levantine elite, as did, in fact, all the other minorities, far more quickly than the Moslem majority did. Many such communities around the Mediterranean basin had never completely lost touch with the Western world, through their fairly close contacts with other Jewish communities in that world and through Jewish emigration from Europe to the Middle East.

The accelerated Westernization started under the impetus of Crémieux and the Alliance Universelle Israélite,* which created efficient schools, propagated the ideals of the French Revolution, and instigated a movement of social and intellectual progress outside the ghetto and toward a Western way of life. The Alliance played a tremendous role in forming this Jewish elite, and broadened its base to include an ever greater number of people who were to play a dominant role in the countries where they lived. They were the ones who established commerce and industries and provided the much needed and well-trained technicians. This elite cooperated with the Western powers, at least the older generation did.

At the outset, this lack of a Middle Eastern Jewish elite in Israel mattered relatively little, for the dominant group of the new country was too intoxicated with its extraordinary victory and accomplishments to permit the rise of any rival leadership from among the newcomers, who themselves needed time to adjust to their changed environment and find their way in their new surroundings. The problems connected with the coexistence of people from different backgrounds living in the same national and institutional framework were made more acute by the lack of a communal elite, which might have provided leadership, or models of successful integration, in this period of transition.

The oriental Jewish community in Israel, with its lack of technical skills and insufficient basic education, was in a position that resembles a colonized people toward a dominant group of a different culture which holds power, imposes its concepts and forms of social organization, and disposes of and directs people to further its own ends in the name of its own ideals and goals. This means that the less technologically developed group has nothing to do but to learn, obey, adapt, and be absorbed or integrated into an existing structure, thus, presumably ideally, losing its own identity. The myth or hope of Jewish unity within the Jewish people in Israel has been so strong that this colonial aspect was blurred for both groups. The dominant group long denied that any problem existed, or that, if it did, it was all the fault of the newcomers.

* Adolphe Crémieux (1796–1880) was a French statesman and Jew who founded the Alliance Universelle Israélite in 1860.

The latter hoped that it would not only soon attain the highest possible level within the dominant group, but would also be fully accepted by them. At the same time, they did not spare criticism of the dominant group for not living up to the high ideals of the pioneering democracy they had inherited.

Indeed, after an initial period of imitation, passive acquisition, and acceptance, the oriental communities finally began to assert their own unique identity and demanded changes for their own benefit. Even in the absence of a Westernized oriental Jewish elite, which could have served as a bridge between these two main groupings, the process of Levantinization or cross-fertilization nevertheless continues. A new oriental communal identity is emerging, patterned neither on the Jewish past nor on the dominant group, which is beginning to develop an elite leadership able to compete with the latter. Because they have improved their standards of health, education, and income, the wish of these various oriental communities to progress more rapidly, to define and assert themselves, is gathering force. As in the colonial era, the pressures, frustrations, and the sense of having been excluded from the undeserved benefits and largesse dispensed by the dominant group, and the desire to make Israel more responsive to their needs, including the need for self-expression, have helped crystallize this new Levantine personality emerging in our midst. Communities which were set apart with some degree of hostility toward each other have lately begun to realize that they do have a common past; a somewhat different concept of Jewishness, which Zionist ideology in no way reflects; common goals; and realizable aspirations for the immediate future.

Israel is in the unique position of having this process of mutual influence and transformation take place within the same country: Levantine, due to its geographic location between East and West, and through the very mixture of its people. It can thus reconcile its two main component groupings into one dynamic, creative unity which, because it must fit together and fuse conflicting elements, can strive toward universality, as did the great Levantine (Byzantine and Islamic) civilizations of the past. They, too, represented a composite of peoples and cultures, indeed, the same as did Western Europe in its early formative period. The best thing that has happened in Israel is that the oriental communities are no longer passive but vitally interested in what they will make of their future in Israel. The path ahead is far from smooth, but the real catastrophe would have been if those communities had not had the impulse to grow, reach maturity, question, challenge, influence, and transform the wider reality of Israel.

This state of unrest, which is not limited to one community, is full of hopeful possibilities, even if it still represents only a sporadic and unorganized impetus. If only the dominant group would understand and sympathize with this process of self-liberation, and would be mature enough not to regard every criticism as callous ingratitude, while itself directing criticism at others. And, if only it would recognize that assimilation is a two-way process, that change is both natural and necessary, and that to make it possible, it must discard many of its own prejudices and misconceptions and renounce its almost exclusive monopoly over its party and state institutions. Then only would this evolution take place in a society not torn by internal strife, mutual suspicions, and fears. The more this process of change is consciously desired and controlled, the better it will succeed; the greatest danger is that, owing to its own prejudices, habits of thought, and a desire to cling to its position of authority, the ruling group will resist change or, worse, give way arbitrarily to the most vociferous and least educated pressure groups.

The hope for active cooperation is very much alive in what is now called the Sephardic community, but it is possible only if the Ashkenazi community abandons some of its negative attitudes and narrow-mindedness. Among these negative attitudes, I would list racial prejudice first, and an intolerance toward anything different, which often translates itself into an odd combination of bad manners and self-glorification—defense mechanisms which disguise a deep-seated sense of injury and inferiority, and a lack of confidence. (But this takes time to find out.) I presume that the masses of European Jews needed both aggressiveness and aggrandizement to defend their egos in a society where they were treated as foreign and inferior, and worse, where they were actively persecuted. In their isolation, they believed that they were the one and only Jewish people. The Eastern European Jews in America, as well as in Israel, almost never realized that Jewish communities existed, and even flourished, elsewhere, and that there was no reason in the world why the members of these communities should speak Yiddish.

I once got lost in a Jewish neighborhood in Chicago and asked my way of a passerby, who answered in Yiddish. When I told him I did not understand, he asked me suspiciously what I was doing in that neighborhood if I wasn't Jewish and, if I was, how come I pretended not to know my *mama loschen* [mother tongue]. I launched into some explanations, at which he remarked, "You're kidding, lady! You don't look like no Arab to me." Before I knew it, he had attracted a crowd, interested in the phenomenon I represented, and after having found out whom I was going to see and why, and that I might therefore be Jewish in spite of it all, I was directed to the house I was seeking. I had found this puzzling, until I realized that our two historical communities were almost completely ignorant of one another. Many people in Egypt believed that most Ashkenazim were dangerous terrorists and revolutionaries and attributed this presumed violence to the fact that they were late converts to Judaism from savage "Khazar tribes." I called it quits in Chicago.

The fact is that abroad, Jewish solidarity is paramount. Among young Jewish university students in America we soon discovered much that we had in common—our own intellectual sympathies and aspirations, the gap between two generations that did not have the same culture, the ambition of our parents, and the conflict that arose with them the moment the children began realizing those ambitions and drew away from the family. These second-generation American Jews had lost some of their parents' aggressive defensiveness but still were fighting for status in American society. "Progressive-minded" as a minority, they made every effort to combat discrimination against all other minorities, since they would be directly affected by racial prejudice. They wanted to Americanize with no sense of guilt, as we in Egypt, for instance, had wanted to Europeanize. In so doing they had discarded many elements of their Jewish culture, which did not appear to them as the pinnacle of world culture. Many tended to be pro-Zionist so as to solve the Jewish problem.

People who came to Israel from Eastern Europe with similar backgrounds made far fewer attempts to overcome or understand their own prejudices, because even if they no longer were the absolute majority in terms of numbers, they were still the dominant group in terms of power. In Palestine, the early Zionists were a positive, though somewhat intolerant and narrow-minded force, and it was Bialik,* I believe, who joked that what he disliked about Arabs was that they reminded him of Sephardic Jews. In the case of many of his contemporaries, there was no external pressure to make them overcome prejudice against another culture or people—quite the contrary, the pressure was to accentuate Zionist Jewishness in the face of the Arab and the non-Zionist Sephardic Jew. The Zionists conceived of Judaism as a nationality, the Sephardic Jews, as a religion based on Messianic hope. Because they were geographically closer to Palestine, and culturally and ethnically to the other people of the Middle East, they did not need to consider the return to Zion as a physical necessity for the survival of an exiled and persecuted people who had to reconquer their lost birthright and pride. Also, the Sephardic Jews were often reproached for not having been Zionists, without realizing that Zionism was no more relevant in Cairo, Baghdad, or Constantinople at the turn of the twentieth century than it was in Vienna or Berlin in the "assimilationist" period.

These attitudes were perfectly understandable in their historical context, and it was normal that Zionism, as a revolutionary movement, was intolerant of anything different from itself. It is a shame that these veteran Zionists so often refused the opportunity to know the Levantine Middle East from the inside, instead of clinging to the misconceptions of the Europe they had fled. They seem to have assumed that there was a complete void in the region between the destruction of the Temple up to the Zionist era. They came and lived in the Middle East as foreigners, with a different culture and language. That was perhaps inevitable, but what is more surprising is that for all the remarkable accomplishments of Zionism in creating a viable Jewish state, so many of these old defensive attitudes continue by force of habit.

The suspicion and intolerance toward newcomers from oriental countries derives, in part, from the attitude toward the Sephardic community which prevailed half a century ago. The result is that even

* Hayim Nahum Bialik (1873–1934) was a major Hebrew poet who is often referred to as the national poet of Israel.

the third- or fourth-generation sabra of oriental origin has not been completely "absorbed," so that one cannot claim, as so many old-timers do, that the problem will not exist in the next generation, a dangerously wishful thinking.

Eastern European Jewry was too hard-pressed, too involved in its struggle to be of help, or even to be able to understand the problems, interests, and evolution of another community, just as the oriental communities were either too remote, too poor, or too involved in their efforts to adapt to the modern world to be totally concerned with what Herzl or Pinsker wrote.* But, after all, years have passed, Israel exists, commands the loyalty of its citizens of whatever country of origin, and has helped crystallize a feeling of Jewish identity and unity. The time has come for these two broad currents of Jewish history to be more objectively appraised, particularly in relation to each other.

A critical reappraisal of Zionist texts and actions, in the light of the total experience of the Jewish people and the history of not only Europe but of the Middle East, may open a rich new vein to young scholars and sweep away the stale old platitudes, refreshingly. After all, this was done in America toward the Founding Fathers without destroying the Republic.

The Ashkenazi community in Israel, in identifying itself completely with the struggles leading to the establishment of the state, considered the state as its child. It is now imprisoned by a kind of parent complex, aggrieved when the child in growing up asserts its independence. Were it more firmly assured of its accomplishments, its attitude would be more rational and less emotional, and more understanding of the growing pains of another, newer section of the population. The perpetual bragging about the sacrifices of the pioneering generation, whom the newcomer sees living quite comfortably as an upper class in spite of the Socialist trappings, makes the latecomers feel not so much deficient and guilty, but resentful. The kibbutz is definitely not proletarian compared

* Theodor Herzl (1860–1904) is considered the founder of modern political Zionism. His writings include *The Jewish State* (1896) and *The Old New Land* (1902). Leo Pinsker (1821–1891), a Zionist leader, published the famous pamphlet "Auto-Emancipation" in 1882.

with the *ma'abara*. Its members know where the next meal comes from and represent, paradoxically, a conservative force which defends the status quo together with collective property, and above all, cling to an ideology rooted in the Socialism of Eastern Europe of some fifty years ago.

It is also quite understandable that after years of danger and deprivation old-timers now wish to enjoy more comforts, but the moment society in general is no longer egalitarian, it loses its appeal for those who believe they have rights to conquer rather than to defend. This higher standard of living and the old-timers' social prestige (but not their provincialism and intolerance of whatever is different from itself) can be accepted as the reward for past achievement, but is not defensible when they and their descendants claim that they still live according to pioneering precepts.

Today, paradoxically, the hard labor of building up new settlements and developing the arid Negev devolve, in fact, upon newcomers, most of whom are of oriental origin. The old-timers of Ashkenazi origin, because of their experience, constitute the managerial class. Although the harsh conditions of the new settlements are softened by the welfare state, the young Oriental who aspires to social recognition is too often denied appreciation by his fellow citizens for the tremendous role he plays. In spite of all appeals, it is not the settled population on the whole which goes to live in and build up the land, but the newcomer, who surmounts his first fears and disappointments to grapple with its starkness, and who, in doing so, has a claim to his country's gratitude.

There may be no reason why the sabra who has the means to study at a university should not do so, and it is normal that he should aspire to knowledge, position, comfort, and money and enjoy the opportunities his parents created for him. But he cannot at the same time be presented as an idealist as well as an austere pioneer. For the Moroccan youth, for instance, who works in Sdom, in the Negev mines, or on the building of a water pipeline, this can only create frustration and a sense of having been wronged.

Less self-idealization and stricter intellectual honesty and criticism would help in bringing together these two segments of our youth who, whatever happens, must continue living together in the same country. Should they join each other, help each other, through direct contact to free themselves from the myths which they both, in different forms, have inherited from their different pasts, they might start a fruitful pioneering era of their own. The sabra, who half consciously rebels against the parent generation, often wants to live in a spiritually wider, less intolerant Israel, but he or she has also inherited many negative prejudices and fears from his or her parents.

Like the parent generation, the sabra is often narrow-minded with outmoded myths about "Levantinization," and he fears the "lowering of cultural standards" by the newcomer. The latter has been presented to the sabra as a potential threat to all that has been built, not as a partner, humanly as well as materially, in what still has to be built. This indeed is the most promising task facing Israeli youth of whatever origin. For this, the sabra too has to examine his own complexes, including the self-image of a "liberated Jew" without any "diaspora complexes," which he does not at all seem to be, and a sense of inferiority regarding the Western world, or his aggressive contempt toward Jewish communities in the diaspora. He must rethink his reasons for feeling cooped up in a small embattled country, which is neither part of Europe, nor of the Middle East, nor even really Jewish, since he has thrust aside all Jewish experience in two thousand years of exile with a feeling of rebellion and shame. This leaves a sectarian nationalism as the only acceptable solution, which a young person, aspiring to a wider, more generous conception of himself in relation to the world, cannot countenance without an unpleasant feeling of being cut off from a fuller and possible development not only as an Israeli, but as a human being.

The first step in reaching this greater maturity is to become conscious of racial prejudice when it is there and work at getting rid of it as something unnecessary and harmful. It is after all not the oriental Jew who called himself "black," because it never occurred to him before coming to Israel that his coloring was not "normal," as indeed it was in the Middle East, peopled by Arabs, Armenians, Greeks, Italians, etc. A mixture of races in the Jewish stock should therefore be accepted by both communities as natural, and even as a positive asset, since the sturdiest stocks are the crossbreeds, and not the purebred. The myth of white superiority should be discarded as brutishly senseless when applied by one section of this very same people to the others.

The further myth of the Israeli Jew as the defender of a superior European culture impedes the creation of a single Jewish people in Israel, free to develop an identity and personality of its own. The Eastern European Jews and their descendants, for all they have accomplished in Israel, play the part of the superior European, because it seems they are still ashamed to recognize that they derive from a subculture and they still have not overcome their feeling of inferiority toward the brilliant, richer life of such centers of culture as Vienna, Berlin in the old days, London, Paris, and New York in the present. Their past still seems too painful. This inferiority complex is totally unnecessary for a people free in their own country and free to use the widest eclecticism in creating their own, original, many-stranded culture. This sense of inferiority is so deep that it has led first to curious imbroglios between Eastern European and German Jews and, later, to a no less odd idealization of the "Anglo-Saxon" immigrant—whose grandmother was often a fine but almost totally illiterate woman from a village in the Russian Pale of Settlement. In England and America one speaks of "English-speaking peoples"—representing a community of language and culture—and not of Anglo-Saxons, representing a nonexistent racial community descended from Germanic tribes which invaded the British Isles in premedieval times. The "Anglo-Saxon" immigrants themselves are often so insecure in their "Nordic" ancestry that they do not joke about it. But as for newcomers undergoing a similar, equally painful cultural transformation in the present, nothing would help more toward integration than a dose of good old Jewish humor, instead of our lofty national ideas covering up, as best they can, our big and little human foibles.

This need to identify with a culture or people considered superior and the inhibition to draw from this and many other cultures with an independent, critical mind are characteristic of the first, negative phase of the Levantinism which is so feared in Israel because so many people are afraid to recognize it in themselves. The old sense of inadequacy has caught almost everyone in Israel playing at being more "European" than the next fellow, without noticing the absurdity of it all, much as one did in Cairo thirty or so years ago. The "real" European, at least, has far fewer inhibitions about admiring, enjoying, absorbing, drawing from many other cultures. In France, for instance, there is a wide movement of interest in comparative religions—Christianity, Judaism, Islam—with particular emphasis on the latter and on the young generation of Moslem writers, while to the average Israeli the picture of Islam is still that of a paradise full of virgins promised to the faithful. Few want to know anything about Islam's history and accomplishments, including its appeal to many races, its lack of prejudice, and its extraordinary tolerance in the past. They still hold to a grossly distorted image current in Europe fifty or so years ago.

This "European" obsession is so strong that many old-timers protest that they "do not want to become Arabs," as if there were no other choice. They consider intermarriage between the young of different Jewish communities as a near catastrophe and express the hope that Israel, with its lively landscape, so harmoniously unique unto itself, should become a little Switzerland. Bulldozers erase delicate contours to give rise to buildings which can be seen anywhere in the world and have no particular relevance as an expression of this land and people except that they are "modern." The charming old parts of Jaffa rot away because we cannot accept their "alien" beauty. Despite this frenzied building activity, Tel Aviv does not look like a "little Paris," but like a dozen other Mediterranean cities, nonchalant, dirty, pleasure-seeking, with crowded sidewalk cafés and pretty women parading in the latest fashion—in a word, Levantine, much of it mixed with the drive and energy of a diverse, active, intense people.

The negative aspect of Levantinism is something the oriental Jew has not been alone in generating. Israel could be Levantine in a more constructive sense by assembling its tremendous richness of backgrounds and cultures to create an art, a style of thought and living, a personality more truly its own. For this, an active, conscious intellectual and moral reappraisal of what makes Israel would open new paths. There is nothing to fear from this type of Levantinization, to which we are destined by our very origins and composition, except this inhibiting fear itself. In effecting this new cultural synthesis, there is no model but what we make of ourselves by living together and attempting to find workable solutions to the problems confronting us. Our various pasts cannot be changed, but none was valueless since some impulse brought us all, through different roads, to live in the same house. We tend often to be driven by the obscure resentments this past has left in us, when a detached, objective sympathy could bring us closer to a greater esteem for ourselves and others. For this past was not without its pride and its beauty.

The European Jews in Israel have brought with them a wide experience in technology and science and they have created institutions which attempted to reconcile economic needs with a just social organization more responsive to other human needs. But these frameworks need not be so rigid, as if all the answers had been given, allowing for no possible change. Between conformity and rebellion there is place for adaptation, mutual influence, and acceptance—for growth. To those who must make a cultural transfer in order to adjust economically to the modern world, this margin of freedom and self-expression becomes increasingly important as they get closer in their way of living and in their ambitions to those of the dominant group, because in the process they become more self-assured in their personalities.

Our national entity is in the making; it cannot be poured into a mold and come out as identical little statues. Because in a living society there are always a large number of defective pieces which live, react, suffer, hope, rebel, and cannot be disposed of. But the old and traditional leadership is wasteful and limited so much that it cannot survive. But as it recedes, no one should be made to believe that this transfer to a technological society itself can bring happiness.

Not only are the oriental communities changing their way of living and to some extent forming groups of a mixed culture, but the dominant group is forced, through their pressure, to revise many of its conceptions; particularly among the young, it would appear that they are awakening to a new independence of judgment and new and wider interests. The sabras too ask questions and seek answers which are not always those of their fathers.

That this transformation is happening, although it may be painful, is healthier than continued subservience to the ideals of a dominant group, particularly in a democracy which prides itself on realizing, as a social reality, the egalitarian ideals of the Jewish ethos. This means that in Israel the dominant group cannot sentimentalize, as did the colonizers of the past, about old native cultures while exploiting them as a source of cheap labor. There is no choice but to help those unacquainted with Western skills to acquire them, and the non-European element itself desires this. Its protest is based on the feeling that it is not given full opportunity for doing so, or for solving the many problems of its adaptation to the modern world connected with this culture change. But, as the European feared the Levantine who had successfully bridged the gap between two cultures, the dominant group in Israel seems uneasy about the formation of a young Levantinized elite which would pull together people of various origins, including the Israeli-born, drawn together by a likeness in ideas, tastes, interests, and goals rather than by country of origin or party affiliation. The parties will have to be a reflection of the new population and its state of mind, but the impulse is to come from people who, in defining themselves and their aspirations, may crystallize a still unformed public opinion.

Keeping some communal ties—occasionally speaking the languages of one's past, even if it is Arabic rather than Yiddish, Russian, or German and to express something of oneself—no longer seems uncivilized or vaguely treasonable, just because it resembles another kind of community now groping for self-expression, as did the old Yishuv in its time.

*

The well-established old-timers in Israel often express the view that there is a kind of battle being waged that, if the Ashkenazi does not win, and if Israel does not preserve its essence, not only as a Jewish state but also as a stronghold of Western civilization, then Israel will become "Levantine," disintegrate or "sink to the level" of the surrounding Arab states, and in this way will be swallowed up by them. This leaves out the possibility of active cooperation, which may face tensions and crises but which includes all those concerned with the living search for an ideal applied to the reality of everyday life. The wider our concept of Jewish or Israeli identity, the more strongly will people have the feeling that they have something that is theirs to defend, not only through arms, but through a clear, dynamic ideal, which can be respected for its independence, integrity, and originality, regardless of the doubts it is bound to provoke.

The Arab states have also made great mistakes in underestimating the value of Levantinization and they, too, have reached an impasse because of this confusion. In their reaction against the West they have stressed Arab nationalism and Islam, while no longer being the least orthodox or strictly observant in their religion, much as has been the case with a majority of the Jews in Israel. But, like us, they too have been influenced by the European concept of the Levantine, who is now considered in the Arab countries as a despised crossbreed which must be eliminated. And this at a time when these countries are modernizing and therefore are becoming more Levantine in their social structure, thought, and aspirations, as they must adapt to and adopt Western concepts and techniques. Islam at the height of its influence was a Levantine empire, for it was shaped by the civilizing influence of Byzantium on the Arabian conqueror, and its attraction for such vast numbers of people was not due simply to a power enforced by arms. Even when Byzantium fell, the Greek in the old Levant never lost his identity, nor did the Jew. They not only survived, but in spite of tensions accepted each other and were accepted by Islam. Even the most fantastic tales of the Arabian Nights recognize four types of subjects: Moslem, Christian, Jew, and Sun-Worshipper, and the Moslem religion concedes that every honest man or woman can be saved, whatever his or her faith. This old tolerance has given way to the modern passion for a monolithic unity, or for a type of unity which excludes all variation. But it is not impossible that the old deep-rooted habits shall one day come to the fore when everyone gets tired of upheavals, bloody purges, wars, hatred, and revolution. Then cognizance will be taken of new national identities replacing without extinguishing the old religious or communal ones.

Israel, of course, cannot go it all the way alone, nor can it make peace with avowed enemies still in the explosive stage of self-creation. But, in the measure that it does not fear its own Levantinization, it may pave the way for some kind of future peace, wherein many people can cooperate—if not always actively, at least more tolerantly of their differences. Israel "wins" if it becomes the model of a well-integrated Levantine country, which refuses neither side its inheritance in creating its own values.

Much of today's history is born of the hidden rebellions of our youth, and to one who so well remembers their genesis, and the struggle involved in keeping one's own identity, with a stubbornness characteristic of Jews and Levantines, it is perhaps not forbidden to hope that if the young today aspire to friendship and a fuller, more harmonious development of themselves in a world that is friendly and not torn by strife, something of this can reflect itself in the world of tomorrow. To help toward this is a task not unworthy of a generation of Levantines, scattered across many borders, not only in the Middle East, who have now reached maturity and remember with tenderness the peace of an old world of serenity, that of our ancestors, whose inheritance we, too, need no longer fear to accept.

## *Seventeen*
# To Remember Alexandria

*Unlike the other examples of Kahanoff's fiction, this short story engages with both the lost past of Egyptian Jewish life and the realities of contemporary Israel. Published in 1976 in the Israeli women's magazine* La-Isha, *this story is set in the years between the 1967 and 1973 Arab-Israeli wars. Antonia Ferrar, a middle-aged Jewish woman born in Alexandria and living in Italy, is battling cancer. During a recuperative visit to Israel, she encounters a young Israeli pilot, Josh. The unlikely romance between the frail, aging Levantine, nostalgic for the past, and the patriotic Israeli youth, looking toward the future, develops against the backdrop of Israel's dramatic military victories in 1967, which as Josh expresses, thrust Israel into the Levant.*

Ever since he was a boy, Josh loved this beach, the wide soft curve of the bay, flanked to the right by the promontory jutting out into the sea. He loved it best in the fall, when the summer vacationers had gone, and there lingered a gentle, reflective luminosity that softened the sharp outlines of this Mediterranean landscape: Asia Minor, really, neither Europe nor the East, but the place where they endlessly confronted one another, repulsion and attraction inextricably mixed. He remembered when the kibbutz children had come down to the beach, how alien they had seemed, those small Arab boys, mending the nets spread among the scraggly palm trees; alien, wild, yet native—native in a way kibbutz youngsters could never be, he had felt, for their parents were pioneers from Russia and Poland who had come to redeem their ancient homeland.

He had wondered at the strangeness of it, that they, the kibbutz-born children, were named after the cactus, *tsabarim*, while it was really the Arabs who were natives in that wild prickly way. He had felt a grudge against the founding generation. As if, having discarded their Eastern European ghetto culture, their children, on this land, were bound to return to the wilderness. "Sweet inside, prickly outside," the parents had defined them, but as a boy, Josh had wondered why the pioneers could not have named their children after some cultivated native fruit—the pomegranate, for instance, juicy, ruby red, full of secret life juices.

Well, the fishermen had gone. Some of their children, now grown men, were engaged in the terrorists' hit-and-miss war against Israel. Feeling perhaps toward the half-remembered kibbutz children the same jealousy, obscure, repressed, which he had felt toward them, but in reverse; each to the other both native and alien, incomprehensible.

Josh climbed the cliff. Down below, among the rocks, washed by the sea, great slabs of stone and broken columns bespoke what had existed long before his parents had settled in the kibbutz, a few miles up the Carmel range. Caesarea was close by on this stretch of coast where each civilization had toppled under the next to come. With time, their remains blended: Persian, Greek, Roman, Byzantine, Turkish. Only the Jewish presence was different, different in its very essence, its hold precarious yet stubborn, maintained through desperate victories and the mesh of memories that linked this people to this land, present to them even when they were absent from it. "Nobody will erase the history we are making here," Josh thought, and in his anger, kicked a stone. "Throw us into the sea, would they? Well, if they didn't know this was a people who returned, here to stay, too bad for *them*."

June 1967—he had taken off from his base nearby, and the land of Israel emerging from the transparent mist had shone with a beauty so resplendent that it hurt. Flying low, almost grazing the rooftops, he had thought of the many families he knew in these modest suburban homes where women kept guard, alone with their children. The faint shadow of the plane cast on the intense blue of the sea, fringed with emerald, lapping the golden beach . . . Not all his friends had returned alive. And yet, the war was not really over. Perhaps would never be . . .

What was this bundle on the edge of the cliff? Madras slacks, neatly folded. Boy or girl, he couldn't tell; they dressed so much alike these days, especially the coordinated youngsters from abroad. But Madras indicated a more conservative taste. He doubted she was an Israeli. She? So he thought the invisible person down there might be a she? Perhaps the lady he had run into, coming down the Zikhron Ya'akov road almost at sunrise, on his way to his base. He had honked, and she had skipped to the side of the road, throwing away the flowers she was chewing. A handsome, graceful woman, elegant in a restrained way. He had stopped. Her brown green-speckled eyes had appraised him coolly, amused. He had asked in English, "May I drop you somewhere?"

"Are you dropping or picking? I'm not sure I approve of either." She smiled at him, her finely chiseled mouth ironic, yet tender.

The play of words, her composure confused him, annoyed him. He almost drove off, in a huff, but something about her smile, her eyes, held him. A kind of defiant lassitude, a quivering grace. She had the appeal of some women, proud of their independence, who did not renounce their femininity, but were distrustful of it. Her eyes seemed to say, "You're thinking, young man, that here's a presentable woman in her forties, rather lonely, more than a little scared. You're absolutely right! But there's a pride in me, you see, so much stronger than I am! It just won't let me make a fool of myself with a boy of twenty."

There was a kind of mockery in her smile, whether at him or herself, he couldn't tell. She had bowed, with mock formality, saying, "Thanks anyway," and picked her way down the hill, not caring in the least whether the thistles scratched her leg.

She had intrigued him, this early riser, who confronted the dawn so truthfully, without a trace of make-up on her face, and he had watched out for her when he traveled the Zikhron road. He had been on night duty, but wasn't sleepy. Exhilarated, rather. He'd wait to see whether the lady he thought Italian was the owner of the slacks. She was totally unlike Tsippy, unlike the kibbutz women of his mother's generation, square and solid in their ankle-high laced boots and white aprons, unlike the stolid German Jewish ladies with cropped gray hair, checkered no-nonsense dresses, and folksy necklaces of beans, carved wood, and Hebron glass, resolute nature lovers who stomped these hills.

It was the Italian lady! She emerged from behind the rocks, a Madras shirt over her bathing suit, her bag slung over her shoulder. A very nice pair of legs. Her foot stirred the sand in the small pools enclosed in the rocks. Tickling crabs, was she? As if aware of a presence, she turned round, saw him, shrugged in annoyance, and oddly, buttoned her shirt up to her collar. She tied on her sandals. Hesitated. To go round the promontory, or climb up the steep cliff, she seemed to ask herself, her head thrown back, gauging the height. She decided there was no point going all the way round to avoid him since she'd have to get her slacks anyway.

He stood his ground, his hands on his hips. She started up but it was clear to Josh she had embarked on an impracticable course, and also that something impeded her movements. He shouted, his hand cupped around his mouth, "To the right there's a narrow ledge where you can hang on to the rocks."

She shouted at him, "Thank you, again! But wouldn't you rather go away?"

"No," he said firmly. "That's a bad spot. So do as I tell you."

"Ay, ay, captain," she called out, mockingly saluting. But followed his advice. Halfway up, she seemed to have trouble with her right arm, unable to go on.

"Hold on, I'll be right there," Josh called out, and in three leaps was down, steadying himself on the rock above her. "Give me your hand. First the left, then the right. There's nothing to it." He could see the beads of sweat on her forehead and upper lip.

"I can't make it. I just can't. Oh, let go, let me go!"

"Don't be silly! Just relax," Josh said sharply.

It was a bit tricky, but he was back on the cliff, and with a backward jerk, swung her up, dumping her rather unceremoniously on the ground. She let out a gasp of pain.

"Are you all right?"

"Yes, yes, thank you . . . I . . . I had a dizzy spell." She forced a smile. "Middle-aged women have no right, really, embarking on idiotic adventures, to be rescued by Israeli pilots, who surely have more important things to do. Even during the cease-fire."

"How do you know I am a pilot?"

"I noticed the wings on your visor, the day you stopped to pick me up. It was in the back of your car."

"Well. Well. An observant lady!"

She picked up her slacks, and slipped them on, embarrassed. She wasn't left-handed, he noticed, and inquired, "What's the matter with your right arm? Did you have a cramp? Yes? Why don't you take your shirt off? It's drenched with sweat. A swim will refresh you. You know how to swim?"

"I'd rather not, thank you." Her hands trembled slightly as she gathered her long, light brown hair, which had come loose, into a scarf. She remarked, impertinently, "Your English isn't bad. But you make typical Israeli mistakes. Particularly in regard to the infinitive. Your usage of it must be a literal translation from the Hebrew."

"You are an English teacher?" Josh was a bit disappointed. "Anyway—a lady of great temerity, who overestimates her power." He blushed at the clumsiness of his remark, furious at himself, her teasing.

"Don't be embarrassed! Please. I'm the one who should be! Indeed, there comes a time when a woman should not overestimate her power. Definitely not. Relax! I'm terrified by those bristling, bushy, eyebrows of yours. You must have a dreadful temper . . ."

Josh smiled. "I can also be very sweet."

She laughed. "I know. A sabra. Prickly outside, sweet inside. Still it is the spikiest fruit in the whole Middle East. Incidentally, I'm not a teacher, but an accredited interpreter and translator. Simultaneous translations for international organizations. The Common Market, UNESCO, FAO, the ILO, that sort of thing.* I suppose my training has made me a bit pedantic about language."

They walked down toward the beach.

"How did you come from Zikhron? That is where you are staying, isn't it?"

"Yes. A taxi comes down at nine, full of ladies who take a solemn health dip in the sea. We're picked up at noon. Sharp."

"Allow me to run you up in my car. It was written in the stars I'd give you a lift."

* The Food and Agriculture Organization (FAO) and International Labor Organization (ILO) of the United Nations.

"What star, I wonder?"

"My lucky star, of course."

She blushed deeply as young girls no longer did. "Well, Mr. . . . Mr. . . . ?"

"Josh."

"Just Josh? You can never be too careful in the IDF I suppose.* How do you do, Mr. Just Josh? My name is Antonia Ferrar."

"A beautiful name . . . I thought you were Italian!" He would have liked to ask her if she was Jewish, but didn't. In Europe, he had learned, one didn't ask people personal questions. But then, what did one talk about, how did one get to know people if one didn't ask personal questions? They walked down the hill in silence, and at last he asked, "Are you alone? Or with some friends? And where are you staying in Zikhron?"

"I'm alone. Staying in Beit Daniel."

"Isn't that a little boring and old-fashioned for a woman of the world like you? All those aged professors and their ladies, speaking German?"

She laughed. "But I am old-fashioned, too, you know. It's a beautiful place, and quiet. I needed the rest. Would you mind waiting a few minutes? I'll tell the ladies not to wait for me."

As he started the car, Josh asked, "What draws you to hills, cliffs, rocks?"

She smiled, a little mysteriously. "This is a kind of parting."

"A parting? From what?"

"Does one know what one parts from in life until it has departed? One's youth, for instance. Or a great love. I . . . I was born in Alexandria, grew up there. But I can't go back to Alexandria. Nor do I really want to. The Alexandria I knew is dead. So I came to Israel as the closest thing to home. I wanted to see this side of the Mediterranean once more. On the European side sunsets are all wrong. One never sees the sun sink below the sea, never feels one's heart sink with it. I missed my sunset blues. Here, as in Europe, the stars are so close, so luminous. I wanted to see again a flying comet and make a wish. Even if I know wishes seldom come true. Wanted to see again that green streak of light in the sky, after sunset. See again these beaches, the tiny crabs scuttling

* Israeli Defense Forces (IDF).

under the crevices of the rocks. The incandescent intensity of sea and sky. They don't need us humans, to be. Simply to *be*. Somehow, it's comforting. They exist beyond the bloody froth of history, indifferent to what human beings create and destroy. Do the waves care about the ruins they roll over? But, as a pilot, an Israeli, you're bound to take a more optimistic view of human history."

"When did you leave Alexandria?" Josh inquired. He was asking questions after all.

"Oh, long ago. In 1948. I knew Alexandria was doomed. Or at least, we were."

"So you settled in Italy?"

"That would have been too simple! No. I married a German Jewish surgeon, precise, efficient. We settled in San Diego. A raw, fantastically ugly place. We had a daughter. We divorced. My daughter has a doctorate in chemistry. Teaches in a college in Colorado. Has three kids, a physicist husband. She's very much at home in the brave new world. The antipodes of Alexandria."

"So tell me about *your* Alexandria."

She said, dreamily, as someone too long alone, who needed to speak. "It smelled of salt marshes, flowers, dust, rot. San Diego was no less corrupt, but smelled only of money, oil, and booze. Alexandria was a city where Greek and Jew met to create the frail miracle of civilization. Constantinople was once such a place. Every few hundred years, the Levant flowers in one city. Much like those cactuses which produce just one, magnificent, infinitely complicated, short-lived blossom. The modern world has no patience for that sort of thing; it forces growth, in quantity. The Alexandria I knew was very nearly that event's latest incarnation. But it didn't have the time to flower before being destroyed. The effort of generations to push back the lethargy and fatalism of the desert, they came to naught. My great-grandfather had come from Italy, at the invitation of the khedive to establish a modern hospital—modern by the standards of the time, of course. We had four generations of doctors, in my family. But all that is gone. And I wondered if Israel would take over where Alexandria left off. Israel is hard and vital, where we were not. Really believes in its survival, where we perhaps did not. The Levant must always be saved by one of its minorities, against itself."

Josh was startled that she should echo thoughts expressed in discussions he sometimes had with his friends. He remarked, "Our parents came from Russia and Poland to build a Jewish state. They thought of rescuing the Jewish people, not the Levant. But perhaps this last war has involved us in the Levant more than we knew or wanted. . . . You remind me of Durrell's *Alexandria Quartet*. You have something of Justine, and something of Clea, too. Does Durrell reflect the Alexandria you knew?"

"You mean you have actually read Durrell? You, an Israeli pilot?"

"Why not? Do you take us to be a new breed of barbarians? The Cossacks of the air, cum technology?" Josh was angry.

Her lovely mouth quivered. "I didn't mean that at all. But you all look so—healthy, so sure of yourselves, so cocky, never doubting . . . I couldn't imagine . . . people here might be more complex than they appear."

"Sure! What do you think? We have our existential problems, too."

They laughed. "Well, tell me about your existential problem."

Josh frowned, explaining, "Those of us who were born here are fascinated by—how shall I say—not the Arab-Moslem world, so much, but by all that happened here, that is beneath, behind, and around us. You've perhaps heard of the Israeli craze for archeology? We seek the traces of our past, but it turns up mixed with those of so many others! Canaanite jars, Persian coins, Greek inscriptions, Roman amphitheaters, Byzantine mosaics. What you call the Levant stirs beneath the Israel our parents created. It does in Caesarea. But nowhere perhaps more than in the Old City of Jerusalem, now open to us—by right of conquest we became aware of all that happened in these parts, between the ancient Israel and the new. It's a dimension we lack, which tempts, fascinates, repels, intrigues. How can I explain it? Masada is one temptation. You've never heard of it? It's about the last-ditch Jewish resistance against the Romans in Herod's abandoned palace, by the Dead Sea. They killed themselves, men, women, children. Then the commander, the last survivor, killed himself. They did not surrender. The other temptation is . . . Alexandria. To compose differences in the Levantine way. The Jerusalem we call reunited is an unresolved confrontation not only between Arab-Moslem and Jew, but between the Levant and Israel. The temptation is within us, always to be overcome. You are on the other side of the coin—that Mediterranean world we once belonged to. Will you visit Jerusalem with me, Mrs. Ferrar? Antonia Ferrar of Alexandria."

She did not answer outright. "What about the gap between generations?"

"Forget about it."

She laughed. "Drop me by the bank. I'll deposit twenty years . . ."

"You don't need to. You're very attractive, Mrs. Ferrar. Also, a woman one can talk to. Our Israeli girls, are all more or less on the same model. Ideally suited to our new suburbia. Where an older generation of women was fleshly and Spartan, our girls have discovered femininity as advertised in magazines. They can't move without tubes of face cream, bottles of suntan lotion, and the proper picnic equipment, including inflatable rubber mattresses. They are devoid of that something unpredictable which makes a woman something other and more than a good chum, with whom one settles down to raise a family."

Josh stopped the car up the hill, to show Antonia the view, over the fish ponds shimmering under the sun.

"Aren't you being a little unfair?" Antonia asked. "After all, you men go abroad on courses, missions, and all that. So you have a greater experience of the world, are occasionally attracted to what appears to you as a more sophisticated type of woman. Few of your girls have similar opportunities. And I imagine you find those who have studied abroad a bit pretentious, too self-conscious. Actually, they are on the defensive. . . . You forget all you owe to your women, here. Israel has shaped a really fine type of woman, attractive, balanced, self-reliant, reliable. I expect the demands of life here force your girls to conform more or less to the same type. They give—and give up—so much. But you are the heroes. And it mustn't be so easy to be your steadfast companions."

"You're perceptive. Have you met many Israeli girls?"

"Only casually. I've observed them in Rome, shopping. So eager to get what's fashionable, and get the best value, too."

Josh thought of Tsippy, who'd never miss a party where the *hevre* met, of the soldier girls at the base, quietly dependable, of all his chums who had already settled with their girls into marriage, as he might yet settle down with Tsippy. He ought to. Yet at twenty-four, he wished to know a feeling at once more sensual, poignant, and tender, wild and wayward than Tsippy's idea of love. She cared about her comfort, Tsippy, while he loved to love out in the open, under the stars. So Tsippy complained about crawling insects, or the sand scratching, getting into her hair. . . . Hence the rubber mattress, which had to be inflated at the most critical moments. It . . . deflated him. Josh scowled.

Antonia Ferrar observed him, amused. They smiled at one another, understanding much that was not said.

"May I drop in this afternoon? Then we'll plan our trip to Jerusalem. You agree to come? I'm free on Saturday . . . unless . . ."

"I understand perfectly. You have your duties. It's strange . . . I used to wonder what Israeli pilots were like. They did such a thorough job, I didn't expect them to be so young. In 1967 you must have been . . . twenty. During those terrible weeks of waiting, which preceded your lightning victory, I couldn't bear to think Israel might be destroyed. I had never been a Zionist, hardly even Jewish. Ours is a family with many mixed marriages: we took our Jewishness rather casually. But in those days the Jewish part of me twitched like a raw nerve. When Israel won, I wept from relief. But then . . . then I saw the places I had known and loved in Egypt from above, as they might look on an aerial map: objectives to be destroyed. Burning . . . and I could see the faces of people, looking up to the sky. It was June, when the tiger lilies are in flower, and I could see the border of flame-colored flowers, rising like swords around the pond in my grandfather's villa explode, burst into flames. The house was sold long ago, and may have been torn down to give way to an apartment house . . . but I could not help it. That is what I saw . . . the garden busting into flames . . . the beaches, my school, the Nouzha Gardens where we played, the Sporting Club, the races, aperitifs at Pastroudis, all that had been Alexandria superimposed, or rising from under the image of the war I saw on the television screen. I rejoiced for Jerusalem, but I wept for Alexandria . . ."

Josh was angry. "We did not bomb Alexandria. What did you expect us to do? Wait to be destroyed? We only hit military objectives. Not civilians. Who risks war, or provokes it, ought to know it's not a game that can be called off. War is not a game, you know, although one calls it, quite wrongly, the war game. There's Egypt posing as a victim. Had *we* been the losers, would Nasser have accepted to call off the game? You can't be sentimental about war, Mrs. Ferrar."

"Rationally, I know that. But feeling is not rational. And I can't help it, I feel both ways. I cannot identify wholly as you do. As you must. You are totally engaged. I'm not. I can't be . . . I think you had better know it. Because I will not see Jerusalem with your eyes. I was there before, you know, long ago when you were only a small boy. In June 1967, I thought God had to be, simply had to be with Israel. I don't know where God is anymore, why there must be such terrible retribution hanging in the balance, for either people or both. Must there be again the Ten Plagues over Egypt for Israel to be Israel because Pharaoh is still Pharaoh? I flee from the confrontation . . ."

"We'd be in a pretty pickle if Egyptian-born Jews who settled in Israel and serve in the army felt as you do! Or those who come from Russia right now. And what about the Syrian Jews, the Lebanese Jews, the Iraqi Jews? Where would we be if they felt both ways, as you do, I ask you?"

"That is precisely why I could not choose Israel. Rome is my refuge. I love it but I'm not involved. Besides, neither Syria, nor Lebanon, nor Iraq has a mythical dimension, while Israel and Egypt do. A war between them is different in its very essence from, say, a war between Germany and France. In their very essence, the two countries are different from, say, the United States and the Soviet Union. Those are only empires, powerful, but transient, as the Roman, the Turkish, the British empires were. Israel and Egypt, each in their own way, have outlasted them all, witnessed their downfall. Because both Israel and Egypt partake of a mythical reality, another dimension of being, rooted in eternity."

"That's a beautiful, poetic idea . . . but who remembers? Only Israel remembers! The new myth of humanity is to colonize the moon, not the Old Testament stuff. *You* remember, Mrs. Ferrar, because in your own way, you are more Jewish than you realize. And Egypt is a Moslem country now. It is steeped in the Quran, not the Old Testament. We don't begrudge Egypt its past, its ancient temples, its pyramids or its mosques. But they, they do deny us the Temple Wall. So after two thousand years of vainly waiting, praying, and weeping we *are* in Jerusalem.

By right of conquest. It is just what you call our mythical reality that others begrudge us, that Egypt will not recognize. How can we make her do so? Just tell me how."

"I don't know . . . I remember at Passover, I used to sip a fifth little glass of wine, on the sly, and pray that there be a new covenant between Israel and Egypt. But prayer does not help. I find it awesome to be Israel. I do not have the strength to be Israel."

"Still, you did come to Israel, now."

"I told you, this is a kind of parting. How can I explain? Some accounts with one's self have to be settled, and I wanted to touch all the dimensions of the past buried here. To remember. For we were all here before. Here and in Egypt. And so I wished, crazily wished to plant a seed of Alexandria in the soil of Israel, for Alexandria was once almost as much a Jewish city as it was Greek. Where else in the world does the street of the Ptolemies bisect Nebi Daniel Street in the heart of the city? Probably their very names have been erased. Those streets are probably now called Liberation Street and Arab Brotherhood Street; the Jewish presence wiped out along with the Greek. I remember those fragile iridescent little vases in the museum of Greco-Roman Antiquities in Alexandria. I used to think they were so much like us, the slow rot of centuries transmuted into that exquisite, iridescent sheen, that phosphorescence . . ."

"There are the same little vases here in the Glass Museum," Josh said excitedly. "I'll take you there."

Antonia shook her head. She said dreamily, "There comes a time when one desperately wants to . . . to remember and be remembered . . . to pass on something for safekeeping. Much as I love Rome, it was here that I had to come . . . to remember Alexandria."

He saw pain distort her face. Thought he understood why she wore that long-sleeved blouse. Would not swim. That sudden fear in her eyes. He asked gently, "Is there no one to make you take care of yourself, Alexandra? Antonia Ferrar, of Alexandria? You shouldn't be gamboling down those hills . . ."

She saw his eyes rest on her breasts. "It isn't there," she said, "but started in the glands under the arm. I have good friends in Rome. Elicia. She's also from Alexandria, half Greek, half Italian. We laugh a lot together. . . . I am not sure I want to live, care to live on and on. The best of life is gone, and what is broken can never be repaired. And yet I am scared. Abjectly scared. What does it matter if I live or die? Who cares? So many are stricken down in youth! Yet part of me wants to live, savagely, instinctively. Although I know it's not really worth the bother anymore."

"You must fight to live. Want to live. As soldiers do. We fight to live. Where would we be without the will to live? We are not the ones to choose when to call off the game, Antonia of Alexandria, Antonia Ferrar. Rather than think such gloomy thoughts, come with me to Jerusalem. You will tell me what it was like when you came from Alexandria to Jerusalem, in those days when one could cross the canal as if there was nothing to it. Tell me about it."

She smiled. "One arrived in Qantara West, by train, crossed the canal in a ferry boat, and took another train in Qantara East, at midnight. The train stopped at dawn in a huge palm grove, on a cliff above the intense blue sea. I'd like to see that place again . . . I don't remember its name. The criss-cross of palm shadows on the sand . . ."

"That must have been El Arish. It is a beautiful spot. But I would not take you there right now . . ."

"The train stopped ever so often among the orange groves. The people working in them, kibbutz people waved. It was lovely, that scent of orange blossoms in the spring . . ."

"Well, we'll sit on the terrace of the King David Hotel, facing the Old City, and you'll tell me what it was like then."

"Is there still that street, in the Jewish quarter near the Temple Wall, full of little synagogues? At Passover, the street was full, of the clamors and changes of all the tribes of Israel . . . there were much more than twelve. In one of them, people were wearing extraordinary, magician-like costumes of velvet and brocade."

"Those must have been the Bukharan Jews. You can see those costumes in the Israel Museum . . . the street is still there. The Arabs occupied it after the Jews had to leave in 1948. But it is now being restored. You see, the future is still full of strange surprises that sprout out of the seed of the past. You must believe in the future, Alexandra."

"I shall try. Josh . . . ? You're young, and attractive. You know that, surely. What drew you to *Alexandra* Ferrar? Your tongue slipped. Alexandra is what you called me."

"It was as if I recognized you, had known you before, Antonia Ferrar. Don't ask me to explain. If we met twice—although you tried to avoid me—it was perhaps due not to mere chance. So accept it, as I do. . . . How long will you be in Israel?"

"Another week. I must be back for tests . . . and treatment."

"But you will come back, safe and sound. So let's make the most of what little time we have now. May I come to see you this afternoon? We can just sit and talk, or say nothing. If you'd like to, we'll go for a drive. I'll show you a little of my corner of Israel."

"I'll be ready, whenever you come." Lightly, she kissed his brow.

He watched her depart, fine-boned, light and graceful. How strange life was! Often had he dreamed of the woman he would love, emerging from the sea, like Venus full of its secrets. They would love, rocked by the sound of waves, attuned to the multifold rhythms of nature, part of the mysterious harmony of the universe. They would be Adam and Eve, full of wonder, awakening with the fresh dawn, cleansed by the sea. . . . And so she had come, Antonia Ferrar, Antonia of Alexandria, warm, marble-made flesh, a statue of stricken flesh. He longed to kiss her sinuous lips, run his fingers, ever so lightly, over the stitches of her scar, as if that could make her feel whole again, alive again, loved. She had come.

*

Antonia reclined in a deck chair on the lawn, watching the doves fly in and out, under and around the iridescent arcs of water gushing from the water sprayers. She saw him come. "Hello! How nice you look in civilian clothes! And even younger."

"I plan to get older; it just takes a little time," he replied, dropping to seat himself on a low rock at her feet. "How elegant you look, in a ladylike way. It looks perfect on you, that pale yellow linen. And the accessories match perfectly, yet discreetly."

"Aren't you inordinately interested in women's clothes, for an army man?"

"Well, they tell you a great deal about a woman, her clothes do. And I won't be an army man all my life. I'm studying business administration at the university. Anyway, I detest those flashy psychedelic prints.

And I have my doubts about the minis and the hot pants, all that flesh flung into every man's face, so overtly inviting, reducing the feminine to the female."

"If I were young, and had the choice, I might prefer to be simply female. Girls nowadays are so much freer, more self-reliant. Less sentimental, too."

"But too matter-of-fact. Love is reduced to sex, a consumer good—the more of it the better. Are people any happier?"

"They aren't necessarily *more* unhappy. I wouldn't set up my generation and its hypocrisy as an example. Not as it was in Alexandria. In a pioneering society, like yours, it was different! When we were girls, we were told, 'First you marry, then you do as you please. It's your husband's affair.' In Alexandria, in a certain milieu, most Jewish women had Greek lovers. There must have been many illicit half-brothers and -sisters between the two communities. Yet if a Jewish girl had a love affair, what a scandal. Particularly if it was outside the community. Then marriage was out of the question. She was very nearly a social outcast, but considered fair game by any man."

"Was that what happened to you?"

"Yes. We went swimming and sailing. . . . We knew that coast so well . . . it was as if we were born from it, Constantine and Antonia. I remembered that in Tantura, the sea, the rocks, the sky, the fluttering wings of sailing boats . . ."

"Do you still see people from Alexandria?" he asked.

"Only a few close friends. Then we talk mostly of memories, and it's rather depressing. Fortunately, I work. This year, I had to take time off. But in October and November, I'm booked. I didn't cancel my engagements. Work will keep me going. I'll be in Geneva, in Paris . . . I hope."

"If you let me know where you are, perhaps I could join you."

"Are you planning on a trip to Europe?"

"Well, one never knows."

They watched the doves dash in and out of the luminous arcs of water. Like star ballet dancers, each bird in turn did a solo performance. The others sauntered on the grass, loudly expressing their admiration. Then another bird dashed in, to praise the setting sun.

"I call that flying! Do you fly like that?"

"No. Birds can afford to fly for pleasure only, for the pure joy of being. We fly with an objective in view. Still, I wonder how they learned such tricks!"

Somewhere the gardener turned off the water. The birds protested raucously, fluttered about agitatedly before taking off to their treetops. Silently, Josh and Antonia watched the shadows lengthen, the incandescent trees turn dark, the sun sink below the horizon in a violent paroxysm of color.

"Did you make a wish?" Josh asked, taking her hand.

"Could I wish for more than what is now?"

In the darkness, Josh took her hand, brushed his lips against her palm. "Come," he said.

"I'll just take a sweater . . . all those ladies staring. I'll say I won't be in for dinner . . ."

They went to the beach in Akhziv, and as they passed the localities he knew, Josh told her about them, his childhood, events along the years. "I know this coast as well as you know that of Alexandria. But I was never really in love, before."

They went down the cliff, and sat, their feet digging deep in the warm sand, listening to the sea, to the multitude of sounds heard only when all is silence. Then they stretched, side by side, with the stars above them. Josh felt Antonia's body quiver. Spasmodically her hand clung to his, at once drawing him to her and pushing him away. Gently, he kissed her, felt the salty brine of tears.

"You're crying, Antonia!"

Suddenly, she turned away, and sobbed.

He held her heaving shoulders. "What is it Antonia? What has distressed you so?"

"To love and be loved, one must be whole. Young, beautiful, healthy, and whole. Otherwise it's repulsive. Simply repulsive. A woman clinging on and on. Wanting more. Wanting to be young again . . . wanting yet to fill the emptiness of years, the emptiness in her, the hunger in her. Wanting. Greedily wanting more! more! more! Wanting to feel alive once more. You could be my son, and I desired you as my lover the very first moment I set my eyes on you. *You* should find it repulsive! Unless it is pity. . . . I don't want pity! No, not in love. Aren't there enough pretty girls of your age in Israel that you let yourself be seduced by a woman who is probably older than your mother?"

"What pride you have, Antonia! Do you really think you seduced me? I seduced you! Rather, we were mutually seduced. And I'm not a boy, not making love to my mother or just any pretty girl. But to you, to you as you are now. Why you, just you? I wouldn't even begin to explain. Explanations aren't that important, anyway. We'll have time for that. You have the pride of beautiful women, who want to be like goddesses. Perfect. So you aren't perfect, Antonia of Alexandria. You are you, and that is enough."

The sobs slowly subsided. "I thought I had come here to find detachment, forgiveness, peace. To make my peace with myself. But what I really wanted, was a lover. A last feast . . ."

"Why the last? Something in you wants to live, that is stronger, much stronger than what wants to die. Stronger than you know. So accept it with wonder and thankfulness and humility, even, for the life in you is stronger than your will."

He heard her sniff, then blow her nose. She sighed. "I never expected to be given a lesson in humility by an Israeli Cossack of the Air!"

She turned round, came close to him. "I shall be humble, Josh, and thankful for the miracle of you."

*

When Josh came to fetch her that Saturday, Antonia saw immediately that something was amiss. "What is it Josh? What's wrong?"

"I can't take you to Jerusalem today, Antonia. I must go . . . in a little while."

She said, very slowly, "You must go . . . now? You will be gone . . ."

"I do not know, Antonia."

"And you knew . . . you might be going?"

"I did not think it would be so soon. And I could not tell you about it. I mean . . ."

"Yes. I understand. The army . . ."

"Antonia, what can I say?"

She smiled. "Dear boy! What could you say? Josh. Mr. Just Josh . . ." She framed his face between her hands. "The face of Josh, with its bushy, fiery eyebrows. The eyebrows are those of Esau but the eyes are the eyes of Jacob. Josh, you gave me all the beauty there is in the world in one embrace. I couldn't ask for more. Not any more. . . . So go now, dearest."

"What will be with you, Antonia? May I come to see you if I pass through Rome?"

"Yes, dearest . . . but go now, go quickly Josh. Without turning back . . . go . . . be happy . . . marry your girl."

He kissed her lips. Gazed at the face of Antonia Ferrar, of Alexandria. "Take care! I'll write. You'll write?"

"Yes."

She watched him go. Then stretched out, in a deck chair, looking up at the stars through her tears, listening to the soft breeze in the pine trees. How long would it take? One year? More? Less? Josh had suggested that she stay in Israel. But of course all her medical and social security arrangements were in Italy. One had to go through the motions of treatment, with its indignities, its cruelties. Lie, not under the trees, but in a proper administrative hospital sickbed. The file had to be closed.

So be it. There had been life and it had slipped through her fingers. But there had been the grace of Josh. He would write. She would write. Then the time would come, in all probability, when her hand could not hold the pen. Another operation. And then . . . ?

*

Tsippy, after those long dark months, finally found the strength to go through Josh's desk. She knew he would never return. His plane had been shot down over Syrian territory in the Yom Kippur War. Outside, her little daughter played with the sprinkler. A war orphan. A war widow. There was Josh's diary. A few letters. Were they hers to read? A card slipped to the floor. Tsippy read the uncertain distorted script.

"To remember Alexandria, Antonia Ferrar."

Below this, someone called Elicia had written, "She asked me to send you this with the little antique vase, when it was over. To be remembered by . . ."

Tsippy stared at the card. Antonia? Who was Antonia? And where was that vase? Whoever she was . . . perhaps that Italian woman?

Because of whom Josh had disappeared for a few days . . . or so she had thought. But then, when he had returned from his mission abroad they had married. So—there was no Antonia. There was no Josh to "remember Alexandria." Slowly, she tore the card into small bits, threw it, stamped it under her heel. Then her head in her arms, leaning against the door, she sobbed.

The child outside called, "Imma!"

Well, she had more to think about than Alexandria. On her way out to the small garden she glanced at the picture of Josh, the deep-set eyes under the flaming eyebrows, smile, gentle, yet ironic. . . . Something in him which had never quite been hers, which escaped her. . . . No, no, no! *She*, Tsippy, would most certainly *not* remember Alexandria. Tel Aviv was the place for her. Definitely.

"Bibi!" she cooed.

The little girl with the red curls ran toward her.

*Eighteen*

# My Brother Ishmael

## *On the Visit of Anwar Sadat*

*The state visit of Anwar Sadat, the president of Egypt, to Israel in November 1977, and the subsequent peace negotiations between the two countries had momentous regional political repercussions. The prospect of peace between the former enemies was of particular personal importance for Israeli Jews who had once lived in Egypt. In this spirit, this essay attempts to replace the shared Abrahamic narratives, which dictate the dominance by one brother over another, with an inclusive narrative about a healthy sibling rivalry. This piece, one of Kahanoff's last, appeared in the Israeli women's magazine* At *along with reflections by other prominent Israeli women on Sadat's visit.*

Sure, Anwar Sadat is an astute politician. Still, he found a way to appeal directly to the hearts and imagination of people, in Israel, in Egypt, throughout the world. Remember the slogan of French students in those heady days of May 1968: "L'imagination au pouvoir!" That hope faded, as did Dubček's Prague Spring and Mao's Thousand Flowers.* And young people have not really shown much more imagination than

* Alexander Dubček (1921–1992), the first secretary of the Communist Party of Czechoslovakia from 1968 to 1969, undertook reforms known as the Prague Spring that were crushed by the Soviet Union. Mao Zedong (1893–1976), head of the Chinese Communist Party from 1935 until his death, served as the first chairman of the People's Republic of China (1949–1959). The Hundred Flowers Campaign (May 1956–July 1957) briefly opened the doors to public criticism of the Chinese Communist Party's policies. Kahanoff repeats a common mistranslation from the Chinese in identifying the movement as the "thousand flowers campaign."

their elders, except in the new sophistication of terrorism. But there is nothing particularly imaginative about murder—it is as old as Abel and Cain. Anwar Sadat is, to my mind, the first world leader to have shown imagination in speaking directly to people, his and ours, by appealing to our common humanity. And they responded. Owing to him, through the mediation of the television screen, we and Egyptians communicated, living through this extraordinary event at almost the same time. Surely it did not leave Egyptians indifferent to witness visually how their president was greeted in Israel, not just by our government, but by thousands of people who crowded along the streets. And the smiles on the faces, including that breaking out on Haim Yavin's face on the television screen.* Nor did it leave us indifferent to see the enthusiasm with which Anwar Sadat was greeted by his people on his return. Somehow he embodied hope. Saturday night, as we were glued to our television sets, the streets of Tel Aviv were deserted—as before Yom Kippur some said. But the streets of Cairo were also deserted—as before Ramadan they said. It is perhaps without significance that both people referred to the religious event that carried the most meaning in our respective faiths. The intensity of the emotion felt was a kind of communion of people reaching out to express their startled recognition of a common humanity.

It was as if behind the bluster, fears, distrust, and prejudices of all these years, at a deeper level, a hidden continent of other feelings began to emerge: a need for hope, forgiveness, reconciliation, love. This man, Sadat, was perhaps most imaginative in sensing this undercurrent of feeling and giving it a concrete form that all could understand and respond to. I've heard our skeptics say that the prize Sadat is entitled to is not the Nobel Prize for Peace but an Oscar. Yes, there is something of the showman about him. So what? Gandhi too was a great showman, but he knew how to reach that deeper core in a people's soul imprisoned in its hard defensive shell. Gandhi failed, as I hope Sadat will not. May the ferment continue to be active in the hearts and minds of human beings, way beyond our borders. Not that the Arab rejectionists are prepared to abandon their set postures, as the vehement

* Haim Yavin was the anchor of the main Israeli evening television news broadcast.

anti-Sadat propaganda in Libya and Syria clearly shows. But even there, there must be people who wonder if it is necessary to go on with all that hatred, if accommodation and reconciliation are not after all more of the essence of life than war and destruction.

It is not the least irony of history that Menachem Begin, who has always believed the borders of biblical Eretz Israel should be those of modern Israel, was the prime minister who welcomed Anwar Sadat and his entourage. Whatever the final decision, it will be a fateful one, and our prime minister when taking it is no less alone than Egypt's president was when he took his to come to Israel. History has placed these two protagonists face to face on the world stage, and as in an ancient drama, we the people are the chorus. As if, beyond irony, there may be a divine design in all this. I imagine it was intentionally that Anwar Sadat chose to come to Jerusalem and pray in the al-Aqsa Mosque on the day of 'Id al-Adha, which commemorates Abraham's willingness to sacrifice his son Ishmael in the Moslem tradition and Isaac in ours—at the calling of his God. Whatever the security precautions, the risk was staggering, especially since the envoy from Egypt requested that all should be allowed to pray in the mosque. Seeing him in al-Aqsa at 6:30 in the morning on the television screen, I trembled for his life.

It was an almost indecent violation of privacy to watch this man pray under the pitiless glare of television lamps, mopping his brow, offering his face to the millions who watched as he lifted his eyes to heaven calling "Allah Akbar!" But it was a sacrifice to which he had consented, and the only adequate response seemed to be to pray with him in the language of one's own soul. I was moved to the core of my being to see this man pray, partly, no doubt, because having been born and grown up in Egypt, to hear "Allah Akbar" clamored by human voices, echoing in the stillness of the air was so familiar—heard daily from the mosque in our neighborhood. But there was more, much more to it than that. It was as if this man was offering his life in sacrifice for some higher purpose, beyond his natural affection and loyalties, as if, for once, the Father offered himself in sacrifice so that the son—or sons—would live. And the call seemed to have been answered at least insofar as Anwar Sadat is alive.

Jews and Moslems both share and are divided by this ancient Semitic myth about a father ready to offer the flesh of his flesh to his God. It is a powerful symbol of these crucial moments when a man is alone with his conscience, or God, and in solitude, goes beyond his purely human nature to obey some higher purpose. But this myth separates us since it is not the same son that is saved in the nick of time to hold down one or the other version of the Abrahamic revelation to the holders of both faiths, each of which has rejected and ridiculed the other's claim to be the one and only true heir. Nor does it really matter what son was saved, born of what woman's womb, as long as both sons—or all the sons—live. Actually, both Israel and Ishmael are very much alive.

The important thing Sadat seemed to be saying is that the sons should live and recognize each other's legitimate rights and birthright and simply live. He was saying it not only to us, but to his fellow Moslems and Arabs—hence the furious reaction of some of them. They call him a traitor because he innovated, and his message is a revolutionary one, in terms of both Islam and Israel, for it calls for the recognition of Israel and Ishmael by one another, and their reconciliation—hence Anwar Sadat's insistence on sparing the sons' lives, on sparing the women who bore them, on the rights of young men and women to happy family lives. The message was not wholly explicit in words, but implicit in his very acts. I saw the man Anwar Sadat pray, and because he is so obviously a believer, I believed him.

Then I heard him in the Knesset. True, he did not give an inch on territories, or the rights of Palestinians, but he did say what no other Moslem leader had ever said before, that he recognized us as Israel, and our legitimate right to be here. This was confirmed by his visit to Yad Vashem where he took cognizance of the indelibly traumatic Jewish experience of the Holocaust.* One can only begin to imagine the impact of this in the Arab-Moslem world, since Arabs have claimed that they did not have to pay the price for Europe's extermination of its Jews. I think it was a mistake to ask him to put on a *kippah*, and he refused, I think, very much as most of us would have refused if asked to cross ourselves if

* Yad Vashem, the Holocaust Martyrs' and Heroes' Remembrance Authority, was established in 1953 by act of the Israeli Parliament. A visit to the Yad Vashem Memorial Museum in Jerusalem is included in the itinerary of foreign leaders on a state visit.

attending a ceremony in a church. We are not always as sensitive to the sensibilities of other people as we wish them to be toward our own.

True, we do not need, at least in our own eyes, Arab recognition to legitimize our right to be here. But in their eyes we were aliens and usurpers, and after all these years and all these wars, it is at least clear that we should have accommodation and reconciliation, we do need this recognition by our neighbors that our presence here is as legitimate as theirs. (I prefer to use the word *peace* sparingly; it has become a shoddy word from use and misuse, and too much lip-service. Perfect peace and harmony do not exist, not between individuals, and not between nations. They are simply ways of accommodating one's self to others that make life mutually tolerable, and we should not ask for more.)

I suggest that behind the modern political parlance taken over from the Western world (as when the Palestinians speak of a lay, secular state, or we of equal rights for all our citizens when we don't even have the right to intermarry) our dispute is a very ancient one, born of another, Semitic, sensitivity and identity, and far more bound up with religion and theology than either Jews or Arabs would admit to. The conflict was dormant in the Islamic world, partly because Jews were too few in number to present a real threat. It found expression in the inferior status of Jews—as of Christians—with the difference that their claim to be the exclusive heir of the Abrahamic special connection with God above subjected Jews to greater pressures and persecutions (according to time, place, and the outlook of the ruler), who moreover often enjoyed the protection of powerful Christian European nations. The Jews continued convinced, covertly, of their superior status as Abraham and Jacob's one and only legitimate heir, and the Moslems, overtly, of theirs. We are all thus trapped in this patriarchal tradition where one son, and one only, is heir. Nevertheless, in the Moslem world, Moslems and Arabs did consider themselves as belonging to the same family—which does not mean necessarily that members of a family get along. Still, when Jewish survival was most threatened, Islamic countries offered an abode. It was the case with the Ottoman Empire, at the time of the Inquisition, taking in the Jews expelled from Spain. Similarly, Morocco's Mohammed V during World War II protected "his Jews" against the French Vichy regime.

Zionism and the rebirth of Israel confronted Moslems no less, though differently, than Christians with the question of the right of this son of Abraham to claim and reconquer his inheritance. To admit the rebirth and triumphant return of this downtrodden son of Abraham returning as a refugee from concentration camps challenged the belief of Islam and Ishmael as the one and only legitimate heir. The presence of this reborn Israel was all the more difficult to accept when Arab countries were undergoing their own national awakening and struggle for independence. The opposition and the rejection were couched in modern terms of nationalism, but its roots are ancient, in the mythology and theology of both protagonists. The two movements of national revival were born at approximately the same time, one supported by Europe, the other rebelling against European colonial domination. The latent Ishmael-Isaac myth was more or less consciously revived, and behind the modern political parlance motivates many postures on both sides.

The diffused, blurred—but secure—identity of Ishmael acquired a precise contour as the exclusive heir to this land, and more particularly in the case of the Palestinian Arab, who became, in his own eyes, Ishmael, cheated out of his legitimate and exclusive right, totally and utterly rejecting that of Israel. The "no recognition" proclamations of Arab summits offend our deepest sensibilities, making our nerves twitch, but then, the declaration of our leaders that Palestinians do not exist and that Arab countries could have absorbed the refugees makes a raw nerve twitch in Moslem-Arab sensibilities regarding their idea of Ishmael's identity. Ishmael was reborn together with and because of Israel, and it is striking in this connection how many themes of Zionism the Palestinians have taken over just because the dispute is couched in terms of these mythical ancestors, each of which claims an exclusive right and totally rejects that of the other son.

Anwar Sadat is the first Moslem Arab leader, and a devout one at that, who did recognize the legitimate right of Israel to be here after so many years of rejection, and it is a radical, indeed a revolutionary departure, not only from the stance of Arab nationalism, but from that of Islamic primacy. We are no longer the alien usurper, but one of the legitimate sons. In a way Sadat has broken, implicitly, with the Abrahamic tradition whereby only one son is heir. Hence the uproar in much of the Islamic world following upon Sadat's radical departure from accepted belief, and the embarrassed silence of Saudi Arabia—the center of Islamic faith—before this proposal of recognizing the legitimacy of Israel.

We are surprised that it is suddenly important for a Saudi Arabian ruler to pray in al-Aqsa, while it wasn't for all the years when Islam held sway—Mecca being the center of Islamic pilgrimage. He is forgetting that from the moment Israel is reborn, not down below in that narrow alley of the Temple wall at the foot of al-Aqsa, but ruling, Islam is shaken in its conviction of its own primacy and obsessed by the need to re-attest its exclusive right. What Sadat was saying to us, and to his fellow Moslems and Arabs, was that there are here two rights, which had refused to recognize one another—I do not think we accept Ishmael as brother any more easily than he accepts us—and we should do so, to spare the sons. And to affirm further that "Allah Akbar," beyond each and every specific faith, he also visited the Church of the Holy Sepulcher.

No doubt the president of Egypt had more immediate political considerations, which is only natural. But to me, the pledge of Anwar Sadat's sincerity is in the enormity of the risk he exposed himself to and is still exposed to. Our legitimacy will be recognized on condition that we accept the reciprocal recognition of the legitimacy of the Palestinians. It is the price to pay for accommodation and eventually, hopefully, reconciliation. This readiness to recognize Israel as legitimate if not exclusive heir is one we should consider most seriously. Should the overture be rejected, then the rejection of us by the Islamic countries is reinforced and in their own eyes justified. We should not let that happen. Curiously, it is Anwar Sadat who is the first to have radically departed from the patriarchal tradition which says that only one son, the eldest, has rights, to assert that all have rights—and he seemed to say—daughters and mothers too. Can we follow suit?

*Nineteen*

# Welcome, Sadat

*This piece, Kahanoff's last, was composed as an afterword to the 1978 anthology of her work published in Israel under the title* Mi-mizraḥ shemesh [From East the Sun]. *This essay reflects upon her earlier writings about her childhood in Egypt, with particular reference to "Passover in Egypt." As in some of these early works, Kahanoff here reimagines biblical narratives to suit her fancy. In this essay she also likens Nasser to the Pharaoh of Exodus. Yet her imagination—and the changed political environment—permit her the possibility of rewriting the story's ending, favoring reconciliation and coexistence over displacement and the separation of peoples. Kahanoff's papers show that after Anwar Sadat's visit to Israel, she sent this article in English along with a copy of the book in Hebrew to Jehan Sadat, First Lady of Egypt.*

How strange it is when the world of reveries you inhabited in your childhood hovers over the margins of reality—clear, if as yet not quite tangible—as though it had been some sort of early prophecy about the future in the reinvented past. A reconciliation between Egypt and Israel, in which each is emancipated and returns to the essence of its selfhood—such had been my dream, and now it is about to come true. Ever since the very first Passover seder in which I took part, I was filled with fear lest the story in the Haggadah repeat itself once Egypt and the Land of the Israelites were reborn, but I was also filled with hope that this time, in our own time, the end would be different.

The story "Passover in Egypt" is included in this selection. In it I ignored one important aspect: the anxiety, and even the terror which I felt in my childhood. The terrible events described in the Haggadah were all too real for me, no less real than Egypt, no less than that seder during which my grandfather Jacob sat at the head of the table while my father Joseph explained to me those events, which took place a long time ago but were liable to happen again to us and to them in our own time. That night I tossed and turned in bed in such a state of excitement that I fell from my bed more than once, haunted by dreadful, unbearable fantasies: the murky waters of the Nile overflow, turn into blood, flood the country, people are trapped in whirlpools, famine and plagues devastate the land . . . the Hebrew slaves flee in dread bearing with them their *matzah*—was that how we were going to leave Egypt?—Pharaoh's chariots in hot pursuit, the sea parts to open a dry passage, and then the huge billows close over and drown Pharaoh's army. And all of this because one stiff-necked Pharaoh forbade the Hebrews to return peacefully to the land that had been promised to them!

Most people summon up the "Exodus from Egypt" one week a year; I bore it within me every day of the year, riddled with doubts concerning the Lord's grace and love. Why should innocent fellahin have to pay such a heavy price for the Hebrews to be set free, while it was certainly in the Lord's power to demand of Pharaoh to listen to Moses and let the Hebrews go? It seemed to me that the matter was not only cruel but a huge waste. Ever since that first seder I always made sure not to take part in the saying of the "Ten Plagues," and when the time came to read out loud *Dayenu* I would pray silently, "Enough, that's really enough! If only such things would never happen again!"

During those years, while Israel and Egypt were still at war or on the verge of war, I was deeply disturbed by the fact that "they" ignored our legal rights, but I also feared that under dire straits and at the limits of despair, having run out of options Israel might deal Egypt a blow not unlike the Ten Plagues. It might, for example, bombard its dams and inundate the entire country. Nor did I dread any less the possibility that we too would be subject to some disaster of biblical proportions. God did not always do us good in our long history. After Sadat's visit I can admit to such qualms, especially since it now seems that at last there may be an alternative to war and destruction.

Perhaps this time people would be smarter and less vengeful than the same implacable and wrathful God—being born a woman I could not but doubt in His wisdom, sense of justice, and even in his common sense—I was just like Kadreya, my Moslem playmate, who regretted that God was not "a bit of a woman." I often saw her in my mind's eye as my silent ally over there in Egypt.

Ever since that same first seder night the Egyptians and Hebrews were linked in my mind as people who belonged to another time dimension, different from those young European nations like England and France (America was not included yet on my horizons), whose history one learned in school. Egypt and Israel had been there from the start, from the very onset of things, before history. They still existed, even if they had lost some of their greatness; together they would rise again and flourish long after Britain's and France's strength had waned—like Rome's power had waned before them.

I would weave every fortuitous bit of knowledge I gathered into the stories I told myself in which the Egyptians and Hebrews returned to their past glory, not as adversaries but allies. We the children would play by the banks of the Nile and I would slip away and peek through the papyrus that still grew by the water. In my imagination I saw the daughter of the Pharaoh drawing from the water the infant concealed there. But I replaced Moses with another child. My hero was Joseph, for he was judicious, good-hearted, and intelligent, and although devoted like Moses he was not hot-tempered and harsh. I was proud of Joseph, who had saved Egypt from famine. And now a Pharaoh as smart as that first Pharaoh might listen to a person like Joseph. When the Pharaoh's daughter became the king's chief consort, like Nefertiti she brought her Hebrew son, the second Joseph, to her brother and made sure they would find a sensible arrangement. The Hebrews returned home in peace and Joseph solemnly proclaimed he would never wage war against his mother's people, but would rather lend a hand against their common enemies, while Pharaoh promised in turn that his army would help the Hebrews fight against their adversaries. The common foes were the light-skinned, fair-haired foreigners who had infiltrated into the ranks of the army and police. Accordingly, negotiations were conducted in the utmost secrecy in the queen's inner chambers. And to prevent these arrogant officers from doing any harm, an order was issued to arrest them in the dead of the night, lock them up in chicken coops, and then send them back to the king of the cold and dark land of the north from where they had come. How I laughed at the thought of the British officers in chicken coops!

I would gaze at the green and fertile fields on the other side of the river and think to myself that the chain of events in the Bible did not have to repeat itself in the same manner. It was certainly clear that years of plenty came in the wake of lean years; things did not always proceed from the good to the bad but also from the bad to the good. Otherwise the world would revert to chaos. Hence perhaps this time a benevolent Pharaoh would follow a malevolent one, and Joseph would come not before Moses but rather after him. The problem was that King Fuad did not resemble one bit that same bad Pharaoh, and in Israel Chaim Weizmann did not resemble Joseph.*

And then Nasser rose to power, and he was indeed that Pharaoh who knew not Joseph. Perhaps we are unable to avoid the ancient myths that close in on us. And so, in the *ulpan* in which I studied Hebrew in Israel we were taught the song "Weep, Rachel, Weep." I was shocked. What mother with half a brain in her head wouldn't have been delighted that her son succeeded in fleeing from his brothers who'd plotted to kill him and then sold him off as a slave? And yet Joseph prospered in Egypt and eventually forgave his brothers, and when there was a drought in the land he even welcomed his brothers there. The same applies to the good and the bad years. Are we to regret that Joseph benefited from Pharaoh's friendship? What nonsense! He was the best of them all, in his intelligence and his down-to-earth wisdom—and God was good to him too. Hence I hope that when our representatives begin negotiating in Egypt, they will remember Joseph as well.

I don't know whether Anwar Sadat listens to his wife, Jehan, but her words and deeds remind me of the same daughter of Pharaoh that I conjured in my heart. However, in my wildest dreams I never dared picture in my mind that Pharaoh would actually come to Jerusalem in order to sign an agreement with Israel. Yet, this is what happened. Now everything can start here anew.

*Translated from Hebrew by Gabriel Levin*

* Weizmann (1894–1952) served as first president of Israel from 1949 to 1952.

# Afterword

## *From East the Sun*

*In reflecting upon the new geopolitical realities confronting Israel in the aftermath of the 1967 war, as well as the ongoing political realities of the Cold War and Arab nationalism, this essay represents Jacqueline Kahanoff's concerns at a specific historical moment. In a post–Cold War world, where militant Islam has replaced Pan-Arabism as the primary ideological threat to Israel, this essay could, upon first reading, appear somewhat dated. Yet it represents an important shift in Kahanoff's thinking about Levantinism in light of Israeli territorial conquests. She also presciently defines Levantinization as what we would now call a postcolonial construct, pinpointing issues about immigration, difference, and cultural integration that at present occupy European nations.*

*Kahanoff wrote this piece in 1968 as the introduction to a planned collection of essays in English. When a book of Kahanoff's essays was published in Hebrew in 1978 under the same title, this essay was not included. This piece has never previously been published in any language.*

These loosely connected essays, articles, and autobiographical fragments written over the years do not have, I know, the formal structure, unity of theme, and continuity of a book written from one particular point of view on one particular subject. Yet the pieces presented here have a kind of unity, for they spring from a rich and ancient subsoil, both mythical and real, although with no clearly delineated contours in time or space. This somewhat haphazard juxtaposition reflects, perhaps, the many facets and complexities of the Levant, where, as in an archaeological dig, various fragments, relating to different people at different times, are unearthed simultaneously.

I seek to discover traces of my own past here. But they cannot be separated from the history of other peoples who lived in or passed through this region; their roots and ours are intertwined, and so are our lives today, through the very intensity of the conflict that locks us in combat. In a sense, this is my dig, through many dimensions of human time, started way back in childhood, in the hope that from my own broken little Jewish-Oriental fragment, I would be able to reconstitute a living whole. Whether we want it or not, Israel is now part of the Levant as it was in ancient times, and is shaping the destinies of the people in this area as they are shaping ours. I believe that the experiences described here, despite their ambiguities and contradictions, may prove helpful to readers.

Were I to write this book today, it would be different, less hesitant, more assertive. But in my youth I experienced the falling apart of traditional ways of living and thinking, and a tentative, half consenting half rebellious adjustment to Western culture. My formal education is Western, my deepest sensitivities are not, and as in the case of a great many other people, I have always been confronted with the need to reconcile the Western superstructure with an identity whose roots are not in the Western world.

The need for adjustment to the modern world and attachment to one's specific past are quite naturally first perceived in terms of conflict, which is frequently expressed here. All around us, people are having a similar experience, striving to retain their identity and yet to belong to the twentieth century. Some, drawn to the Western world, shed their past identity as a worn, discarded garment. Others cling to the past and turn their backs on the challenge of anything new. Still others, having experienced the Western world, yearn for some remnant of their own past, but transformed, and projected in a new dimension of the future. This is essentially what Israel has done in relation to Jewish tradition. It is a valuable experience because, while Israel has to some extent disengaged itself spiritually from the Western world, it is perfectly capable of making the most of its intellectual, scientific, and technological tools. This may be the promise it holds out to other people living in the Levant's essentially Semitic tradition.

But because Israel has succeeded—and at what cost—we tend to overlook the fact that other people around us are still in the throes of a traumatic experience, which, through force of circumstance, has been rendered more acute. For instance, Arabs are thought to be "irrational," without an attempt being made to understand their motivations, which stem from a logic of passion, doubt, fear, and despair. But this despair is bound to affect us in the future as in the past, for we are periodically involved in the tragedy of war. No matter how many wars may still have to be fought, we shall need to work out some alternative to warfare if we are to have a common future in this part of the world.

I am not a historian, archeologist, philosopher, or sociologist, so at best I can only describe the experience of having lived in a certain dimension of the past which may be relevant to Israel, at a time when Israel is more deeply and directly involved in the destinies of the people surrounding it. As with many Jews who came to Israel from so-called oriental countries, my attachment to this land owes little to Zionism but is steeped in an awareness that we are native to the Levant, quite as much as the Moslem-Arab is. Indeed, the Hebrew people, or, if one prefers, the Jewish people, are natives here no matter how long they were absent before returning; their roots are here.

But, along with many others, I was disconcerted by the frame of mind, the pervading culture, which made Israel appear antithetical to the Levant and contemptuous of it. The pressures toward the integration, or assimilation, of new immigrants from non-Western countries are enormous, and difficult to withstand. Obviously one needs to adapt, but not necessarily to renounce one's own past as irrelevant. That would jeopardize the integrity and very existence of Israel. Though one realizes that Israel is surrounded by many enemies, threatened and besieged, one is not always sure it can, or should, find its place in the Levant. Is there no alternative to a permanent state of siege? A whole new set of questions arises as to one's perspective toward Israel, and of Israel's relationship to the other peoples of the region. Some of the essays included here reflect this dilemma. In view of the fact that we are not allowed to live in a secure little Jewish ghetto untroubled by our neighbors, we are, by necessity, involved with the people around us. If Israel represents a revolution in Jewish existence—and it does—as with all other revolutionary processes, it is bound to have an impact on others. Since we are here and intend to stay, then we will have to propose to the other people in the region some viable alternative, something which Zionism alone cannot do. Zionism was essential in building Israel, but it has little or no meaning to non-Jews, nor does it want to. No matter how many Jews settle this country, Israel will still be in this part of the world, and therefore the question of its relationship to the other people in the area is the one which should concern us. A modernized Levantine framework, comprising people who are different, equal, and equally native, might provide a workable—not perfect, but workable—pattern for coexistence.

*

I would like to clarify the notion of "Levant," which in Israel acquired a pejorative connotation because unthinkingly we adopted European attitudes rather than regarding ourselves as a native people returning home. The Levant is a land of ancient civilizations which cannot be sharply differentiated from the Mediterranean world, and is not synonymous with Islam, even if a majority of its inhabitants are Moslems. The Moslems themselves belong to different sects—principally the Sunnis and the Shi'ites—and not all of these are Arab or even Arabic-speaking. Turkey and Iran, for instance, have no claim to Arabism, nor do Pakistan and Nigeria, even if they practice Islam. The Levant has a character and history of its own. It is called "Near" or "Middle" East in relationship to Europe, not to itself. Seen from Asia, it could just as well be called the "Middle West." Here, indeed, Europe and Asia have encroached on one another, time and time again, leaving their marks in crumbling monuments and in the shadowy memories of the Levant's peoples. Ancient Egypt, ancient Israel, and ancient Greece, Chaldea and Assyria, Ur and Babylon, Tyre, Sidon, and Carthage, Constantinople, Alexandria, and Jerusalem are all dimensions of the Levant. So are Judaism, Christianity, and Islam, which clashed in dramatic confrontation, giving rise to world civilizations, fracturing into stubborn local subcultures and the multilayered identities of the Levant's people. It is not exclusively Western or Eastern, Christian, Jewish, or Moslem.

Because of its diversity, the Levant has been compared to a mosaic—bits of stone of different colors assembled into a flat picture. To me it is more like a prism whose various facets are joined by the sharp edge of differences, but each of which, according to its position in a time-space continuum, reflects or refracts light. Indeed, the concept of a continuum is contained in the word *Levant* as in the word *mizrah*, and perhaps the time has come for the Levant to reevaluate itself by its own lights, rather than see itself through Europe's sights, as something quaintly exotic, tired, sick, and almost lifeless.

The rebirth of Israel radically transforms the relationship of the Levant's populations, for it represents a dynamic new entity sprung from an ancient myth, whose origins were here. The people of the region need to come to terms with the meaning of Israel and Israelis today—not just theologically, but also with the new image of the Jew, which has undergone so startling a transformation. The prism has turned, presenting a hitherto dark facet to the light, so that the position of all the other facets has changed accordingly.

The very intensity of the present conflict makes us see Israel as a small Jewish enclave surrounded by an Arab-Moslem sea ready to engulf it, but behind the façade of Arab nationalism there still exist many cultural, political, linguistic, ethnic, and religious entities, which are neither Arab nor Moslem, nor Arabic-speaking, although they are as native to the region as Moslems and Arabs are, and have just as much a right to be here.

Reconstructing a pluralistic Levant may offer a workable alternative to imperialism, neocolonialism, Christian, Moslem, or Great-Power rivalries and domination, by suggesting a framework in which people have the right to be free, different, and equal, rather than one in which the "superior" would subject, eliminate, or at best tolerate others in the name of universalism.

We tend to forget that the Levant had a long and complex history long before the Moslem conquest, and that many of its people never renounced their specific identities, though they may have adapted in some ways in order to survive. The Druze and the Maronites in Lebanon and Syria, the Kurds and Nestorian Christians in Iraq, the Copts in Egypt, like the ancient Jewish communities scattered from Yemen to Morocco, are just as native to the region as those who converted to Islam. Are they all to be stifled and suppressed under the outmoded conformity of Islam dressed up in the new garb of Arab nationalism? Some, like the Kurds and Israelis, resist. Others, like the Copts, must at present lie low. But few, if any, consent simply to disappear.

Behind the dramatic Israeli-Arab confrontation the fate of many other people and the future of the region itself hang in the balance. The Kurds have a better chance to achieve their independence as long as Israel constitutes a major preoccupation for the Iraqi rulers; the Maronites in Lebanon cannot be absorbed or eliminated by the Moslem majority as long as Israel is there. Some of them surely know that, even if a deep-rooted anti-Semitism has prevented many groups struggling for their own survival to fully appreciate the significance for their own sake of Israel's existence. The grave mistake of Syrian and Lebanese Christians might well have been to support Arabism for the immediate advantage it gave them over other minorities (Greeks, Armenians, Copts, and Jews) who had no claim to "Arabism," while forgetting that their own survival hinged on a pluralistic Levantine framework rather than on a monolithic Arab or Moslem one.

We have all clung to old hostilities from our pasts—ethnic, theological, and national—and made no attempt to reinterpret them in terms that would be mutually inclusive rather than exclusive. Reviving the notion of the Levant as a geographic entity, comprising many genuinely native peoples and cultures, may help us to create a consensus between Israel and other people in the region that stems from the acceptance of diversity not as an inevitable evil, but as a necessary good. Our own fears about assimilation and Levantinization have prevented us from stressing to best advantage the importance of a strong, independent Israel in the Levant, which can have a dynamic impact. The very fact that we are intensely particularistic as regards our own history, language, and culture provides an assurance that what may be termed our "expansionism" and "imperialism" cannot be indefinite, but will be limited in time, as was the case with Byzantium and Islam. A Jewish Israel promises the best guarantee for the freedom of other people in the region who are just as particularistic and are no more prepared to be absorbed by us than we are to be absorbed by them. Even those now in the grips of revolutionary Pan-Arabism may yet discover that a pluralistic Levantine solution is a reasonable alternative to the anarchy created in the name of an all-embracing, if largely illusory, Arab unity.

The concept of a reconstructed Levant may help us to redefine ourselves in relation to others. While Zionism has little meaning for the people in the area among whom we live, an independent Israel which defends its right to be itself may have far greater impact. But Western concepts, unfortunately, often prevent us from finding a language that expresses our perception of ourselves, and we may need to circumvent them in order to communicate directly in terms of our own historical sensitivities.

The concept of the nation-state appears modern or advanced in regard to the Levant's hodgepodge of communities, but in global terms nation-states may be already obsolete. Yet, psychologically, human beings still feel the need to belong to smaller, cozier communities, and still care about their personal pasts. Strikingly, while Europe unites, the Bretons, Basques, Welsh, Flemish, Irish, and Scots assert their own cultural autonomy against the all-inclusive nation-state. Furthermore, newer groups crystallize, as a result of immigration following the breakup of the European empires—Africans, Pakistanis, West Indians, Indochinese, Algerians, etc. They constitute new social and cultural enclaves in Europe—much as Jews almost exclusively once did—with no territorial claims in their new surroundings. They are not, and do not want to be, totally integrated or absorbed in the nation-state; they maintain ties with their countries of origin. They constitute *ummot*—folk—much on the old Levantine pattern. In other words, the Western nation-state itself is being Levantinized. Various types of communities, incorporated in a wider, rather loosely organized entity, might provide a solution in the many cases where different people have to share the same geographic space. Human groupings thus comprise concentric, intersecting, and overlapping circles, and ethnic, spiritual, or cultural identities do not and can not correspond to neatly fixed territorial units.

Significantly, Israel has as yet no fixed or recognized boundaries, so that, while some may debate whether we should exist at all, Israelis argue about the fate of Hebron, Shekhem, and Jericho. But what to us is Shekhem is Nablus to others—who have forgotten that its name is not Arabic, but derived from the Greek Neopolis. Nowhere is the tight knot of conflicting feelings toward our mythical ancestors more evident than in Hebron—al-Khalil to Moslems—for there God befriended Abraham. We differ sharply as to who is the favorite son, and from what wife. The issue is still emotionally loaded for the children of both Israel and Ishmael. To dismiss these notions as irrelevant, outmoded superstitions, and to advise the formation of states on the European model, makes little sense, since both Jews and Moslems in their conscious and subconscious associations are deeply attached to their conflicting interpretations of the same basic myth. It is rather in the context of their dispute that a solution may be found—from the moment each recognizes the other as a legitimate heir, entitled to a share of the earthly and spiritual inheritance.

Time and again people have had to learn to live together in the same territorial and mythical space in order to survive. This is perhaps the great historical lesson of the Levant, as each entity has had to renounce part of its claim to an all-embracing universality—so often synonymous with imperialism, oppression, and suppression. Pluralism here is the indispensable antidote to mutually exclusive territorial claims based on an obsessive concern with monotheism—in a multiplicity of forms—each of which sees itself, rather arrogantly, as the only entity with whom God is on speaking terms.

*

Israel is part of the Levant, and might become an important factor of its rebirth by fostering an association of diverse people native to the region who want to maintain separate cultural or ethnic personalities while sharing in the benefits of a planned economic development in place of the anarchy, social disintegration, and economic ruin the present Arab regimes have precipitated. Transforming the Levant into an association of free and independent peoples, with each ready to renounce its exaggerated claims of nationalism and to respect the rights of minorities in its midst, might help defuse the continual crises which endanger the stability and prosperity of the whole region. This framework need not be zones of American or Russian interests but could organize its own resources more economically than heretofore. It is an idea Israel should advance, for in the long run we all stand to lose by being drawn into the vortex of Great-Power rivalries playing on our mutual enmities, but finding agreement among themselves. Our best chance for peace and survival may be to transform the Zionist revolution into a Levantine one.

This need not necessarily be at the expense of our Jewishness or of our links with Jewish communities outside Israel. After all, Jews are bound by spiritual affinities, much as Moslems and Catholics are, and feel attachment to Israel, as Americans of Greek, Italian, or Irish descent feel toward their old countries. Jewishness is obviously our deepest concern, but it need not be exclusive of all others. From the moment we became a territorial and political entity we needed allies in our immediate area just as much as great nations do. The question of how long we can survive alone while winning wars, but not the peace, is one which ought to preoccupy a new generation whose problems and interests are rather similar to those of other minorities and other non-Arab or non-Moslem people in the Levant.

The fact that Jews and Greeks could maintain themselves and their cultures in the Levant for centuries, without being absorbed, or absorbing one another, while their economic and cultural levels were on a par, may provide an interesting model for us now and calm our fears regarding assimilation or Levantinization. The Greeks, much as the Jews, long the Levant's main protagonists and rivals, have constantly shuttled back and forth across the Mediterranean, at times in possession of their homeland, at others not, but never wholly contained in it. The Greeks provide an illuminating example of the constant transformation of a people who, through time, still maintain some unchanging elements. The culture of ancient Greece penetrated Egypt, Palestine, and Asia Minor. In the Hellenistic culture of Alexandria, Jew and Greek met, and their dialectical disputations provided the intellectual base from which Christianity, and what is now considered Western civilization, sprang. Greek and Jew also confronted one another in Judea, where the Hellenistic influence was by no means insignificant. Greek, the language of civilization, maintained itself in the Levant long after Greece became a province of the Roman Empire, and the Greek Byzantine Empire became the center of the civilized world after Rome fell to the barbarians of the north. When Byzantium's emperors opted for Christianity, Greek rather than Latin prevailed and became the liturgical language of the churches now considered Eastern.

Even as Byzantium fell to Islam, large Greek-speaking populations persisted within the Ottoman Empire and in Mediterranean cities, much the same as did the Jews in Eastern Europe. The Renaissance was directly connected with the exodus from Turkey of Greek and Jewish scholars who, taking old manuscripts with them, brought new cultural influences, those of antiquity, to bear on Western culture.* Thus, the Levant's culture, an ever-changing synthesis of many strains, flourished in several cities; Constantinople took over where Alexandria left off. Venice and Ravenna, Toledo and Cordoba during the late Middle Ages, embodied many aspects of the Levantine culture on the fringes of the Christian world, somewhat as Alexandria, in modern times, briefly incarnated the Western aspect of Levantine culture on the fringes of the Moslem world. That latter-day Alexandria was a Levantine city rather than an Arab one, a city where Greek and Jew renewed their dialogue at the crossroad of streets called Nebi Daniel and Ptolemy. These ethnic groups were a Western-oriented and semi-native or Levantine element, which might have put the Levant back on the map of the modern world as a reality. But the Arab revolution destroyed that possibility, and at present it is rather Tel Aviv which incarnates the Western aspect of the Levant's culture on the fringes of the Moslem world. Israel is now the carrier of a vigorous new culture, made up of many strains, all of them with origins here.

Surprisingly, just when Western cultural influence is at its lowest ebb, and the Greeks almost totally disengaged from the Levant, the Hebrew people, who constitute the second semi-native, more widely traveled and experienced element in the Levantine process of transformation, are active again. Modern Israel, representing a scientific and technological culture, and a far-reaching social revolution, is bound to have an impact, for it poses a direct threat to the static conservatism to which Islam clings behind its revolutionary Arab façade. Science and technology give us an opportunity which never existed before, of beating back the desert that threatens to cancel the gains made by the activists, of

* Contemporary scholarship discredits this notion.

the contenders who challenged the prevailing fatalistic view of human experience. Jacob in the Hebrew tradition—somewhat like Prometheus in the Greek—is an archetype of this challenge. Jacob does not submit to the will of God, nor is he defeated by the gods, but establishes an active partnership with the divine will, as a chosen—and self-chosen—instrument. God speaks to men and women who interpret his commands, rather than to those who passively listen and obey, in order to establish a covenant with them. Is it not the very act of contending both with and against the apparently blind will of nature and the apparently arbitrary will of God which is the very essence of a revolutionary process—as well as one of constant transformation in attempting to resolve the contradictions of human existence through a dynamic creative effort, rather than through passive submission?

Israel is at the forefront of that revolutionary struggle, but it can hardly be the torchbearer for itself alone. Perhaps because it is inherently a part of the Levant, Israel inevitably universalizes its experience by practical means. Thus, for instance, Arab farmers in the West Bank and Gaza are learning new techniques of agricultural production, and Arab laborers from these areas working in Israel are being paid at Histadrut rates. Arab women are included in this labor force, and the fact that they enjoy an independent income is certain to change their way of life, as it did among the oriental Jewish communities, although here the change is bound to take longer and be a greater source of conflict. This trend toward equalization, however tentative and fraught with difficulties, spells the downfall of the feudalistic middle class whose obsolete means of production is profitable only because it is sustained by cheap, unskilled labor.

The secondary school youth in these areas, most of middle-class background, are torn between conflicting impulses, between nationalism, class interests, and a genuine desire for change. They may not know what they want, except that they do not want their elders to settle matters for them. Often they find themselves in direct confrontation with Israel. Girls are politically far more active than in the past, and although their protest is directed against Israeli occupation, it is doubtful that they would ever willingly return to the social status quo which prevailed before June 1967. Paradoxically, it is the Israeli presence which has given these young people the opportunity to act together.

Societies living at different levels of development but in close proximity cannot simply ignore one another; when no other relationship exists—for lack of communication—the confrontation is bound to be violent. The terrorist organizations are able to capitalize on the discontent of the Arab population but have no program to offer, except for the return to a utopian Palestine which, should Israel somehow disappear, would be plagued by internal contradictions of Arab-Moslem society vis-à-vis the modern world, a problem these revolutionaries studiously ignore. Our best way to counteract them may be to launch practical schemes and ideas for the social, economic, and political reconstruction of the Levant. The Palestinians would find their place in it but not in the framework of Arab hegemony denying the freedom and rights of non-Arab people in their midst.

We may have to think in terms of long-range alternatives, if only because the effects of the internal problems of Arab-Moslem societies will affect us for a long time to come. Events have proved that Israel cannot insulate itself from the region in which it finds itself, so that a consciously planned social revolution may offer an alternative to war, by transforming the Zionist revolution into one which would involve all the people of the Levant, no longer bound together exclusively by the Israeli-Arab conflict.

Technologically and materially, the United States and the Soviet Union have more to contribute to the area than Israel does—particularly weapons—but their joint presence means keeping the Levant as the theater of their rivalries. This may be to the advantage of the present Arab leadership and the Moslem middle class that supports it, but it is not to the advantage of the people in the region. The alternative can be stated clearly: progress and independence with Israel, or wars and new forms of colonization without it. The Six-Day War has catapulted Israel as a force in the Levant; whatever arrangements are finally made about our as yet unrecognized borders, the imbalance between our different societies remains, leaving us little choice except to modernize the Levant while remaining respectful of its diversity.

The present conflict tends to make us feel encircled and isolated, so that we cling all the more tenaciously to Jewishness as our main human dimension. In a way this constitutes the most effective weapon of psychological warfare that the present Arab leaders and their allies have against us in their arsenal. Still, our survival is directly linked to Levantine diversity in a modern framework, in a joint fight against any dominant hegemony. What prevents us for the most part from taking the lead in propagating the ideal of a Levant Federation is our particular—and particularly painful—Jewish experience. Israel is as free to want a predominantly Jewish immigration as Iraq, say, is free to open its gates to an Arab-Moslem one. It is only in the framework of Arab hegemony that Jewish immigration has to be eliminated.

Another psychological barrier which impedes us in the Levant is that we all live by mutually exclusive concepts of historical time, all of them emotionally charged, which are part of the way we perceive ourselves as people, as we uncomfortably coexist in the now. According to the Hebrew calendar, we are in the year 5729 (1968), while the Moslem calendar, starting with Mohammed's flight from Mecca, stands at 1348. Christian time dates all events as BC or AD, as if whatever happened before or outside Christianity was of secondary importance. Jerusalem is the symbol of this time collision based on divine revelations, with claims to be absolute, exclusive, and universal. Thus, to many of us, Jerusalem has never been anything but Jewish, even when usurped by others; for these others, we were considered virtually nonexistent.

The reconstruction of a pacified Levant requires not only accommodation of diversity in space, but also adaptation to these human dimensions of time. We need to reevaluate these psycho-historical time reckonings as related and relative, rather than as separate, antagonistic, and absolute. If we were to start out with the study of prehistory, Judaism, Christianity, and Islam would appear as branches of the same tree which continue to grow, and grow apart, but it is still one whole tree. There is hardly an educational system that does not indoctrinate youngsters to blindly support their own ideological family and reject all others. It is here perhaps that change is most called for. As space contracts, accommodation in regards to historical times, and the value we attach to them, becomes more important.

Our myths are part of our political conflict: Ishmael and Israel belong to the same family, but as enemy brothers. Yet the myth, dormant as long as Jews were an oppressed minority, has been reactivated by the very birth of Israel. According to the patriarchal tradition only one son may be blessed; to supersede him the other son must either eliminate or dominate him. But a patriarchal society is not the one most of us would choose to live in today, probably not even the Palestinian Arabs, for whom the conflict is all the more acute as they are still so close to it. Hence, we might rewrite the story of Ishmael and Israel—and of their respective mothers—to give it a happier opening onto the future.

Sarah and Hagar were rivals and victims within the framework of a patriarchal society, and while they are still among us, nothing prevents them from establishing a new covenant for themselves and their children. We need not be bound forever by the terms set by our ancient myths and holy scriptures. While recognizing the crucial role they play in shaping us, we might interpret them within the context we now live in. By objectively prodding those areas where our myths clash, we may become more rational in appraising the passionately irrational element at the core of most human actions, where the feeling of identity is concerned. Arabs are irrational, we say, because they do not recognize facts, but Jews have hardly been more rational in the course of their history. Israel itself does not owe its existence to rationality but rather to the use of rational means to attain an irrational end. If we create new facts, these might include the facts of a culture which includes, but is broader than, any one of our particular identities or their manifold components.

Zionist ideology, born in the Eastern European environment, as a Jewish response to it, has not been able to relate itself to the history of this region or to the people who have lived here from earliest antiquity and have undergone many transformations. Perhaps in its formative period this ideology needed to stress its uniqueness. The founding fathers of Zionism seem to have acted on the assumption that, as far as Jews were concerned, there was a total void here from the destruction of the Second Temple to the Second Aliyah.* Even as regards those periods when Jews lived here in a sovereign state, our history stresses the hostility of others, our stunning victories and desperate resistance ending in

* The destruction of the Second Temple in 70 CE by the Romans marks the symbolic beginning of the second Jewish exile. The Second Aliyah refers to the second wave of Zionist immigration to Palestine (1904–1914).

suicide or exile. We stress destruction, persecution, massacres, passing over in silence the long periods of fruitful exchange. We overlook that even Pharaoh's Egypt was quite friendly to the Hebrew people for a long time. So was Spain, so was the Ottoman Empire, and the Jews were not the only victims of persecution.

Our case is different, mainly in that we have been far more stubborn than most in not wanting to disappear and not letting ourselves be absorbed, so that this history of persecution has repeated itself in varied contexts. But even this is not entirely true in the Levant. The Greeks, with or without territory, have not disappeared, and people like the Armenians have known massacres, exile, and dispersal. The last-ditch resistance of Mosaddeq is reminiscent of Masada.* Our history is not all that different from that of many other people, but we cannot possibly find friends and allies as long as we wish to remain in every respect "unique." We ignore the fact that Jews have always lived in the Levant and around the Mediterranean basin since ancient times, and that the Jewish ethos itself was not born in a vacuum, in the abstract of a divine revelation, but emerged from a long, slow cultural development. We have every right to be proud of it, attached to it, but we must also see it as one particular development within a larger context.

This refusal to acknowledge anything we might have in common with other people in the region is reflected in the name given to the native-born children of Eastern European parents. They were called *sabras*, while other native-born children were *yelide ha-aretz*. It was as if returning here they could only identify with the prickly fruit of the wild cactus, a godlike creation contending with the wilderness. But it left their children with no way to relate to the other children. Cultivated fruits of the area, so often mentioned in the Bible and used as decorative motifs in exile—the vine, the fig, the pomegranate—were ignored, as if any shared symbol linking us to the past had to be rejected. But if

* Mohammed Mossadeq (1882–1967) was prime minister of Iran from 1951 to 1953. Masada is the site of a Herodian fortress on a butte overlooking the Dead Sea, as well as the site of resistance by Jewish zealots against the Romans during the first Jewish-Roman war. After a siege in 73 CE the community committed mass suicide rather than surrender.

we refuse a common past, we can hardly have a common future and are consequently bound by the terms of the Ishmael-Israel dispute: one brother eliminating or subjugating the other, and the other people in the family having nothing to say about it.

Actually, it should be no shame for any of us here to be called *yelide ha-aretz* or native, which we are in different but related ways. Between absorbing or being absorbed, dominating or being dominated—or eliminated—there remains the alternative of establishing a mature, civilized relationship, that of recognition between free and equal people who have every right to be different from one another. None of us has yet attained this maturity. But it is an alternative we might foster and offer to the other people of the Levant, in order that together we may form an association of modern people, attached to their own respective pasts but not enslaved by them. The past can be reinterpreted in order to bring people together in a modern, livable, workable, bearable framework. At present, we stress the most negative or backward aspects of our cultures, those that ignore one another in terms of absolutes.

This pluralistic alternative might not prevent the next war, or the one after that, but, in the long run, it might help Israel integrate in the Levant. Not in the sense that new settlers were supposed to be integrated into Israel, losing every shred of their own identity, but as enlightened and adult people, with a proud past—but also with a present and a future to be lived and shared with others.

*

As I write this, I know the reader will find that this [afterword] is not a summary of the contents of the book. [The above essays] reflect ambivalence toward a past still not disengaged from the Levant of the period between the two World Wars, or the dilemma of a new immigrant from an oriental country who wasn't all that enthusiastic about being "absorbed." The pieces included here look backward, rather than forward, questioning all the way. The Six-Day War transported us back into the Levant, to become one of the main forces disrupting the old order, but, hopefully, also a positive force which will contribute to replacing the old order with a more modern and progressive approach. We certainly cannot live in a vacuum.

I have tried to explore in a personal way many dimensions of the past with their unresolved contradictions. But the Levant looks very different to me now than it did at any time in my own past, whether in Egypt, in France, in America, or even as seen from Israel only ten years ago. Israel is now a factor in the Levant, confronted through its victory by new problems which are no longer exclusively Jewish ones but involve the relationship to be established with other people in this specific region as well. The reader may wish to reflect on this in order to better comprehend the world around us—not only the Arab-Moslem world, but perhaps also a world in which the rebirth of Israel heralds both hope and promise for a reborn Levant.

# *Glossary*

*ʿarousa*: [Arabic] Bride.

Ashkenazi: [Hebrew, sing.; pl., Ashkenazim] Descendants of the Jews of Central and Eastern Europe.

*Bairam*: [Turkish] Muslim religious celebration, corresponding to the Arabic term *ʿid*. In Egypt it refers particularly to *ʿid al-fitr*, the festival marking the end of Ramadan.

*dafina*: [from Arabic *dfina*] Traditional stew made for the Sabbath by the Jews of North Africa.

*Dayenu*: [Hebrew] Traditional Passover song in the Haggadah; literally, "it is enough for us."

Eretz Yisrael: [Hebrew] Literally, "the land of Israel."

fellahin: [Arabic, pl.] Peasants.

felluca: [from Arabic faluka] A traditional sailing boat of the eastern Mediterranean.

Haggadah: [Hebrew] The text read on the eve of Passover to commemorate the Exodus from Egypt.

*ḥamin*: [Hebrew] Traditional stew made for the Sabbath.

*ḥara*: [Arabic] Urban quarter or neighborhood, usually referring to older, traditional districts of the city. In Egypt the term also signifies an alley.

*ḥarat al-yahud*: [Arabic] Cairo's poor Jewish quarter.

harem: [English; from Arabic *ḥarim*] The women of a traditional Muslim household as well as the portion of the house reserved for women. Kahanoff also uses the term to refer to the practice in Egypt of designating a tram car for the use of women passengers only.

*ḥevre*: [Hebrew] Group of friends.

Histadrut: [Hebrew] Founded as the General Federation of Laborers in the land of Israel in 1920, it went on to become a powerful organization of trade unions after the establishment of the state of Israel.

Holy Carpet: *Kiswa* [Arabic], the covering of the *Kaʿba* in Mecca, traditionally provided by Egypt. There was an annual ceremonial processional called the *maḥmal* during which the *kiswa* was paraded through the streets of Cairo on an elaborately decorated litter atop a camel.

*inshallah*: [Arabic] God willing.

kaddish: [Hebrew] A prayer in the Jewish liturgy that is recited in memory of those who have died.

khedive: [From Turkish and Persian] Term used for the ruler of Egypt; recognized by the Ottoman government in 1867 and used until 1914.

*kippah*: [Hebrew] Skullcap worn traditionally by Jewish men. Also known as a yarmulke.

Ladino: The old Castilian dialect used by Sephardi Jews whose ancestors were expelled from Spain in the sixteenth century.

*ma'abara*: [Hebrew] Transit camp constructed in Israel during the 1950s to provide temporary housing for new immigrants. A great number of the camps' residents emigrated from Arab countries.

*maktub*: [Arabic] Destiny. Literally, "it is written."

*matzot*: [Hebrew, pl.; sing., *matzah*] Unleavened bread eaten during the Jewish festival of Passover.

mitzvah: [Hebrew] Commandment; refers to the commandments in the Hebrew Bible. Kahanoff uses the phrase "to do a mitzvah," which means to fulfill a commandment or do a good deed.

*mizraḥ*: [Hebrew] East.

Mizraḥi: [Hebrew] Jewish immigrants to Israel from the Arab and Islamic worlds and their descendants. Kahanoff uses the somewhat outdated term "oriental Jews" to refer to this community.

*motsa'e shabbat*: [Hebrew] Saturday evening.

*mujaddara*: [Arabic] A popular dish of the Eastern Mediterranean prepared with lentils, rice or grains, and sautéed onions.

pasha: [Turkish] A man of high rank.

*Pesah*: [Hebrew] Passover.

sabra: [from Hebrew *tsabar*] Prickly pear cactus; commonly used in modern Hebrew to refer to native-born Israelis. Kahanoff distinguishes between *sabras* and *yelide ha-aretz* (see below), reserving *sabras* for those of Eastern European descent and applying *yelide ha-aretz* to all others.

Sephardi: [Hebrew, sing.; pl., Sephardim] Descendents of the Jews from the Iberian Peninsula who were expelled in the late fifteenth century. The term is often used broadly to refer to all non-Ashkenazi Jews.

*Shema Yisrael*: [Hebrew] Jewish prayer affirming faith in one God.

*shlishi be-shlishi*: [Hebrew] Third cousin once removed.

tarbush: [Arabic] Fez; a traditional red hat.

*tsabar*: [Hebrew, sing.; pl., *tsabarim*] See sabra.

*ulpan*: [Hebrew] A school where Hebrew is studied.

*ummot*: [Hebrew, pl.; sing., *ummah*] Nations.

*yelide ha-aretz*: [Hebrew] Literally, "those born of the land" (see sabra).

*yishuv*: [Hebrew] Settlement. The term *old Yishuv* refers to the community of Jews, mostly Sephardim, who lived in Palestine before Zionist immigration.

# *Index*

Note: "JSK" refers to Jacqueline Shohet Kahanoff.

Library of Congress Cataloging-in-Publication Data
Kahanof, Jacqueline (Jacqueline Shohet), 1917–1979, author.
[Works. Selections. 2011]
Mongrels or marvels : the Levantine writings of Jacqueline Shohet Kahanoff / edited by Deborah A. Starr and Sasson Somekh.
pages cm. — (Stanford studies in Jewish history and culture)
Includes bibliographical references and index.
ISBN 978-0-8047-6953-2 (cloth : alk. paper)
I. Starr, Deborah A., 1968– editor of compilation. II. Somekh, Sasson, editor of compilation. III. Title. IV. Series: Stanford studies in Jewish history and culture.
PJ5054.K3136A6 2011
892.4'6809—dc22

2010051265